# NEXT STOP, Chancey

1

# NEXT STOP, CHANCEY

## 1

## KAY DEW SHOSTAK

*Kay Dew Shostak*

August South
PUBLISHING

*Have fun in Chancey!*

ISBN: 978-0-9962430-0-1

Library of Congress Control Number: 2015905154

SOUTHERN FICTION: Women's Fiction / Small Town / Railroad / Bed & Breakfast / Mountains / Georgia / Family

Text Layout and Cover Design by Roseanna White Designs
Cover Images from www.Shutterstock.com

Published by August South Publishing. You may contact the publisher at:
AugustSouthPublisher@gmail.com

*To Mike*
*You never doubted*

# CHAPTER 1

So how did I get stuck driving with my daughter, the princess, during one of her moods? Rap music, to pacify her, adds to my sense of disbelief. Carolina Jessup, you have lost your mind thinking this move can work.

Rolling hills of dry, green grass and swooping curves of blacktop lead us to a four-way stop. Across the road, sitting caddy-corner, is the sign I found so adorable last October. When we still owned a home in the Atlanta suburbs and moving hadn't entered the picture.

"Welcome to Chancey, Georgia. Holler if you need anything!"

A scream of "Help!" jumps to my lips, but that might disturb her highness. Maybe she's asleep and won't see her new hometown's welcome.

"Holler? Who says 'holler'? Who puts it on their sign for everyone to see?"

Nope, she saw it.

With a grimace, my voice rises above Snoop Dog, or whoever is filling my car with cringe-inducing music, as we cross the highway. "Honey, it's different from home, but we'll get used to it, right? And Daddy's really happy. Don't you think he's happy?" She dismisses my question, and me, by closing her eyes and laying her head back.

I stick my tongue out at the sign as we pass. I hate small towns.

Savannah sighs and plants her feet on the dashboard, "All my friends back home want me to stay with them on weekends."

Drumming manicured fingernails on the door handle of my minivan she adds, "Nobody can believe you did this to me."

Guilt causes my throat to tighten. "Honestly, Savannah, I'm having trouble believing it, too." Apparently, she's tired of my apologizing because she leans forward and turns up the radio. Rap music now pounds down Chancey's main street, but no one turns an evil eye on our small caravan. Two o'clock on a Sunday afternoon, there's no one to notice our arrival. July heat has driven everyone off the front porches, into air conditioned living rooms. Bikes and skateboards lie discarded in several yards, owners abandoning them for less strenuous activity, like fudgesicles and Uno.

Jackson is driving the rental truck ahead of my van in which our twenty years of life together are packed tighter than the traffic at home. Oh, yeah, Atlanta isn't home anymore. As the truck takes a curve, I have a view inside the cab. With their grins and high fives, they might as well be sitting on the driving seat of a Conestoga wagon headed into the Wild West. Next to Jackson in the truck is our thirteen-year-old, Bryan. Beside the passenger window is our older son, Will. Bryan is ecstatic about this move. Will just wants to get it done so he can get back to his apartment at the University of Georgia.

We slow to take a turn where two little boys in faded jeans lean against the stop sign post. After Jackson passes, the taller one steps toward the road and waves. I press the brake pedal harder and roll down the window. Humidity and the buzz of bugs from the weeds in the roadside ditch roll in.

"Hey guys."

"You moving here?" He punctuates his question with a toss of his head toward the moving truck lumbering on down the road ahead of us.

"Sure are. I'm Carolina and this is Savannah."

The smaller boy twists the front of his red-clay-stained t-shirt in his hands and steps closer. "Ask 'em."

"I am," the speaker for the pair growls as he shoves his hand out to maintain his distance from the younger boy. "You moving up to the house by the bridge?"

"The train bridge?"

He nods and both boys' eyes grow larger. They lean toward me.

"Yes, you can come visit when we get settled."

Both boys shake their heads and the designated speaker drawls, "No, ma'am. Can't." He pulls a ball cap out of his back pocket and tips his head down to put it on.

The little one keeps shaking his head and finally asks, "Ain't you afraid?"

Savannah moans beside me, "Mom..."

"No, we like trains. Well, we'd better be going."

"You ain't afraid of the ghost?"

My foot jumps off the accelerator and finds the brake pedal. My finger leaves off rolling up my window. "What?"

But they don't hear me. The boys are running toward the house sitting in the yard full of weeds.

Savannah grins for the first time today. "Did he say 'ghost'? Cool." She turns the music back up, lays her head against the head-rest and we pull away from the corner.

*Ghost? Like there's not enough to worry about.*

Tiny yards of sun-baked grass and red dirt pass on the left. Across from them a string of small concrete buildings house a laundromat, a fabric store, and Jeans-R-Us. Chancey's version of an open-air shopping mall. Hopefully, Savannah's eyes are closed as I speed up to catch the truck. Over a small hill, the truck comes into view along with a railroad crossing. A smile pushes through my worries as I think of the grin surely on my husband's face right now.

For years, Jackson talked about moving and opening a bed & breakfast for railroad enthusiasts, railfans, in some little town. Now, a lot of people fantasize about living in a small town. I believe those are the people who have never lived in one—like my husband.

Only five weeks ago, he came home with a job offer from the railroad. We'd already experienced life with the railroad in our early married life. When we finally tired of his constant traveling, he took a job with an engineering consultant and we moved to the upscale suburbs northwest of Atlanta. Railroad job, or no, nothing was getting me out of the suburbs.

Then I find condoms in Savannah's purse, freak out, and accidentally make his dream come true. Well, the small town part of his dream, but the B&B is not happening. Things won't get out of hand again, not with me focusing.

At the railroad underpass there is no stop sign or light, but Jackson and the boys are stopped anyway. Arms poke out of both windows of the truck cab. There's no train coming but Bryan and Will spent more father-son outings in rail yards than parks so they could be pointing at one of a hundred things of interest.

At first Jackson's train obsession was cute, but I realize now, I'm an enabler. Like the husband walking down his basement stairs when it dawns on him his den could double as a scrap-booking store. Or the wife suddenly realizing her last ten vacations involved a NASCAR event.

Past the railroad yard and up the hill overlooking town, the harsh sunlight is muted by thick, leafy boughs drooped over the street. Shade allows for thick lawns encased behind wrought-iron fences or old-stone borders. Sidewalks cut through the lawns and lead to deep front porches and tall houses. The houses stand as a testament to Chancey's once high hopes—hopes centered on the railroad and the river. As we come to the top of the summit the Tennessee River runs on our right. Savannah leans forward to look out her window, pushing her dark hair back. Ahh, even she can't ignore the view.

"Mom, you realize we are officially in the middle of nowhere, right? Look, nothing but trees and water as far as you can see. Not even a boat in all that water. I guess everybody's inside watching *The Antiques Roadshow*."

So much for enjoying the view. We turn away from the river and start back down the hill, taking a sharp turn to our right. A narrow road maneuvers through a green channel of head-high weeds. The road and weeds end in wide-open sky and a three-track crossing.

"Great, a stupid train already," Savannah growls. We can't

see the train but up ahead her father and brothers are out of the truck and pointing down the line. We both know what that means.

I put the van into park and lay my head on the steering wheel. My sense of disbelief wars with the memory of the joy on my husband's face. Is it possible for us to be happy here? A train whistle blows as dark blue engines rock past and my head jerks up. Through the blur of rushing train cars I see the other side of the tracks—and our new home.

Frustration cuts through my sadness because someone is sitting on the front porch. Are you kidding me? A drop-in visitor already?

# Chapter 2

My anger at having visitors before we even move in vanishes with the train. The front porch railing, where the man was sitting, is empty. We bounce over the tracks, but my eyes keep flitting to the porch. One of the primary things on my list of things to hate about living in a small town is drop-in guests. My fears must be playing with my mind. Right?

The hundred-year-old house really is beautiful. With the tracks to my back, the quiet of a summer afternoon and whiffs of the musty river make me forget the reason it was on the market for so long—until a train goes past. Now the voice of a pre-schooler in a dirty shirt with big blue eyes asking me about the ghost makes me wonder if the trains were the only selling weak spot.

Three stories built on all those high hopes of yesteryear. Hardwood floors throughout and nine-over-nine pane windows face the tracks in the front and the Tennessee River in back.

It's going to be hard to stay anonymous here. I stare at the house. Three stories sitting on a bluff, in a town with one stop light. And the one stop light thing isn't a cliché—it's true.

Mom and Dad should've lived in this house. My parents, Jack and Goldie Butler, needed a dozen kids to run their circus of a life, but ended up with only me to entertain and help host their weekend houseboat parties. My parents never met a gathering, party, or event they didn't equate with an afternoon on the porch at Twelve Oaks. With the last name "Butler" they carried on as if they were old-South money straight from "Gone with the Wind."

Dad always wanted at least one boy to name Rhett. I spent every day thanking God I wasn't a boy. Being named Carolina Blue Butler was bad enough. Mother had a horrible Aunt Bonnie so at least they didn't give me Rhett and Scarlett's firstborn's complete name.

"Are you going to help or just stand there pretending you're back in Marietta?" Savannah stomps past me, her arms loaded.

Daddy's dark, Rhett Butler-looks and mother's shiny goldness melted together to create non-descript me with hair, eyes and build—much like a brown bear. But their looks interlaced to create my daughter. She has daddy's dark hair and mother's sky blue eyes. And while I've spent my life fading into the background; she claimed center stage at birth. The suburbs allowed me to disappear; for Savannah the monotony soaked up some of her persona. As her mother, figuring out how to reel her in never came easy. She doesn't really intimidate me—but confrontation isn't worth the effort. Which partially answers the question screaming in my head...

How did I let this move happen? Fear of confrontation—and books. My love of books and ability to get buried in them while real life piles up outside the door always keeps me passive and deluded. Fear of losing that anonymity in Chancey makes my stomach churn and ache. Better get moving before Savannah comes back out.

While my daughter finishes unloading the minivan and the car, the guys empty the truck. The kitchen gets all my attention. Pine cabinets with black hinges and pulls are like those in my grandmother's old house. The laminate counter tops are black so I can pretend they're the granite ones I left. Hardwood floors cover all of downstairs, but they're not nice and shiny. These are the color of a cheap, brown crayon, with the sheen of a paper sack. More of the tall, paned windows line the side walls facing out to the river and woods.

Haze from the summer sun shimmers across the field but a spot on the edge of the woods makes me stare. The bushes in that area seem out of focus. And why is the little cloud or fog moving? There isn't a breeze in the entire state today. I grab a towel to wipe the window. Maybe it's a smudge on the glass. Then the smudge is gone, the bushes look normal and nothing is moving. Something was there, I think.

"Can you believe it? A double-stack train on our first day." Jackson enters the kitchen grinning like a little boy, and grabs me when I turn toward him. "The boys are beside themselves. This is great, isn't it?"

His blonde hair looks dark since its cut so short for his first day back at the railroad. The short hair and sparkle in his eyes reminds me of Bryan on his first day of school. Jackson's sweat dampened t-shirt doesn't deter me and I lay my head on his chest. In his arms, everything comes clear for a moment: Our musings about a bed and breakfast for rail fans, Jackson hating the consulting rat race, Bryan's delight at having woods and a river to play in, and our constant worries of having a 16-going-on-25 daughter in the fast-paced suburbs.

"You're the best, you know?" He leans back a little, "So how's Savannah?"

"Oh, she's Savannah. She's got her own little castle up on the top floor." I pull away from him and begin unwrapping glasses, "Maybe we could lock her up there. You know, like a real princess in a storybook tower."

"Then she'd actually have something to whine about." He takes a glass from my hand and steps around me to the sink. "However, if it kept her away from Parker Garrison, I'd install the lock myself." He fills his glass from the tap.

Oh, yeah, Parker.

"Well, back to the truck, but what about feeding all these kids?"

"There's a pizza menu in that top drawer. Let's get pizzas delivered."

Jackson nods and sets his water down. He pulls me toward him again, "Thanks for making all this happen. Did I tell you you're the best?" Nuzzling my neck, he awakens those feelings he's stirred in me since we met in college.

"A hot woman in my kitchen and a double-stacked train

in my front yard, hmm, must be doing something right," he murmurs as he nuzzles his way to my mouth.

I press into him, but he jerks his head back and, with a quick squeeze of my arms, steps away. "There's a train whistle."

He dashes through the living room and out the front door.

With a bend to peek out the kitchen window, my gaze travels the edge of the woods but there's no fog or movement. I straighten and hurry to follow Jackson. The view at the front window stops me. Jackson's hand shields his eyes from the slanting afternoon sun. He stands facing the bridge and Will squats just below him. Bryan is hurrying toward them but looking back over his shoulder, waving at the engineer high up in the cab.

The train races past; the engineer's arm stuck out the window in greeting. Will stands up, leans close to his dad and points at some sandy-colored cars. Jackson gestures toward the cars and cocks his head so Will and Bryan can both hear his answer. They turn when the last car flies by and Jackson lays his arm around Bryan's shoulders. As they watch the train fade down the track, they face away from the sun and it silhouettes them.

Something inside me says this is where Jackson Jessup belongs. And one fact is embedded in my soul—I belong wherever he is.

Two hours of unpacking and arranging the kitchen pass before Bryan wanders in looking for food. I grab the pizza menu and the phone book from the drawer and sit at the kitchen table.

Stick a fork in me, I'm done. Now for melted cheese, greasy pepperoni and a Braves game on TV. My Atlanta Braves are stumbling a bit, but they'll pull it together. They're on the West Coast for a couple of games so that means a late afternoon start.

Watching sports is like watching trains for me—I don't actually have to participate and I get to be with Jackson.

My break lasts only long enough for me to read the front page of the pizza menu and take a look in the phone book. The phone book isn't as big as our suburban high school directory.

"There's no delivery out here in the sticks and the pizza place isn't even open on Sunday." No response makes me fear no one heard my dire proclamation. I push away from the table and in search of apologies for leaving civilization, walk into the living room.

"The pizza place is closed on Sunday. And, yes, THE pizza place. The one and only. Guess I have to go to the grocery store."

Jackson looks up from behind the TV where he and two of Will's friends work on connecting cables. "Okay. But bring back lots of food, we're starving."

"I'm going with you." Savannah yells from upstairs.

Great, another ride with the queen of joy. "Well, hurry."

"I'm ready."

There on the stairs stands sixteen years of commercial watching honed to perfection. Makeup, sundress, tanned limbs, straightened hair, teeth whitened to a glow. I feel like the BEFORE pictures. Way before.

Bryan comes in from the front porch, "Where are you going? I want to go."

"No," Savannah decrees, "You are not coming with us."

"We're just going to the grocery store." I tell him as both hands dig in my purse for keys. "Why don't you stay here?"

"I want to see this Pig store. C'mon, Mom."

Keys in hand, I put my purse strap over my shoulder and sigh, "Okay, but I'm leaving now."

Battle for front seat concluded, we rock over the crossing, weave through the weed channel, and drive down from the bluff. At the bottom, we come to the tracks again, where the road runs along them until Main Street. However, instead of turning left toward the old downtown, I turn right. Development in Chancey is a Dollar General Store, a Mountain Express gas station, Oriental Delights Chinese Buffet and the Piggly Wiggly grocery store.

I park next to the three cars in the gravel parking lot. As we walk across to the store entrance, everything in me wants to compare this to home where the landscaped parking lot is adorned with dozens of crepe myrtle trees, looking like lush bouquets of raspberry-colored flowers. I can almost hear the diners at the outdoor restaurants providing background noise of laughter and clinking glasses. And then that whiff of dark richness at the entrance where Starbucks waits inside.

But let's not think of any of that.

Once inside, the kids sense they're on semi-familiar territory and set off to explore the store. After studying the overhead signs, I head straight to the deli area for something, anything, already prepared.

The deli is closed. A quarter after five and it's closed—if this assortment of lunchmeat and cheese can actually call itself a deli. No rotisserie chickens or specialty salads. No sushi bar or soup pots. I grab two loaves of bread, jars of peanut butter and jelly from the first aisle and then continue down the second and third aisles filling my cart.

On the third aisle, the sheer number of cake mixes available stop me. At home the cake mixes take up three shelves in a section about a yard long. Taking a further look, strange boxes and bags surround me with labels for stuff like corn meal and cracker meal. These people take their baking seriously. At home we're too busy watching *The Food Channel* to actually cook.

Savannah walks up and watches me maneuver around a cart of day-old bakery items at the end of the aisle, readily accessible for when that congealed cherry-Danish impulse hits. She dumps a handful of magazines in with my groceries, "At least they have decent magazines. This place smells. Don't you think it smells?"

"Well, kinda. But it's not a bad smell, just a grocery-store smell." With a smile, I attempt to push aside the fear of having a fearless daughter. "But you smell good. Why did you get all dressed up?"

"I'm not going to let living in a hick town downgrade my style." She lifts her head and straightens her spine. "Besides,

I'm trying to keep my spirits up. This is hard, you know."

"I know, honey."

"And Parker texted me we're only 45 minutes from his Uncle's lake house where his family is this weekend. He might come over tonight."

Oh, that's why she's talking to me. "If he gets there before we get back you know your daddy won't be happy." We turn the corner toward the check-out.

"Parker said he won't get here until around seven. And you and Daddy have to get over this. Those condoms were Sarah's, not mine. I am not having sex with Parker."

The check-out clerk looks up at Savannah's announcement. Midnight black bangs hang over her right eye, completely concealing it. Her left brow sports four rings parked on it, or through it. Black lipstick completes her look and those ebony lips mesmerize me as she speaks.

"Did you find everything you need?"

Before my answer forms, Savannah leans forward. "Absolutely, I'm Savannah Jessup and I'm going to be a junior at Chancey High. Are you in school?"

Who said that? The beauty queen standing beside my cart beams at the vampire-wannabe. What happened to the sulking girl I was just talking to?

"Yeah, um, yeah, I'm a junior, too." Surprise is not a normal vampire emotion.

"Great, maybe we'll have classes together and get to know each other."

Savannah's longing for friendship pours out every lying pore as she catches my eye and smiles. She knows clean-cut, Abercrombie wearing Parker looks like the answer to a parent's prayer next to the girl checking out my groceries. My darling daughter picks up her magazines, bags them, and holds her hand out. "Keys?"

Anxious to get rid of her, I toss her the keys.

Savannah, glances at the clerk's name tag, "See you at school, Angie."

"Mom, can I go to youth group tonight?" a voice behind me

asks.

"What?" Bryan walks toward me, followed by two boys about his age.

"This is John and Grant. They'll be in eighth grade, too. They go to that red-brick church we passed and their youth group is doing this messy Olympics thing tonight. Can I go?"

"Um, hi guys." Leave it to Bryan, he talks to everyone he meets, and not out of selfish intentions like his sister. "Just let me know when and where."

While I pay, they fill Bryan in on the details.

Bryan loads the back of the van while Savannah examines the visor mirror. I slide in the passenger seat and Bryan takes the cart to the banged-up cart corral in the next row.

"Sounds like me and Angie might be good friends, don't you think?"

My eyes roll without my permission. "Did we buy ibuprofen?"

# Chapter 3

Jackson left early this morning for Alabama. I'm enjoying another cup of coffee and watching the boxes sit and wait for me to unpack them. Yesterday's energy from a full house of busy people dissipated overnight. It was easier to be in the flow yesterday, when the house was jumping. Will and his friends left late yesterday for campus. Savannah and Bryan are still sleeping.

Thank goodness, it's quiet this morning. Needing to think, I grip my coffee mug in my hands, rest my elbows on the kitchen table, and close my eyes. When we got home from the grocery store last night someone was sitting on the front porch. This time, I'm sure. As we came out of the weed tunnel, the head lights hit the front porch and a man, one hip hiked up, sitting on the railing. Between looking for trains and the headlights bobbing over the rough crossing, the next time I got a good look at the porch, it was empty. Something seemed odd about the man and around 3:30 it struck me.

He wore long pants. Jackson, Will and Will's friends all wore cargo shorts. We laughed over sandwiches about khaki shorts being their moving uniforms. Plus the man got off the porch in only a second. Where did he go?

Savannah and Bryan didn't mention him and I'm not sure he really was there. Maybe it's the stress. And, Lord knows, sleep hasn't come easy in weeks.

Parker finally left last night at 11:30. This staying up until her midnight curfew is killing me. Since school ended, my surveillance covers seven nights a week. Most every night is survived with flipping channels and finding reasons to buzz by the darling couple.

The condom thing at the beginning of the summer shocked the life out of me. It all started with me needing a phone number from her cell, which was in her purse. I opened the small Coach knock-off and there they were.

They could be Sarah's. Couldn't they?

Anyway, I called the realtor that day. Up to then the debate centered on how to stay put while Jackson took the new job. He'd found out the house beside the tracks we'd seen on our autumn trip to Chancey was for sale.

Jackson even joked, "Maybe we should go ahead and open the B&B now. Think how happy living in the country would make Bryan." To me his joke wasn't funny, since I refused to move Savannah.

Then the condoms.

In the worst housing market in years our house sold in three days. Three days!

Terror at my daughter having sex fueled me for weeks until the consequences of my freaking out hit me—we were moving to the sticks.

Of course, it's not "PC" to love the suburbs, but I loved the suburbs. Small towns are not magical or sweet. Just ask anyone slightly overweight with pimples who grew up in one. Two out of three will tell you small towns are the dumps. Okay, that's a made up statistic.

"Mom, Grant's coming over today, okay?"

Bryan slumps into a seat, stirring me from my silent rant. I stand and head to the coffee pot. The boxes would like a few more minutes respite before being unpacked.

"Sure. Is the other boy coming?"

"No. He has to work today."

"Work? Where? He's only thirteen."

"I don't know. Where's the cereal?"

It doesn't take long to dig out a bowl, spoon, and show him the new cereal shelf. Bryan taps out a tune on the side of his bowl with his spoon then he pulls the cereal box toward him to read. I decide to join him and pour Raisin Bran into my bowl.

He darts a look around his box at me. "Did you hear the trains last night? Isn't that cool?"

See, it's an inherited sickness. Most people don't want to be awakened throughout the night by whistles and bells.

"Yes, they were loud." Wonder how long it takes to get used to the sounds and stop hearing them. Except Jackson will probably wake me up each time one passes to guess how many engines are pulling it. "When you're done eating, take that stack of empty boxes in the living room out to the garage and break them down, okay? When is Grant coming?"

Bryan shrugs and keeps eating.

With breakfast finished, dressing is next on my agenda. In the living room, a look around makes me feel good about what we've accomplished. The furniture is in place and boxes filled with pictures and knick-knacks are stuck in one of the empty rooms off the kitchen. Sunlight seeps in from the back of the house. Opening the front door allows me to enjoy the shadowed front yard. Waiting a few more minutes before getting dressed won't hurt.

Our front porch stretches the length of the house. A white, wooden railing edges the porch on both ends and the front opens in the middle for the steps. A mature maple shades the end of the porch near the driveway. I step onto the porch's wide boards, which are painted a rusty red and walk to the end pointing toward the river. A breeze ruffles the leaves around me and the hills across the river appear alive as the leaves lift, swell, and then fall in the wind. Small ripples appear on the green water and thin, high clouds move quickly across the blue-white summer sky.

My hands pull away from the railing as I turn and suddenly see the porch as it will look one day. Rockers gathered at both ends, small tables holding sweating glasses of iced tea. Rag rugs and pillows adding touches of comfort. Finally.

Finally, some vision of what we can make here is fighting through my panic. Finally, my *good* imagination is kicking in.

My imagination's been working overtime lately, but leaping from disaster to disaster and seeing people and things that aren't there. Frankly, that's been a little tiring.

A blue SUV turns down the hill and crosses the tracks. It pulls into our driveway and one of the boys from the grocery store jumps out. Then, wouldn't you know it? His mother puts the car in park. She turns it off and opens the door.

Just as things start to look up, a drop-in visitor arrives with me still in my robe.

"Hi there, I'm Grant's mom." Dressed in blue jeans cut-off at the knee and a sleeveless, button-up shirt, the woman comes up the side walk and onto the porch. Grant beats her up the steps and I open the screen door for him.

"Hey, Grant. Bryan is inside somewhere." He darts into the house and leaves me with my guest. "Hi, I'm Bryan's mom— Carolina."

"Susan Lyles. Thought I'd stop in, say 'Welcome' and drop off some tomatoes from my garden." She bobs her head at the bag she holds out to me.

She doesn't seem to mind she's found me in my robe and it's really hard to beat home-grown Georgia tomatoes; so I invite her in for coffee.

"Y'all really got a lot done for one day," Susan says as she follows me into the kitchen. She's tall, thin, tanned and her pale hands say she gardens with gloves on.

Setting the grocery sack of tomatoes on the counter gives me a free hand to grab the dish rag from the sink and squeeze it out. "We used to move around quite a bit and we had a lot of help yesterday." The table gets a quick swipe where Bryan ate.

"Oh, yeah, everyone saw the caravan coming through town and then all that food you bought at the Pig. We figured you had a bunch of folks here. Guess that's explains the large crowd at youth group last night. Everyone heard the new kid was coming." She joins me in taking the cereal boxes off the table and putting them away. She waves off the milk and sugar offered for her coffee and pulls out a chair at the table to sit down.

"Bryan did you proud, he behaved just great." Susan leans forward and laughs. "Even with everyone pestering him with questions. Was that your oldest son, Will, who picked him up last night?"

Welcome to life in a fish bowl.

"Yes, that was Will. He headed back to his apartment last night."

"Thought that must be him. Tracey Barlow goes to UGA. Wonder if they know each other?"

"Could be. So, do you have any other children?"

"Law, yes. Griffin and I have three. My sister and brother each have two. Our kids seem to run the high school since they're all around the same age. Grant is the youngest of the seven kids. My other two are Leslie, who's a senior, and Susie Mae, who's a sophomore." She pauses to take a quick gulp of coffee. "Laney's are twin girls and the age of your daughter. My brother Scott's two are both seniors 'cause Ronnie got held back in third grade. Ricky is his other son and he's the quarterback."

It's all coming back to me now—this living in a small town where everybody knows everybody and expects you to know them too. However, names are easy to remember because no one moves in and no one moves out.

"Wow, y'all must be kept busy with all those kids."

"It's fun, though. Nothing's changed in Chancey since we ran Chancey High, except now we sit up in the old people section at the football games!" Susan laughs again and then drains her cup of coffee. I hadn't taken much more than a sip.

She stands up. "Well, I gotta go. Grant said he'll just walk home later. We live across the tracks and up the hill some. Ours is the blue house on the corner with the big garden." She takes her cup to the sink, rinses it and sets it upside down on the counter. "I gotta go get some weeding done before the sun is up full."

I follow her through the living room and back onto the front porch. "Thanks so much for the tomatoes. They look delicious and thanks for bringing Grant over."

Susan leaves—headed for her garden—with me still in my

robe. I pull open the screen door and step back in the house to get dressed before someone else shows up. In the suburbs no one drops in. Some developers are trying to make subdivisions like small towns. Garages and privacy fences aren't allowed. The houses sit close to the road, with front porches and wider sidewalks—all to encourage people to stop and visit—don't think the 'burbs are ready for that.

With the screen door closed and wooden door shut, maybe other visitors will get the message.

The top wooden stair meets sage green carpet in the hall. The same carpet flows throughout the bedrooms on the second floor. Cream wallpaper with tiny sage and pine-green stripes covers the hall, reflecting the light from the window at the end. The window looks out toward the river. The door to the right of the window leads to the master bedroom.

Jackson tried to talk me into taking the room on the front of the house so we could see the trains from bed, but Bryan pleaded his case for sleeping track-side. Thank goodness he won without me having to say a thing. Our room is painted soft green with windows on the side and back walls. Sliding doors from our room open onto a narrow deck that runs the length of the house and ends in stairs to the backyard. But right now, it doesn't look safe to me, so until Jackson looks closer at our bedroom deck, it's off-limits.

My clothes are still in boxes. I locate my shorts from yesterday and pull them on then throw on the first shirt found in the box at the foot of the bed. This summer's anxiety resulted in me losing about ten pounds, but the other extra twenty seem to be sticking around.

Coming out of our room, I stop and listen. Nothing from the third floor. Savannah's tower stairs are at the opposite end of the hall. She gets to sleep-in most all summer because, honestly, that's easier on me. The third floor, Savannah's castle, is open space with half-windows and a small bathroom.

Stacked in the hall in front of me are boxes of towels and sheets for the linen closet. "Might as well get the hallway cleared." Occasionally the boys' voices disturb my quiet work, but mostly the AC kicking on and off is my only company.

The linen closet is one of three closets in the hall. Unlike so many old homes, storage is not a problem in this house. Built-in cabinets and shelves line many of the rooms and downstairs there is a hall of rooms off the kitchen. The wing juts off from the main body of the house on an angle. With four rooms and two bathrooms, it would be a great place for a bed and breakfast. However, since that's at least, *at the very least,* two years away we have lots of room for storage.

An armload of empty boxes leads my way down the stairs. At the bottom, forward progress stalls when the front door flies open and Bryan and Grant storm across the living room. The front door still swings as they hit the back door in the kitchen. Yelling at them would do no good because the Norfolk & Southern engines blaring past my front windows claim center stage. Okay, that's one good point about the trains. They'll cover anything I don't feel like saying, or forget to say:

"'I did too tell you to take out the garbage...'"

"Oh, I told you it was your mother's birthday.' "

Confrontation is not my style. The trains and I might find a happy medium here.

The front door closes with a shove of my hip. Then, despite limited vision due to the boxes, wet towels in the living room floor are avoided on my way to close the kitchen door.

"Okay, why are the good towels from my bathroom wet on the floor?" Once the boxes are thrown in one of the extra rooms in the wing off the kitchen, I pick up the towels and walk through the kitchen holding them away from me. Out on the deck, I shake the towels and breathe a familiar smell. Lake water. Like all those days spent on the lake in East Tennessee as a kid. Yankee Candle will never scent a candle with this smell, but the musty mix of fish, mud and heat relaxes my shoulders. As much as I hated the spectacle of party weekends on the houseboat with my parents and their friends, I did fall in love with the lake. Tucked in a nook with a book, the party always carried on without me. Those days come back with each breath, nose deep in the folds. Then I plant my elbows on the thick cushion of towel and examine my new backyard.

The slope from the house to the river is gentle and the stretch of grass rolls into a green forest, which sways in the morning breeze. A weeping willow promises refuge behind its dancing curtain. My parents' neighbor, Rose, had a huge willow tree for climbing and hiding in when I was a child. This one may prove the perfect escape from drop-in neighbors.

Bugs in the meadow sing and birds swoop over the heat crinkled lawn. I close my eyes but fling them open as the boys run around the corner of the house.

"Wait, where are you going?" I ask before they can get away, or a train comes by.

"Mom, we...uh...we're going back down to the water."

"Well you can use these towels, but don't take any other of the good towels down to the water again, okay?"

"Can we take some food? We're starving."

"Okay, just don't make a big mess in the kitchen, okay? I'm still trying to get it straightened out."

The short conversation took them from the yard, across the deck and into the kitchen. They never stopped moving toward their goal. Maybe they can teach me how to get things done.

We all three enter the kitchen. "Boys, I'm going to town later, but I won't be gone long."

My words are cut short by my cringe when the doorbell rings. Wonderful—another drop in. The closed wooden door keeps me from seeing who's there.

After a quick march through the living room, I open the door and screen door for the older woman stationed there. My smile is tense and business-like, "Hello, can I help..."

"Good morning, I'm Mrs. Francis Marion Bedwell and I want to welcome you to Chancey on behalf of the Women's Historical Society."

The little woman reaches out her hand and I jump. She has on white gloves! White gloves talk to girls raised in the South. They say, "sit up straight, spit out that gum, quit giggling", and they say it so loud not even the advancing coal train lets me miss one word.

Weakly my fingers take her hand and shake it. She steps toward me, so I push the door open wider and motion for her to come inside. The train continues to clack but her voice carries over it—and she's not even trying.

"Thank you. We're thrilled to have you and your family for neighbors. I'm sure you'll do this lovely home justice."

I close the door and turn around to find she's already seated and looking very much at home in the center of the couch. Her white gloves rest on her lavender skirt as her gloveless hands unpin the straw hat from her hair. She lifts her hat and lays it on the coffee table next to empty pop-tart wrappers and nearly empty glasses of lukewarm milk.

I sink into the easy chair closest to the door, but then leap up. "Would you like a cup of coffee or some ice water or something?"

"No thank you, dear. Please sit down and tell me your *full* name?"

"I'm sorry, that's right. I'm Carolina Jessup..."

"And your maiden name, dear?"

"Yes, Butler."

"Wonderful, where are you from?"

"East Tennessee, near Knoxville."

"Oh, do you know any of the Bedwells there? My husband's family has a branch in the Sweetwater area. Bradford Bedwell was quite a well-known evangelist in that area shortly after World War II. Have you heard of him?"

Oh, Lord. More names. Small towns in the South run on names like the "It's a Small World" ride runs on mechanical dolls and grease. "I went to school with some Bedwells, but I don't know if they're the ones you're talking about." I start to settle back in my chair, but the white gloves catch me.

Her eyes brighten and she nods. Her white hair holds its weekly shampoo and set and doesn't move. "I'm sure they belong to us somehow. What's your mother's name?"

"Goldie Mann Butler." Might as well save her from asking mother's maiden name.

"Mann. Is she related to the Mann's in north Georgia."

"Could be, she's from Copper Hill."

"Really? My second cousin lives in McCaysville. I'll call her this afternoon and see who your mother is." The introductions concluded, she tilts forward and lifts both hands to form a steeple which she points toward me. "So, I want to welcome you to Chancey on behalf of the Women's Historical Society. We meet the second Monday of each month at 10 am in the museum. The committees meet at different times depending on their members' schedules and the committee's duties."

I try to say "thanks, but no thanks", but she sits tall, unsteeples her hands and cuts off my words by flashing her palms at me.

"We are quite busy now as the Tunnel Hill Civil War re-enactments will come up soon and we are determined to build on the activities they already have scheduled. We simply must not let other towns steal the tourists that should be coming to Chancey. It is simply not to be tolerated." She sits even straighter as she makes her speech.

"And your bed & breakfast will be quite a feather in our hat!" She picks up her gloves and actually swats my leg, "Collinswood thought they'd be opening theirs first, but you've beat them all!"

Now *I* was sitting up straighter. *My bed & breakfast?* Why did I let Bryan out unattended last night?

"Oh, Mrs. Bedwell, we're not sure about all that. It's just a dream for someday and probably won't even happen."

"Nonsense. You're the answer to our prayers. I've called a meeting for next Monday at which you can lay out your plans and we will assign a committee to aid you. The mayor is completely supportive." She clicks her tongue against her teeth, "It was all I could do to keep him from coming with me this morning." She picks up her hat, places it on her head, and pushes in the pins to hold it in place.

"Jed has been pushy ever since he won class president his freshman year at Chancey High." She pulls on her gloves as she locks steely eyes on me. "But don't worry, I won't let him push you around."

"Oh, okay, thanks," I say as she steps past me. I rise and follow her to the door.

"So, I'm sure you know where the museum is and we'll see you there at 10 am Monday. I'll let you decide when you are ready for a tour of your B & B, but I would like to get the tour on the calendar as soon as possible." She stops just as she reaches the porch, "You know this area was integral during the Civil War. General Sherman marched his men along these very tracks on his way to Atlanta. Many men gave their lives attempting to stop that advance and I wouldn't wonder if some lost their way home and still roam this area." She ends her conjecture by clamping her lips together and piercing me with a questioning look.

"Do you mean ghosts?" Horror dawns on me as I think back to my porch visitor and the gauzy looking thing at the edge of the woods.

Triumph lifts the corners of her mouth and she crisply nods, "Exactly. We will see you on Monday morning. You do understand any sightings of our poor lost boys from The War would greatly interest the historical society? Notification would be appreciated."

Feebly I nod and say, "Of course" while scoping the woods and weeds on the other side of the tracks. "It's nice to meet you, Mrs. Bedwell."

And she was gone. She could put those ninja people Bryan watches to shame with her stealth moves. Speaking of Bryan, he's going to need some good ninja moves when I get hold of him. As for ghosts? Nope, not thinking about that. The screen door swings shut and punctuates my voiced decision. "No ghosts. No way."

"So, why do people think you're doing this hotel thing now?" Savannah steps out of the shadows at the top of the stairs, making her way down as silently as she apparently had been sitting there listening.

"Guess Bryan mentioned it last night. Don't really know."

"Well, it's not happening until I leave for college. Hope you know that."

Someone has apparently died and the Princess now thinks she's Queen.

I close the front door and lean back against it, "Your Dad and I will do whatever we think is best."

"Oh, yeah, like you thought moving here was best? You're along for the ride just like me, except I get to leave in a couple years."

A train whistle blows as an exclamation point and sucks every bit of fight out of me until she sashays past in her cami top and pajama pants. A little of Mrs. Francis Marion Bedwell must still hang in the air because I stiffen my spine and say in tones clear enough to be heard over the passing train, "If we want to open a bed and breakfast tomorrow, we'll do it young lady, and you'll be washing sheets and flipping pancakes right beside me."

Savannah turns and stares at me.

I lift my chin, pivot in my pink flip flops and ascend the stairs. The true Queen has spoken.

# CHAPTER 4

Getting out of this Bed and Breakfast situation occupies my thoughts early Monday morning on my way to Mrs. Bedwell's specially called meeting of the Historical Women's Museum Club Society thing. Be firm, but don't stand out. Speak up, but not loudly. Just get in and out. Go home and get back to being anonymous. The word "no" sticks in my throat so usually I stay far enough removed to never be asked anything. I learned that growing up in the Butler Never-ending House of Fun. You can't be asked to show off your dive from the back of the houseboat or entertain the Cline's 12 year-old twins, if no one can find you.

Susan Lyles, Grant's mom, called yesterday to say she'd meet me in front of the gazebo in the park and walk with me to the museum. Did I mention the museum is in the old train depot? Or that Jackson thought opening the B&B as soon as possible was the greatest idea he's ever heard? Also, Savannah is no longer speaking to me?

See, there *is* a bright lining to this cloud.

I'm joking, kind of. We've never talked much, but this intentional silent treatment hurts, especially since Parker is spending this week at his Uncle's. We'll probably see him every night. She went over there yesterday and supposedly his Aunt and Uncle were there the whole time, but how do I really know that? Like my dad said once about me hoping to have my kids ready to make adult decisions by time they were 18. "Carolina, you don't have until they're 18. Once that driver's license is in their hands you don't really know where they are or what they're doing." And, honestly, I'm worried about them being at his Uncle's house, but what about the 40 miles between here and there? What about the hour-long walk they took down to the river? Where is the nearest convent? Do you have to be Catholic for your daughter to be a nun?

And why didn't all this drive me crazy when Will was 16? Those poor mothers of the girls he dated. Maybe I should write them apology letters.

"Boy, you're sure lost in thought." Susan leans toward me and waves her hand. "Planning what you're going to say at the meeting?"

"No, not really. Hopefully, that will come to me once we get in there. Can't stop thinking about Savannah and her boyfriend. Thinking, but mostly worrying." Our feet crunch on the gravel path to the depot.

"You might want to plan what you're going to say, because this is the biggest thing that's happened in Chancey since state playoffs last year. You're the main attraction. You even made the prayer requests during church yesterday."

"No way. The prayer requests?" My heart sinks, prayer requests spoken during the service are serious business in a small town. "But...but I don't have any idea how to run a B&B. I'm just going to tell them I'm not ready and they'll have to wait."

Susan raises her eyebrows, "And you say you've actually met Mrs. Francis Marion Bedwell? Good luck with that plan."

"What is her first name anyway?"

Susan stops walking and grins, "You're going to love this. Her family's greatest fame comes from Sherman taking over her family home as headquarters when he came through Chancey on his march to the sea in the Civil War. Her great-great-grandmother or something like that was a teen-ager and thought Sherman the most fascinating man she'd ever seen. She fell in love with him. In pure orneriness, she set it up so the family inheritance is dependent on every child being named after William Tecumseh Sherman, the most hated man in the South, well at least Georgia. Mrs. Francis Marion Bedwell's name is Shermania." Susan's scrunches up her nose like the word smells. "From the day she got married she has called herself by her husband's name. No one uses her first name. Everybody—even her husband—calls her 'Missus.' Hey, there's Laney, my sister. She can't wait to meet you."

Laney Connor and her family spent last week at Hilton Head so we hadn't met. However, in only a week I'd met more people than in all my years in the suburbs. We also had enough tomatoes to start our own ketchup factory. Let me tell you, Southern hospitality is alive and well in Chancey, GA.

Folks wave and call to Susan as we wait for Laney to catch up.

"Hey, so you're Carolina. Susan's told me so much about you." Laney's beauty queen hair bounces around her as she skips up to us.

Of course, grown women don't skip, but she's not walking and she's not running and she reminded me of a little girl. Deep brown curls swirling over her shoulders pick up shafts of light like she's under a spotlight. Blue as the delphiniums surrounding the gazebo behind us, her eyes reach out to grab my eyes, just as her hands close over mine. She moves close and then drops my hands as she hugs me.

"I hope you just love it here." Syrup seeps around her words and glistens in drops on her lips. She releases me and steps away.

I take a breath, shake my head and watch as Susan is enveloped in her own hug. Their mother had not been fair in dispersing of curves to her daughters. Susan reminds me of a Midwest map with straight roads intersecting at appropriate junctures. Laney is like a drive through the lush rolling hills of north Georgia leading to the rising mountains of Appalachia. Rising mountains which threaten to spill out of the white, button-up shirt. The shirt is knotted at her waist above a short denim skirt. Tanned legs make her white tennis shoes look whiter and the tiny silver ankle chain with a single blue stone winks at me as I force my eyes back to those blue eyes staring at me.

"Did I tell you Laney was Mrs. Whitten County last year and a runner-up in the Mrs. Georgia pageant?" Pride pours from

Susan. "Her Jenna is sure to be named Miss Whitten County at the fair next month."

Beautiful people ring my suspicious bell. I don't trust them. But Laney didn't cause my pretty person alarm to so much as ding.

Laney grabs her sister's arm and leans toward her, "Oh, shush. I want to hear about this B&B. I love Bed & Breakfasts. I always, *always* stay in one when we're in Savannah or Charleston. Are you going to have feather beds? Are you worried about the trains waking people up? Are you going to have a grand opening? Can I cut the ribbon?"

"You know, Laney sure is great at cutting ribbons and that would get you on the front page, you know." A little man steps from the sidewalk and inserts himself in our conversation. "I'm Charles Spoon, editor of the Chancey *Vedette*." He talks around the unlit cigar clenched in his teeth. As he studies Laney's greatest assets, her ribbon cutting hands I'm sure, Mr. Spoon pulls a business card from his shirt pocket.

He turns to me, searching for the assets I brought to town, but with a sigh and an upward glance, simply hands me his card. "I'd like to come out and take some pictures, before and after, you know. This is, you know, big news 'round here. So, you know, how have things been out there? Anything interesting?" He leans in a little too close and I step back.

"It's fine."

"You'll call if anything, you know, happens, right?" He's looking at me like I should know something.

"Well, you know, I'll let you know." Can't resist. You know.

"Okay, gotta get inside see if Missus is there yet." He scuttles off, kinda like a crab. He actually walks sideways.

Laney wraps an arm around one of mine. "We need to hurry if we're all going to sit together." She smells like peaches and I have to stop myself from leaning into the mass of curls lying on our shoulders and taking a deep breath.

Susan steps a little ahead of us and opens the heavy door leading into the depot. We enter the room where Jackson spent a Saturday afternoon last fall. I'd only ventured inside once that day to see if there was a bathroom. While he examined the Civil War and Railroad exhibits, I sat in the car reading a cozy English mystery. Everybody was happy.

When the kids were little we'd pile the coolers with lunchmeat, cheese, and fruit drinks. Put a loaf of Sunbeam bread and bag of Wise potato chips in a grocery sack and head out for the day. My job was to feed the kids, sit in the front seat, and nod in agreement that the hump yard was pretty amazing. Oh, what's a hump yard? Later. I need to concentrate on the meeting right now.

Two-foot-tall windows line the top of the thick walls and streams of morning light fill the air above our heads. Dust, decades of floor wax and lots of old stuff fill the space, the perfect setting for a small town museum and historical society. About 25 wooden folding chairs occupy the center of the room facing a podium and table. Behind the table and facing the audience are five chairs.

Mr. Spoon apparently located Missus seated in one of the five chairs. He's leaning over her, thrusting the corner of his note pad at her making some point. Her white glove magic isn't intimidating the editor. I turn to ask Laney what the deal is, but she herds me toward a middle row of seats. Everyone wants to talk to us as we scoot past the folks camping out in the end of the row chairs. Laney sheds her grace on all for both of us and Susan answers questions behind me. In the center of the row we finally settle into three chairs.

"Hey, Carolina." And suddenly it's obvious that sitting right in front of me is the answer to how everyone knows about the B&B. I owe Bryan an apology.

"Good morning, Retta." Retta Bainbridge, our realtor.

"So how's the house? Don't you just love it?" Retta wears the same outfit I saw her in the two other times we'd met. A royal blue polka-dot blouse and skirt set with at least seven strings of red beads hanging down her front. Her lipstick is just as red as her beads and she smells like gardenias—hearty, never-dying gardenias. "You're all moved in? I can't wait to hear what you have planned." She's talking loud so everyone *knows* we're best friends.

"Retta, we told you the B&B plans aren't for sure. And they definitely aren't happening anytime soon." I speak for all to hear, too.

"Aww, you're going to need something to keep you occupied out here and besides you don't want your daughter with too much time on her hands. Seeing as what you found in her purse." Retta, arches her eyebrows at me, glances at both Laney and Susan, then turns around.

Why did I tell her about that? So many years in the suburbs where people have their own lives and don't really care about yours made me careless. Higher personal boundaries are needed here.

I hate small towns.

Laney and Susan are doing that sister thing of communicating without speaking. The air vibrates around us. My hands are clammy, so while searching for something to say, I rub them on my khaki capris. Fortunately, Missus stands up and clears her throat

"Thank you for coming to this special meeting of the Women's Historical Society. We will still have next week's regularly scheduled meeting, so have your committee reports ready at that time. Today's meeting is to hear from our newest resident and her plans for the Cogdill house out at the railroad bridge. I'd like to..."

"Now, Missus, you know we ain't called it the Cogdill House for years." The portly young man in the blue oxford-cloth shirt and khaki dress pants seated toward the end of the table leans forward so he can see Missus as he addresses her.

However she doesn't look at him. She lifts her chin and stares straight ahead. "Jed, that's the most historical family that's lived there. It's only fitting we call it the Cogdill House."

Susan leans over to whisper in my right ear, "Cogdill is Missus' family name and after that Sherman stuff, it's taboo around here.

"The mayor's right, nobody's going to call it the Cogdill House. You might as well get over it," declares an old man in the front row. His bushy hair is white and red suspenders curve over his shoulders. He's angry and his accent is thick as peach jam.

Laney pats my knee, "That's Mister Missus."

"You just hush, FM. You aren't on the board. You aren't supposed to be talking." Missus flushes as she points a gloved finger at her husband. "Besides we all want to hear from our special guest."

"Don't be telling me to 'Hush'. We don't need no fancy motel in Chancey. It'll just bring in people who don't like the way we do things. Like this girl, here," he flings his thumb over his shoulder toward me. "She ain't been here a week and she's got everything all stirred up!"

Laney pats my knee again, but around me heads bob in agreement. I need to say something, "Wait a minute, I don't..." But the mountain of blue polka-dot polyester lumbers to a standing position in front of me and interrupts.

"The Jessup's are nice people. I handled the sale of the Varner house to them."

Susan whispers at me, "Varners were the mayor's wife's people."

Retta continues, "And they are moving out to the country because they've had enough of living in the suburbs with no one watching the children and them getting into who knows what. Mrs. Jessup gave up a good job, a *good* job with the Public Library to move out here and get to know her kids again after, well, a few problems. So she needs this business venture, because if they can't make payments on their home, we'll have it back again on the market. And you all know it'll just sit empty again." Heads nod around her.

Mine drops.

"And you know the only folks that are going to be interested in buying this particular house are gonna be outsiders. Since, well, you know."

My head jerks up at that. "Know what?" I mouth to Susan. Susan just shakes her head at me.

Retta pauses to let her 'you know' comment sink in and facial expressions change as folks come to terms with her words. "Mr.

Jessup works with the railroad and is going to be traveling a lot which leaves Carolina here," she turns and extends her hand toward the subject under discussion, me, "to take care of her children and this new business by herself. My Chancey would want to help this family. The Jessup family needs us. How can we turn our back on them?"

People actually applaud.

"Well, I have a couple of questions for Mrs. Jessup," growls the short, crab-like newspaper editor.

Missus speaks up, "Perhaps Mrs. Jessup should make her presentation first. Then we'll open the floor for questions." She darts her head toward her husband, "You hear that, FM? You're the floor." Then she nods at me and sits down.

Gripping the back of the metal folding chair in front of me, I slowly stand. "I'm not sure I have the answers you all want...."

Missus waves her hand at me. "Carolina, honey, you need to come up here to speak. Several folks have hearing aids and they need to be able to see your lips moving."

I step over Susan's legs and those of a young couple on the end of our row and walk to the front table.

"If you have any drawings or papers you can put them right here on the table," a woman in a Braves t-shirt and jeans sitting at the end says as I come around her.

"Okay, thanks." At the podium, my hands curl around the sides. That's pretty much all I remember from my public speaking class freshman year of college, holding on to something solid keeps your hands from shaking.

"Well, first of all, we are glad to be here in Chancey. Everyone's been real nice." I looked down to smile at Mr. Missus, but all I see is the top of his shiny head.

"As for a bed and breakfast, we don't even know if that's something we want to do at..."

"See, y'all've scared her off. Now Collinswood will beat us and they'll get the grant money," a man in the back catastrophically predicts.

"No, we're not scared off, we just...."

Missus put her hand on my arm, but speaks to the audience.

"That's good. See even with all this controversy the Jessups aren't scared off. They're just not the kind of people who can be rousted from their dreams by some stuck in the mud naysayers. Go on, Carolina."

"You see, my husband is a Rail Fan, his hobby is going around and watching trains and well, the railroad bridge by our house is just a great place to watch trains and so we came and visited last year. We went out on your walking bridge, and with the fall colors and the river, well it was just a very special afternoon. And then Jackson spent hours here in this very room looking over your collection." With nods to folks on both sides of me, I add. "You've done a wonderful job with your museum."

Prideful nods and smiles meet my statement. "When Jackson changed jobs we decided to move here and maybe someday open a bed and breakfast place for rail fans who want to watch the trains."

"Train watchers?" The lady in the Braves shirt at the end of the table waves her hand at me. "Why would people want to watch trains?"

"I've heard of this," the mayor answers. "Lots of towns have built platforms for these train people or even bridges so they can see the trains coming through. Folkston's is big business."

"But can't you just watch trains anywhere?" the woman at the table scowls at the mayor. He shrugs, then looks at me.

"Not really. Some places don't have many trains going through so you have to wait a long time. Some places, like Chancey, have several trains an hour so chances of seeing one are greater. Also two railroads have lines in this area, so there is even more traffic. And then some places have a greater variety of trains and engines."

"But the railroads are dying, aren't they?"

"Not really." How do I know all this? "The railroads went through some major downsizing several years ago and now are running more efficiently. And as gasoline prices rise, rail becomes an even better way to ship goods and even to move people." Interested faces encourage me to go on, "And the history of the railroad is attracting more attention, especially in places like Georgia where the railroad changed history during the Civil War." Jackson would be so proud of me.

Missus stands up next to me, "I say we form a committee to help the Jessups' however we can. All in favor, say 'Aye'." Aye's rise from around the room as Laney waves and winks at me. "All opposed, say 'Nay'." A couple nays rise from the people, but the ayes clearly carry.

To be involved in a victory like that shoots a thrill through me. We won. Wait, we won?

"So when will you be opening your doors?" asks the Braves fan at the front table. "I'd suggest the first part of September as that is when the big re-enactment in Tunnel Hill will be taking place."

"This September? Like, in a month and a half?"

Missus leans behind me, "Jed, do you see any problem with getting her business license or anything?"

"Nope, none a'tall. First of September sounds very doable." He beams at me and then hefts himself up from his seat. "Mrs. Jessup, we're thrilled to have you in our community. I'm Mayor Jed Taylor and here to help you achieve your dreams in any way. Any way at all."

Small talk flits through the audience, but Missus quiets it. "Okay, everyone settle down. Who wants to serve on the committee? Put your name on this clipboard. If you know anyone who couldn't be here but would like to help, put their name down. The board will select the chairman and officers for the committee at our board meeting Thursday. This meeting is dismissed."

Handshakes and congratulations warm the flush of victory through me again until there are only a couple people left and I realize what just happened. They're serious? Only people left are Missus and Charles Spoon and they're once again in a private conversation, back by the display cases against the wall. Both look serious and a little mad. I'll talk to her later and set things straight. In a daze, I leave the gloomy building and return to the bright sunshine of a July morning.

"Hey there she is, congratulations!" Susan and Laney's

energy levels run high. Susan's energy is efficient and controlled, like a runner. Laney reminds me of kids on the first day of kindergarten. My mouth hangs open and I want to demand a recount or a time machine, but they sandwich me between them and we clip down the gravel path toward the gazebo.

"Y'all want coffee? Let's go to Ruby's, okay?" Laney pulls her hair back in her hands and then lifts it off her neck. "It's going to be hot today. We should go swimming later."

"I think Grant was going to see if Bryan wanted to go swimming at your house this afternoon anyway. Savannah could come and meet the rest of the kids." Susan pulls her phone out of her shorts pocket. "Let me call and see if the older kids are going to swim today."

"Oh, I shouldn't make plans for Savannah. Her boyfriend is nearby this week. Umm, let me go call. My phone's in the car. But wait, what was Retta talking when she said people from here wouldn't buy our house?"

Susan sighs and her shoulders slump, "There's been talk this summer about a ghost along the river. No one's seen anything, but Charles, the newspaper editor, is obsessed with ghosts. He thinks he's one of those ghost hunters like you see on TV. He's been to Charleston, Savannah, anywhere ghosts are supposed to be."

Laney waves off Susan's explanation. "He's a kook, a bored old kook that needs to get a life. Now I'm going to Ruby's before all the old people get out of the meeting and take the good tables." Laney points across the street we're facing. "Just meet us in there. I'm not going to work today 'cause of those piles of laundry from vacation. So between washer loads, I'm hanging out at the pool this afternoon. So if y'all, or whatever kids, want to come over, that's fine."

We head off in separate directions. My car is parked across the tracks at my car; I unlock it and sit on the edge of the seat. The phone is too hot to hold, but wrapped in an old McDonald's napkin it's okay. However, it just lies in my hand. My attention drifts off. Why am I considering going to Laney's pool? Parties or get-togethers aren't my style. Things are not going according to plan. Where is my head? This will just encourage them to think I want to get together for cook-outs and talk on the phone and have coffee.

I should go home. By myself. Alone. Just me and the ghost.

The phone rings and I jump. Now it rings from somewhere on the floor of the van. "Great, where is it?" I push my hand around the gas pedal and finally find it over near the emergency brake.

"Hello?"

"Mom? Its' Bryan. Can I go to Grant's aunt's pool? He says we can walk. His mom called."

"I guess. We're all invited. Is Savannah there?"

"Are you going?"

"Maybe. Is your sister there?"

"Cool. Here she is." And he leaves the phone.

The two of them talk, but I can't hear what's said. After an audible exchange of "okays", Savannah lifts the phone.

"Hey. So Bryan says you two are going to a pool or something?" Doubt slows Savannah's words.

"He is. I'm not sure. You're invited, too. They have high school kids."

"Why are you invited?"

"Why not?"

"Yeah, right. A pool party is so you. Parker is here so maybe we'll go for a little while later. I'll check with him."

"Parker is there? Why is he there this early? Why didn't you tell me?"

"If you carried your phone, you'd know. I left you like a million messages. We're going out now. We'll drop Bry and the other kid at his house and they can show us where the pool is."

"I'll be home soon, you know."

"Whatever." And she hangs up.

Oh, to be back working at the library! Lots of books, lots of quiet—and limited phone calls from home. Okay, that sounds bad, but not knowing beats having the pictures now circling in my mind of them in every bed in the house.

I shove the phone in my pocket, throw the wadded up

napkin in the floorboard and step out of the car. Going home is a stupid idea.

# Chapter 5

Back across the tracks, the gravel path leads back to the gazebo. Straight beyond that on the other side of the park a row of antebellum houses stand, some run-down, others refurbished. At the flower garden surrounding the gazebo, I turn to my right, headed toward an old, weather-beaten row of stores huddled inside stern, dark-brick buildings. The depot where we had our meeting is literally behind me. Now, I'd really like to put what happened there out of my mind, except when I do, worries about Savannah and Parker take center stage.

So, I'll concentrate on the dark red buildings facing me. They're two-story and attached to each other. At each end of the row are old houses. Ruby's Café, my destination, anchors the middle.

Jackson wanted to stop in at Ruby's when we were here last fall. No way. I reminded him he's not from a small town and doesn't understand that the people in there wouldn't leave us alone. They'd want to know everything about us. Waitresses in small towns are the nosiest people in the world and they're proud of it.

However, I willingly walk into Ruby's to keep from having to go home.

Four tables, just like the one my grandmother had in her kitchen, with white glitter-sprinkled tops and rimmed in shiny chrome fill up the middle of the floor. The sides of the room are lined with booths. Not tall private booths, but booths with short backs so everyone in the place can be seen. Turquoise vinyl covers the booth seats. The chrome-rimmed chairs around the tables have seats and backs in either red or yellow. Along the back is a counter with padded stools in front of it, also in red or yellow and rimmed in three-inch chrome. There is no restaurant décor, just what is. My grin won't stop. I've eaten in so many places that spent a lot of money to look like this.

Susan waves from a center booth. "So, Bryan and Grant are at my house now. I told them they needed to weed at least two rows of beans, if they want to go swimming later."

"Who's weeding beans? Bryan?"

"Yeah, Grant will show him what to do. The kids all have to do an hour of garden work every day. Of course, they wait until it's hot and then they complain about the heat, but that's their choice. It won't kill 'em."

"Shoot. I send my kids over there to weed a couple times a week just so Susan'll give me free veggies. You won't catch me putting in a garden." Laney pats the seat in the booth next to her. "Here sit down."

What? Kids weeding gardens? Do the lawn maintenance companies know about this? Aren't there union rules somewhere about teenagers doing yard work? I slide in beside Laney. "You know, I forgot about doing yard work growing up."

Susan laughs, "That's why we had kids, isn't it?"

But I pause and think about my friends back home. Everyone pays someone else to do their lawns. And gardening is a hobby, an expensive pastime.

Susan stammers in my silence, "I'll send Bryan home with a bag of beans, so he'll not be working for free."

"No, it's not that. I just forgot about kids working, chores and stuff. Not much of that back in the 'burbs." I turn over my cup as Susan lifts the carafe to pour.

Laney takes a quick gulp from her cup and sticks it out for a refill. "Janie says she ran into you all at the grocery store Sunday and your daughter was real nice."

"Sunday? It must've been when Savannah was looking at the magazines. She didn't tell me she talked to anyone."

"Janie checked you all out. She's at the register."

"But her name was Angie and, uh, she well...." How do I say there's no way that girl is your daughter?

"That's her. She changed her name back in fifth grade and it stuck, well with everyone but my side of the family. Her whole name is Angela Janelle, but Angela is my husband's mother's name, so I called her Janie." Laney grinned and shrugged, "Angela, Tommy's mother, is kind of out there and Janie adores her. So, in fifth grade, you know when the girls all want new names? Well, Janie renamed herself Angie."

"And your other daughter's name is Jenna, right?"

"Yep, no change there. So, anyway, Angie said Savannah is nice. Pretty, too."

"Y'all eating anything?" The woman standing at our table only has a dish cloth in her hand."

"Ruby? You're taking orders now?" Laney's glossy lips part in a perfect "O" and she bats her eyelids like she's in a *Flirt like Scarlett O'Hara* contest. Maybe she and I were switched at birth, because this is the daughter my parents deserved.

"Yeah, do you want anything?" Ruby darts a smirk at Laney but directs her question to me.

"Um, I don't know. Haven't even look at the menu." But there's no menu in sight.

"Don't need a menu. Are you hungry?"

"A little, I guess."

"'kay, you two want anything?"

Susan lifts her hand and begins to say "No."

Laney reaches across the table and slaps at Susan's hand. "We all want muffins and honey butter." The beauty queen waves a dismissive hand at Ruby. "That's all." She then pulls the metal napkin holder toward her and peers at her reflection on the side.

"'kay," Ruby says, but she just stands there, glaring at Laney. After shifting back and forth for a minute she blurts out, "You can look at that all you want but you ain't gonna find no manners in there. Least none for you. Beauty queen my foot, ain't you ever heard, 'Beauty is as Beauty does?'"

"What do you want me to do? Say 'please' and 'thank you'?

Is that gonna make you any sweeter? You're not looking for pleasantries, you're just nosy."

Susan jumps in, "I'm sorry Ruby. Have you met Carolina Jessup? She's new in town and just bought the house out by the railroad."

"Well, nice to meet you, Mrs. Jessup. Hope you'll stop in sometime when I'm not so busy and we can chat." She reaches out for my hand, shakes it, and then turns, head high, toward the back.

Susan shakes her head at her sister. "You're awful. You know she's going to tell Mama, again."

"Aw, it was funny." Laney turns to me. "Ruby never steps from behind that counter. Never. She usually insults me from behind it 'cause she hasn't liked me since I took Shaw from her precious daughter, Jewel. Those two were the only ones surprised. Everyone knew I was going to marry Shaw." Laney picks up her cup and grins. "She just wanted to meet you. I couldn't resist messing with her."

"Well, Mama won't think it's funny. You just like knowing you're the topic of conversation at their circle meetings."

"Circle meetings?"

Susan looks at me, "It's just an old-fashioned name for the women's groups at church. There are three groups that meet once a month and then all of us get together four times a year for a luncheon. What church are you going to?"

Another thing about small towns in the South, they don't know it's rude to ask where you're going to church. We didn't go to church before and no one noticed, but here they're going to. I know the game and don't want to play. However, there's a strong likelihood we'll be joining a church in the next month because what I want and what I do usually have nothing to do with each other.

"Not sure. Maybe we'll visit with you all this week?"

"Oh, you're Methodist?"

"Sure. Is that your church too?" I ask Laney.

"Nope. Shaw goes there and the kids go there. But not me. I'll probably go over to Dalton to the Catholic Church. I like

50

things to be orderly and dignified. Besides, everyone doesn't know me there."

Susan rolls her eyes as she swats at her sister. "She's a liar. Don't listen to her. She belongs at First Methodist with the rest of us. She's just taking a break."

Ruby approaches our table with a basket the size of a watermelon. Red-checked cloth hangs over the sides with heaps of muffins piled inside—brown muffins, yellow muffins, muffins with nuts on top or oozing melted chocolate chips. Every single one looking like it has my name on it.

"I brought you an extra-large basket so you can take some home. My muffins are famous and if you want to buy them for your inn we can work out a deal." Ruby smiles and sets the basket right under my nose.

"Famous? What makes you think your muffins are famous?" Laney queries in all innocence.

But Ruby doesn't miss a beat, "Shut up. Just let me know Mrs. Jessup."

The basket has my attention, but she's waiting. "They sure smell good. Thanks. I'll let you know." That must've been good enough because she turns and hustles back to the counter, ignoring the pleas for more coffee from other customers along her way.

"Wow, out from behind the counter twice in fifteen minutes." Laney bats her eyes at me. "You're my hero."

"So, you're opening up first weekend of September? What happened to telling them you weren't ready?" Susan asks as she pulls the basket to her.

I lift a ginger-colored one off the top while they are still in my reach. "Who knows? And here I sit drinking coffee and eating muffins like everything's right with the world." The rich muffin breaks open in my hands and steam rises from the moist inside. "Wow, this does smell good."

"Her muffins are fabulous and famous in this whole part of Georgia." Laney says as she breaks open one of the dark, rich ones studded with melted chocolate chips.

"But you said…"

Susan laughs, "She's a liar. I told you. You can't listen to her about anything."

Laney just shrugs at her sister's diagnosis.

"So was the lie that they are famous or not famous?"

"They're pretty famous. The truth just gets so boring, don't you think?"

"Ignore her," Susan says again. "So, the Bed & Breakfast?"

"No way. Not happening. Jackson is never going to be home with this job. Savannah and Bryan start school in a couple weeks and they're no help anyway. I don't have any idea where to start."

Susan's eyes brighten as she leans across the table, a cinnamon-brown muffin in her hand. "We want to help. We talked about this all weekend and we want to be your partners." Susan pinches off tiny bites of muffin and puts them in her mouth while she talks but the pieces are so small they just disappear and don't interfere with her talking. It's like watching a mother bird feed her babies.

Susan continues, "I'm the youth leader at church and can get all kinds of kids to help with the grunt work. Painting, mowing, cleaning. All that stuff. We may have to pay them some, but we might be able to get away with feeding them and having a party or two down at the lake. Laney is an accountant so she can help with all the money things. Plus she's the town treasurer so she has an in with the business licenses or whatever you need. But you heard the mayor—those won't be a problem."

Laney in all this time hadn't taken a bite of her muffin. She cut it open with the butter knife and then buttered each half. (Yes, she buttered a chocolate-chocolate chip muffin) She wipes the crumbs off her fingertips and then picks up a half, but before she moves it toward her mouth she pauses, "I'm sick of working for the town. I'd love to work for a private business." She sinks her perfect teeth into the muffin, eyes closed and cheeks flushed.

I'd buy whatever she's selling. My head bobs in agreement. But wait, the town treasurer is a known liar who wants to be *my* treasurer? Too late, I've nodded.

"Great! Let's get this down." Susan pulls a notebook and pen from off the seat beside her. "Getting a license to serve food is the hardest thing and I found one option is to bring the food in, like muffins from Ruby. You don't have to serve a full breakfast."

"That's an idea." *Maybe one of those golden yellow muffins next.*

"What are the bathrooms like? How many rooms do you have?"

"They're okay, I think. We've not really paid much attention to that part of the house. We could go look at it sometime. What is this muffin? It's got cheese and bits of, maybe bacon?"

Laney leans over, "I think that's the cheese and bacon muffin. Is there something like cornmeal in it?"

"Yeah."

"Isn't that good? Did you put butter on it? It's even better with butter."

Why not? I slice off a hunk of butter with my knife and lay it the other half of my golden muffin.

"What was it that man said in the meeting about a grant?" The butter is already melting on my muffin so that piece gets popped into my mouth.

When I look up, Susan is nodding at her sister.

Laney sighs, "Okay. It's supposed to be a secret until sometime this fall, but of course, everyone in town knows about it. One of the carpet families from Dalton is going to award $500,000 dollars to a town that is actively pursuing tourists. I've been studying up on applying for grants all summer. One major thing Chancey lacks is any overnight accommodations. Believe me, by time I get through with the application it's going to look like we went down to Marietta, found you, and moved you up here in our minivans." She laughed, "That's why folks keep calling you the answer to prayer."

The cheesy bacon muffin didn't look dry, so why is my mouth suddenly like Lake Lanier during the drought? This isn't good. I'm not dealing with bored country folk that will lose interest as soon as football season starts (which had been my latest hope.)

Susan is picking apart another muffin, which apparently

requires her diligent focus. However Laney's blue eyes slant in my direction like a girl on a first date watching the guy's hand on the arm rest next to hers.

"This is bad. I'm not getting out of this, am I?"

Laney grins and shakes her head, "Nope."

Susan finally looks up. "Do you really want out of it?"

And Jack Butler, my showboat Dad, jumps up from the bottom of my stagnant gene pool and blurts, "It might be fun!"

*What!* My hand flies to cover my mutinous mouth.

Laney leans over and pokes my side, "I knew you'd get into it once you realized there wasn't a choice. It'll be a blast. Now, if we're going to your house to check it out we need to hurry. I plan on being in the pool by 2 pm sharp."

Susan wipes her mouth with her napkin, lays it on the table, and closes the notebook. "Okay, let's get going. You all go on and I'll get the bill.

First coffee and now they're coming over? This is out of control and all with my insane blessing. This has to stop before these people nominate me for Mrs. Congeniality.

But how to uninvite them when I never invited them in the first place?

However, something stirs deep in my stomach. Butterflies? Excitement? Suddenly, the image of my mom on those Fridays packing for the houseboat weekends came to mind. She'd be rushing around, packing boxes and coolers. Lists lying everywhere reminding her of menus and guests. Mom completely frantic and worried and, yes, happy.

My sigh goes unnoticed, "What do I owe?"

Laney scoots and forces me to move out of the booth, "Nothing. You got us free muffins." She stands and pulls on her skirt to make sure it's down where it belongs after sliding across the booth. She shouts toward the counter, "Hey Ruby, I'll bring the basket back later."

"It was good to meet you, Mrs. Jessup." Ruby hollers.

Shouting across a room full of diners seems uncouth. I wave and semi-shout, "Thanks."

"Let me know if you want to order some muffins for your

inn."

With a nod, I rush out the door. Ever heard, out of the pan and into the fire? I'm so there.

# Chapter 6

Morning mist rises off the river and above the trees to blanket the bottom of our backyard. As the hill climbs toward the house, the fog weakens. The grass has collected the moisture into tiny beads of water running down each blade. Soon the sun will top the trees on my right and turn the lawn into a valley of rainbows and dripping cobwebs. My coffee is lukewarm, but I curve my hands around the mug, as if it has warmth to give. The mountain mornings are cooler than back in Marietta, but it's energizing. Slippers keep my feet warm and my head rests back against the chair cushion for a few more minutes of relaxation. Once the sun is over the tree tops, the back deck will quickly become scorchingly hot. It is August in Georgia, after all.

We're into the third week of work on the Bed & Breakfast. A dozen teenagers descended every day the first two weeks and I must've cooked five hundred hot dogs. Our house back home was never a hang-out for the kids. They're just so loud and hungry. But Susan keeps them in line and Laney is like their big sister. It took a good week and a half before I got used to coming into the kitchen and seeing a stranger rooting around in my refrigerator. And then school started.

Savannah and Bryan don't seem to be missing their old school. That's a surprise. Savannah's old friends came up several times and decreed the guys, especially Laney and Susan's nephews Ricky and Ronnie, hot. The girls slept over here several nights and were great when it came to picking out paint colors and coming up with decorating ideas for the B & B.

Parker spent the final weeks of his summer at his uncle's, so he hung around here almost every day. Believe it or not I like him. He's funny, and polite. He wants to attend Georgia Tech and study robotics. And he is awfully cute. Of course, the day Savannah found Parker and me in the kitchen laughing was the day she started being cold to him. Who knew it was that easy?

And vampire Angie from the grocery store really is Laney's daughter, whom she calls Janie. Angie/Janie and her sister Jenna are Laney and Susan all over again. Brick house versus summer camp cabin. Jenna's hair is golden brown but fills the room like her mom's and her eyes are as startlingly blue as Laney's. Her personality? As big as her hair.

A problem has emerged, however. Chancey finds itself with two queens—Jenna and Savannah. Kinda like that fight over in England a few hundred years ago between Elizabeth and Mary. I don't think anyone would be surprised to have this battle end in a beheading either. However, like true daughters of the South, their hatred for each other can only be measured in their gagging sweetness. The hugs, kisses and compliments that fling between the two are like mushy, rotten potatoes wrapped in cotton-candy. And the rest of us, being true Southerners, are enjoying the show. Especially Angie. Savannah's comical, and semi-evil, prediction of their friendship has come true.

Who knew teen-agers could be this fun? Me, Laney, and Susan sit back and watch them like this is our own series on *Lifetime*.

But since the kids went back to school, I'm kinda on my own. Susan volunteers at the school and is the paid youth director at church so she's busy getting everything back in motion after the summer. Laney got an old lap top from her husband's dealership and she's setting up files for the B & B. She's also busy shopping for Jenna's wardrobe for the Miss Whitten pageant at the county fair in September. Oh, yeah, and she has her job as town accountant. When she finds time to do that no one knows, but apparently she's good.

There's the sun. It's been creeping up behind the trees, throwing sparkling kisses and flirting with me through the leaves, for twenty minutes. Clearing the last branches, it empties a wave of gold over the field and fills every dewdrop with light. Like discarded hankies, tiny webs become visible as each thread is highlighted in silver. I'm rereading Anne of Green Gables so my thrill at the beauty of nature is heightened. To be a kindred spirit with Anne means to find kisses in morning sunshine and delicate, cobweb hankies scattered on the lawn. Wish I'd brought my book out to the deck. However, getting up to get my book means I should start my day.

My shoulders drop with a deep breath. Once the children are in school, Monday mornings are Happy Hour for stay-at-home moms. The house generally looks like the Rolling Stones used the place for an after party, but there is blessed silence. I close my eyes and soak in the warmth of the morning rays, which will shift from comfortable to hot quickly. God's way of telling me to go clean up the house.

Jackson was in town all last week so he worked every evening on the things the youth didn't get done. We have three rooms ready and we'll open the first weekend after Labor Day. The rooms, of course, have names. Railroad names. After a week of painting all the ceilings in the B & B wing, Ronnie Troutman, Susan and Laney's nephew who is not the quarterback decided the rooms should be named after famous passenger trains. Ronnie wants to work on the railroad and is fighting with his dad about going to college or going straight to work when he graduates in the spring. Susan says the first time the boy willingly sat down at a computer was looking up names for the rooms. So Ronnie came up with a list—he decided on his own that the trains were to be American trains which upset Laney who already had great plans for the "Orient Express" room.

We all voted on our favorites, Will even e-mailed his opinions from his apartment in Athens. Jackson, however, lobbied for veto power saying he got to make all the train related decisions. Whatever.

Our first three rooms are "Orange Blossom Special," "Southern Crescent," and "Chessie." Jackson wielded his veto power on "The City of New Orleans" saying it was nothing more than a glorified commuter train. Susan was vehement that the song alone made it a worthy choice, but Jackson said the railroaders coming to stay would expect "dirty windows, no beds, and constant stops" if they stayed in the "City of New Orleans." So, his veto stands. Susan is determined to fit it in somewhere, so stay tuned for that battle.

Ronnie wrote full reports on each of the names up for adoption and over lunches of grilled hot dogs, Cheetos, and Cokes, we discussed and decided on decorating schemes.

The cordless phone lying on the table rings. Mom always calls early in the morning. I push the button. "Hi. Thought you might call before you left."

"Your Daddy says we'll be ready to hit the road as soon as he gets the water tank full. But, I say we're waiting until traffic thins out. We'll have to go right through Knoxville. Figure if I'm on the phone with you he'll not badger me to leave."

"Where are you staying tonight?"

"We'll be in Akron to see your aunt Lucille tonight, so we'll just be at a small park there. I'm going to love having my own bed in the motor home instead of having to stay in everyone's houses. That just wears me out."

"And when do you think you'll get back?"

"Not 'til late October. Your Daddy has it laid out, but that's all we've talked about for days. So, no more. Finish telling me about your rooms. You told me about the cat one and the dark one when we talked last week. What's the fruit one like?"

"Mom, it's the Orange Blossom Special, you know, like the train?"

"That's right, wait a minute, let me freshen up my coffee. I'll be right back."

Mom thinks we'll disconnect if she walks around with their cordless phone, so she always sits right beside the phone cradle. I take a sip of coffee and wait.

"Okay, I'm back. First tell me about the train itself and then the room. I can't believe we have this trip with the camping club scheduled or we could head south to see y'all. It sounds like such fun! Okay, start talking. I want to picture it all."

Thinking of Mom sitting with her eyes closed so she can concentrate makes me chuckle. She loves details and it's been fun filling her in on every step of the B&B. If not for their camping trip, they'd be right here in the middle of everything.

"Well, the Orange Blossom Special traveled from New York to Miami in the twenties. It specialized in taking wealthy New Yorkers to the Florida sunshine and that clientele expected luxury travel. They even had chefs onboard to cook the meals."

"Oh my. Can't you imagine eating a gourmet meal in one of those fancy dining cars?"

"And everything was fresh. They made special stops for cut flowers and fresh fish. Maybe I should try and have fresh flowers in that room."

"It would get expensive. Maybe look for some nice silk ones. Now you know about the song, right?"

"Oh yes. The kids found several versions and made a cd for us to play in the room. They like Johnny Cash singing it so much that a couple of them downloaded it onto their ipods."

"Last month at the bluegrass gathering up at Cades Cove we must've heard it a dozen times. Every group played it. Tell me about the room."

"We painted it a soft peach—the color of a summer sunset according to your granddaughter. The white gauzy curtains we tied back with little nosegays of silk citrus leaves and orange blossoms. One whole wall is lined with windows and the seat below the windows is cushioned. Did I tell you about the comforters we found on Ebay?"

"You and your Daddy with that Ebay. No, you didn't tell me. What did you find?"

"Whole sets of white bed linens. Must've been a hotel or something that went out of business."

"But white's going to get dirty."

"The price was so good we got several sets, plus I can bleach out stains. We've found colorful covers, afghans, and pillows to keep them from looking so stark in the rooms."

"Now that's a good idea. Looks like your Daddy is coming, so I can't talk long. He's itching to get on the road. We'll meet up with the rest of the club on Friday at Niagara Falls. He's glad we don't have to wait on them to leave, law, some of them take forever."

"Okay, the only thing left to tell you about is the quilt. It's actually a map of Florida. It looks old, but Jackson picked it up for me at a roadside stand outside Panama City. Any quilt, any size is only $29.95. I saw the quilts when we down there at spring break so when Jackson was in that area last week I asked him to stop."

"Is it one of those that looks like a 1950's map with oranges, girls on water skis, palm trees, and alligators? I love those."

"Yep, that's it."

"Well, honey, 'sounds like you're practically ready to open. Why are you waiting until after Labor Day? You're going to miss all the summer travelers."

Why am I waiting? It is almost finished and empty rooms won't help our bank account. But open sooner? A shiver runs down my back. Through the phone I hear their front door open and close. "Tell Daddy I said hi."

She pulls the phone away from her mouth a little. "Carolina says hi. Are we ready?" She speaks up to me, "Honey, we're ready to go. You know your Daddy doesn't like to use our cell minutes for chatting, but call if you need anything. And I think after hearing about all three rooms I want the orange room when I come down there."

We hang up and I smile as I think of them out on the road. Their motor home is as luxurious as the Orange Blossom Special. Maybe Angie can make some cute pillows to match their home-away-from-home. I never know what to get them for Christmas.

Turns out, Vampire Angie is quite a seamstress. She stalked the clearance table in the fabric section at Wal-mart for pillow fabric and sewed them for every room. All the girls helping us want pillows for their rooms so she's built up a nice little business.

While Angie coordinated the bedding and pillows, Savannah and Parker haunted thrift stores and junk stores for furniture.

Of course, we bought new mattresses and box springs, but everything else they drug home in the back of my van.

We're leaking money like those dikes leaked water in New Orleans after Katrina. All the profit from the sale of our old house is gone. This has to work with no more money pumped into it. Has to.

Time to leave the deck, the sun is no longer kissing and flirting. Missus invited me to her home for lunch today. Wonder if her husband will be there? Mister Missus scowls when he sees me. Missus acts like I'm her long lost daughter.

After pushing up from the chair, I pick up my coffee cup and phone and enter the coolness of the kitchen. Movement in the front yard catches my eye as a train blows past.

I didn't even hear it.

Missus' house is one of those restored antebellums adjoining the park downtown. Needing a little walk to calm my nerves, I leave my van beside the railroad tracks on the other side of the park. My white flats crunch on the gravel walkway that crosses beside the gazebo. Thick shade reminds me of the morning coolness. Soon the huge trees will be turning orange, red, and gold.

*Oh, my goodness, I'm going to be living in the mountains this fall.* The thought astounds me and brings me to a halt. On our autumn trips to the mountains for apples and a picnic, I've often envied the people living in the mountains during September, October and November. How did the fact that we are now those envied people not occur to me before?

Chill bumps run down my arms and I remember the sermon yesterday at Susans and Laney's church. The pastor talked about the lilies of the valley and how God takes care of them without them having to worry. That God wants us to relax and let him work in our lives to bring his plan together. Could God be watching me right now saying, "I knew if you ever looked around you'd realize I had a plan?"

Okay, that's just a little too creepy for me. I shake my head and start walking again. I'll be sure and say "thanks" tonight if I pray. I tuck that away on my internal 'things to do' list, then lift my eyes and see where I'm having lunch. My mind darts back to last fall and that first visit to Chancey.

Jackson parked almost exactly where I parked today and we walked through the park. Standing in the gazebo we looked out at the little town. The old depot with its high brick walls topped by little windows and its steep pitched roof situated near the tracks; the line of shops, with Ruby's cafe right in the middle. That was when he'd suggested lunch at Ruby's and I'd explained the facts of small-town waitressing to him. And then we turned to look at the line of four homes sitting on a slight incline, overlooking the park, town and even the railroad.

The house on the end near the row of shops was, and still is, shabby. Bushes pushed overgrown limbs up against the house as if embarrassed at the peeling paint. A faded wreath of orange, yellow, and bronze silk mums hung on the front door so all didn't appear lost, but the battle was not going in a good direction.

The other three houses sat proudly, unabashedly pulling for the corner house to join them in their parade of fineness. Leaning against Jackson, as he leaned on one of the gazebo posts, I gazed at the tall, much-loved homes with wide porches and fresh colors emphasizing intricate carpentry. There's an octagonal window centered above one front door; stain-glass trim around the windows of another house; and deliberate carvings on the porch posts of the third house. My voice dropped to a whisper, "What must it be like to live in one of those houses?"

Now on my way to a lunch appointment in the middle house my next statement to him comes to memory. "It would be wonderful just to be invited to dinner in one of them."

Am I living my dream and fighting it every minute?

Contentment tries to settle over me, but a little struggle holds it at bay until I have time to understand it more. Lunch with Missus requires all my concentration. I've simply got to figure out a way to stop Missus from running over me like a University of Georgia running back against Vanderbilt's defense.

Across the street, the path beckons me up the Bedwell's front walk, lined with short walls of perfectly trimmed boxwood bushes. At the steps, tall snapdragons, in shades of lemon, cream and blush, reach up in welcome. Pots of pachysandra and white impatiens line the edges of the shiny gray porch floor. The salmon-colored front door boasts brilliant brass fixtures. With the chime of the doorbell, footsteps can be heard. Crisp footsteps.

Shoot, I bet she's wearing heels. After debating what to wear, Susan said for me not to worry because I'd be fine whatever I wore. Laney said not to worry because whatever I wore with Missus wouldn't be right.

My hands brush at imaginary lint on my navy and white striped skirt and navy polo. At least, there's the hostess gift. *Wait, where's the gift?* Oh, great. The gift is in my car, which is across the park. But, too late, the door opens.

Missus stands there with her hand on the door knob. She's wearing mauve pumps and a deep-rose linen suit. The suit does have three-quarter sleeves and the blouse underneath is white with cutwork, so it's not too dressy. Dressier than anything I've worn in years, but not too bad.

"It's so good to see you, Carolina. Please come in."

"I had a gift for you, but apparently forgot it in my car."

"Well, lucky that you wore those *darling* flats since you parked so far away."

"I just wanted a little walk in the park before lunch."

"Scared of her, aren't you?" Mister Missus booms from the parlor to my right. "Thought a little walk would boost your courage?" He comes around the half wall separating the foyer from the room. His baggy gray pants are held up with suspenders, strapped over a white dress shirt. His glasses rest on the end of his nose. He holds a newspaper unfolded and stretched out in front of him.

"FM, you are not invited to lunch today. You need to go take a walk."

Missus has turned away from me but I can tell her words are pushed out between taut lips.

"I've decided I don't need no invitation to lunch in my own house." He folds up his paper and tucks it under his arm. "Believe I'll just go set myself a place so I can watch the show."

*There's going to be a show?*

Missus whips back towards me. "Please come in."

My smile and first words congeal with my first step over the threshold and view of what hangs at the end of the hall. Along the sides of the hall are entrances into the parlor on my right, a double-door entrance to a formal dining room on my left and straight ahead is the kitchen. The foyer is two stories tall and on the wall above the kitchen door is a life-sized, or bigger, full body picture of Missus wearing a crown. She's young, maybe 18, but it's obviously her. Obvious not only from the resemblance, but from the way my host openly admires herself.

"I was the first Miss Whitten County."

"She sure was something, wasn't she?" her husband has come back and stands underneath the picture staring with us.

Never has there been an uglier beauty queen. Her blonde hair is pulled tight in a bun and her neck is stretched like an old turtle's. Her complexion is pasty white and the only make-up is blood-red lipstick. She is way better looking now, but I don't think that's an observation I should relate.

"I know what you're thinking," Missus declares.

My frozen wide eyes dart looks between Mister and Missus, their eyes now focused on me.

"Grace Kelly," they say together.

*Are they blind?* I cover my throat with my hand and stare in concentration at the picture. "Exactly."

Mister turns to gaze at the picture again and his voice becomes husky. "She stole my heart up there on that stage, 1954."

"FM was a judge at the pageant. Now, wouldn't you love to have this hanging in your house?"

"What?" Horrified, I turn to her.

"Well, not this one of course. One like it of Savannah. She is destined to be the next Miss Whitten County."

Laughter bursts out. "You're kidding, right?"

Missus pulls herself up even taller. "I assure you, this is no joking matter."

Mister tucks his thumbs through his suspenders and swells his chest with a deep breath. He releases it saying, "And you won't even have to pay me to vote for your daughter like Shermy's dad did."

Let the show begin.

"I'm keeping her stupid hostess gift," I say to the empty car. Dropping into the driver's seat and slamming the door makes me feel a little better. My mood upon entering that house was so pleasant due to my reminiscing in the park. Then they ambushed me with talk about Savannah being a beauty queen. And to find out that while this was *my* first time in their house, apparently my daughter is a regular guest there.

Groans accompany my drive home. Whatever concessions I made to Missus in regards to opening the B & B can only be imagined. All my thoughts centered on my next conversation with Savannah. Like she needs a real crown to think she rules the world.

My foot leaps to the brake when the crossing bells greet my roaring arrival at our driveway. Dust swirls from my sudden stop as the crossing arm descends to block me from my home. The advancing black engines have the Norfolk Southern rearing horse on their noses. The "pony engines" are Bryan's favorite.

As cars loaded with new automobiles fly by I see through them that there are people on my front porch. Could be the mayor, and maybe Laney? Laney knew no one would be home, so what's the deal? Finally the train ends and I cross the tracks.

After some maneuvering the van is finally parked so Laney's car and the mayor's new pick-up aren't blocked.

"Here are your first reservations!" Laney yells.

She has on a light blue cotton sweater that hugs her chest. It hangs loose at her waist and she is wearing white capris that make her behind look bigger than usual. Wish that made her look worse than usual, but it doesn't. She meets me at the top step of the porch and leans over to hug me. Now Laney likes to hug people, but this time I'm sure she's doing it so Jed thinks he's going to get a look up her short sweater. And he *is* looking.

"Jed and his whole family are going to spend Labor Day weekend here!"

Jed grins and nods his big, red head, "Laney convinced me it would be a great PR move and since it's free...why not!"

"But we won't be open until the next weekend."

"Oh, shush," Laney says with a wave of her hands. "It'll be fine."

"Well, I don't want to bring my brother and his family all the way here from Jacksonville if things won't be ready. His wife is, uh, rather, uh, picky." Jed's pink face creases in doubt. "Her daddy is in the Florida Senate, you know. She's used to the best."

Laney crosses the porch to stand in front of Jed. "Jed, we'll be ready. You know I wouldn't let you down, right?" She then pulls her arms up to gather her cloud of hair into a pony tail. Of course her sweater rises.

A tan midriff in his face, Jed blinks. "That's true. That's true." He stands up and works his way around Laney who doesn't move an inch. "So, let me know the details. Thanks, Carolina. See you later, Laney."

He moves quickly for his size and as his truck turns around to cross the tracks, Laney sits down.

"Oh, have a seat Car'lina."

"Should I applaud your show?" I snarl and pull a rocker closer to her.

She grins. "Guys never change, do they?"

"Do they teach those moves at cheerleader camp? 'Cause we sure didn't cover that in the literary club."

"Well, some of it is natural, you know. You can't teach everything."

"You've obviously learned enough. It's not going to work on me though. Why did you make reservations a week early and why aren't we charging for it?"

"Like Jed said, PR. It'll be Jed and his family. You don't think he'll bring his kids, do you? Then there'll be his brother Gideon, Gideon's wife, and Jed's parents, who live in North Carolina. They lived in Chancey for years. So they'll need all three rooms."

Laney jumps up, "Well I'm going to go talk to Ruby about muffins for those mornings. You need to figure out what you'll have for them to do at night, okay?"

"What do you mean at night?"

She shrugs as she swings down the steps, "Like a bonfire, or a cook-out, or picnic in the park, you know. You'll figure it out."

Okay, those earlier thoughts about this being my dream? I was hallucinating.

# Chapter 7

"You want to be in the pageant? This was your idea?"

"Sure, why not. Missus Bedwell says I'm sure to win and there's even scholarship money."

"Oh, don't start on the scholarship money ploy. Is this just about beating Jenna?"

"Some. Everyone's just so sure she's going to win and I can't bear thinking of how impossible she'll be with a crown." Savannah throws herself down in the kitchen chair beside me.

"But she's the daughter of my friend," I whine. "Have you thought of how you'll feel if you lose?"

"Right, like I'd do this if there was a chance I'd lose."

The microwave beeps so I go to it and take out the small pitcher holding family-size teabags steeping in several inches of hot water. Closing the microwave, a smile accompanies a head shake. Where did she get such guts? Sure, my dad was full of bluster, but this young?

"Missus says with her backing, I can't lose."

"Yeah, and when did you get so close to the Bedwells?"

Savannah shrugs. "Me and Angie go over there sometimes."

"Vampire Angie?" Now there's a picture.

"I'm going to take a shower before dinner, okay?" she says as she stands and adjusts the beach towel she has wrapped around her.

"Who were you down at the lake with?" I squeeze out the tea bags and pour the hot liquid from the small pitcher into a gallon Tupperware pitcher.

"People. Just some kids from school."

"People I know?"

She shrugs, "I guess. Ronnie was there. Angie had to work. Susie May and Leslie and some of the other cheerleaders." Susan's girls are both on the cheerleading squad and they'd talked Savannah into trying out.

She's left the kitchen and almost to the stairs when I say, "Oh, yeah. We're opening early. This weekend."

From the stairs she says, "I'll be in Marietta. Have fun."

That's right, she's going back for the first football game at her old high school. Chancey High's first game isn't until the next weekend.

Leslie is senior Captain of the cheerleading squad and told Savannah if she showed up she'd make sure she got on the team. So Savannah showed up at the first practice, tried out using some cheer she'd learned in elementary school and made the team. Her high school in Marietta has almost 1,000 students and making any team requires exceptional skill. There were separate cheer teams for each sport, boys and girls, and then there are the competition cheer teams. But still not enough spots to go around.

Savannah never expressed an interest in trying out before. She probably tried out more because of Jenna's goading than wanting to be on the team. One day as the girls were painting, Jenna announced to her rival, "It's really good that you're not the cheerleader type since your dark hair would look so dull against the new black uniforms." Sweet as the sugar I'm measuring into the tea, aren't they?

With the sugar dissolved and cold water added, the container is full. I push on the gallon jug lid and place it in the refrigerator.

Earlier Bryan took his book bag and snack to the front porch. He's taken to doing his homework out there.

Taking him another juice box, I leave the air conditioned comfort for the humid closeness of Indian Summer, those two weeks in late August when we get our warmest, most humid weather. After placing his drink on the table beside him, I sit on the opposite end of the porch so as to not disturb him.

He is bent over a book in his lap and his book bag is lying against the railing to his left. Papers poke out of the openings. He tries, but school work is hard for him. Will sailed through honors classes, Savannah opts out of upper level classes and is happy with B's, so she sails through too. Bryan's goal is to not get D's.

My nose tickles. "Do you smell that?"

Bryan looks up at me. "Smell what?"

"Smells like a pipe or tobacco? It's not really like cigarette smoke."

He takes a sniff, "Kinda smells like peppermint?"

"Yeah."

Bryan scrunches up his nose and shakes his head. "I don't know."

My feet propped up on the rail, the afternoon sun hits my toes as the sun peeks under the eaves of the porch. Maybe someone smoking a pipe was out walking across the bridge earlier. The railroad bridge across the river was replaced about three years ago. The old bridge wasn't good enough for heavy rail traffic, but the structure was still sound enough for a walking bridge. The town put together a proposal and asked the railroad to help the town take out the track and lay down a boardwalk all the way across. Wrought iron railing lines the sides and antique styled lampposts are stationed every twenty feet or so.

Jackson and I walked across the bridge last fall when we were here. We talked about how the house perched on the hill by the entrance to the bridge would be a perfect Bed & Breakfast for rail fans. Between the front yard and the tracks, a dirt area, about two cars wide, provides parking space at the entrance to the bridge. So maybe someone smoking a pipe parked there earlier, took a walk and I missed seeing them. Savannah and the beauty pageant occupied my thoughts all afternoon.

"Did you find your dad's sleeping bag?" I ask Bryan. Jackson's good sleeping bag from scouting days with Will went missing last week.

"No, I forgot to look for it."

"You boys are not to take stuff down the river without asking, okay?"

"Sure, Mom."

He hadn't looked up at me, so I got the message he was busy. Time to start dinner anyway. Jackson's gone and we're having corn dogs for dinner, not much prep time needed there. Of course, surely there's something to do to get ready for the weekend. But I don't want to do it, whatever it is.

Back in the house, I fill a tall, clear glass with ice and pour fresh-made sweet tea over the ice. Then take a sugar cookie off the plate lying on the kitchen table. The preacher's wife sent them home with us from church yesterday morning. With my book, the fifth in the Anne of Green Gables series, *Anne's House of Dreams*, I head to the back deck. A homemade cookie, sweet tea, and a favorite book—summer in Georgia.

# Chapter 8

"Hey Carolina and Jackson, this here's my brother Gideon Taylor. Gideon, this is Carolina and Jackson Jessup."

Even stretching out the front door trying to reach Gideon's hand we barely touch fingers because between us stands four huge suitcases. He leans forward and our palms eventually meet. Gideon shares Jed's russet coloring, but he's only tilting toward being portly, while Jed has overtaken portly headed to heavy-set. Gideon's sleeves of his white button-down shirt are neatly rolled up. His dress slacks crease sharply and his shoes and belt shine in that dull, rich way good leather makes its presence known.

"Gid spent the day in Atlanta with the governor's people, didn't you, Gid?"

"I had some business to tend to, but let's not get off on all that, okay? Where do the bags go?"

"Here, let me help you with that," Jackson says as he picks up the two closest to the door. Gideon picks up one and Jed grabs the last one. They enter as I hold the door, then we follow Jackson into the kitchen.

In the kitchen, Jackson waves me around to the front. "Here, let Carolina go first so she can get y'all to the right rooms."

The men pull back for me to maneuver around and lead them into the hall. My hand nervously shakes and I grasp the hem of my shirt like a security blanket. My other hand shoots out at the first open door. "This is the Southern Crescent room and Jed thought you and your wife would enjoy it, Gideon."

We all squeeze into the room. "Jed, you and Betty are in the room next door, if you'd like to put your luggage in there."

"Oh, this is all Vanessa's and mine," Gideon says stiffly, pointing at the bags.

Great, our first customers and I've already insulted them, but *four* suitcases for a weekend?

"Are the wives coming up later?" Jackson jumps in on top of my stammering.

"Sure, sure." Jed nods at his brother and says, "Isn't this room grand?"

The walls are a rich green, as close to the color of the famous Southern Crescent train as possible. We decided this would be elegant, as well as comfortable, like its namesake.

When the luxury liner, Southern Crescent, cut from New York to New Orleans in an "unprecedented 40 hours" in the late 1800's, it was the first vestibule train riding the rails in the southern states. Vestibule meant the cars were connected and passengers didn't have to pass outside going from car to car.

"Color picked out personally by the president of Southern Railway in the 20's, Fairfax Harrison," Jackson explains. "Harrison like the two shades of green he saw on the locomotives on a trip to England, so he borrowed it. And here's one for train trivia. The sleeping cars were named for seven distinguished sons of the South from the seven southern states the train traveled through."

"Really? What were the names? I enjoy Southern history and I've never heard that." Gideon asks.

Jackson laughs, "Well, I've not got the names down yet. You *are* our first guests."

"Okay, but next time I'll expect a full report," Gideon says with a wink.

Yep, he's a politician. Winking belongs to preachers and politicians.

"You got it. Carolina and her work crews did a great job on the room, so the least I can do is provide the background." My wonderful husband smiles at me. With a sigh, my shoulders relax. We've done good, the room is beautiful.

The interior of the Pullman sleeping cars were green with touches of gold leaf. Mimicking that luxuriousness, we added touches of gold throughout the room and furnished the room in deep wood tones. Ronnie Troutman sanded and stained the furniture hauled from the local thrift store by Savannah and Parker. Brass lamps, unearthed in Missus attic, sit on the night stands and one hangs in the corner over an embroidered high-back chair—also from the Bedwells' attic.

The white comforter we toned down with a lacy, crochet afghan of ivory thread. Plantation shutters cover the windows, except they aren't *real* plantation shutters. Real ones are too expensive. These Susan had been using in her den, but they were country blue. Before throwing the fake wood shutters out she tried spray painting them a dark brown. They add to the image of a richly appointed drawing car and set an elegant mood. Jed picked it for his brother and sister-in-law immediately when he came to check things out on Wednesday.

"It's nice, real nice," Jed agrees. He seems as proud as Jackson and me. Gideon is twelve years older than his brother, and our mayor obviously worships him.

"Oh, Gid, we left the flowers in the car."

Flowers?

"Is the car locked? I'll run and get them," Jackson offered.

Jed nods, hands Jackson his keys and Jackson leaves.

"Vanessa enjoys fresh flowers in her room and she's partial to roses. We had Shannon at the flower store make sure she had a couple dozen for the weekend."

"Do we need some vases?"

Gideon looks at me like I just asked if politicians need money. "Yes. We need vases."

Okay. Out of the room, I head for the kitchen phone. "Laney? I need vases for roses."

"Roses? Oh, *you* ordered the roses down at Shannons?"

I don't even ask how she knows there are roses at Chancey Florals.

"No, Jed did. For Gideon's wife."

Laney squeals, "Ooo, she must not be happy about coming

here. Men only buy roses when they think they're in trouble. What does she look like?"

"She's not here yet. Just Gideon and Jed and the roses. Vases?"

"Sure. I'll bring them right up."

*Was that a giggle?*

Jackson comes into the kitchen carrying three boxes. These are the flower boxes like in old movies. All the flowers I've ever gotten came wrapped in see-through plastic by teenagers at Kroger.

"So we have our first guests. What do you think?" Jackson lays the boxes on the kitchen counter.

"I'm already tired."

"You're fine. It's going to be fine." He grabs me and kisses me. "I'm excited and the rooms look great."

"They do, don't they."

He leans in for another quick kiss and makes me laugh.

"Enough of that. Laney's bringing vases. I hope she knows how to arrange long-stemmed roses." The doorbell rings and we pull apart. "That can't be her already, plus she'd never ring the bell. You go help get Jed and Gideon settled. I'll get the door."

Late afternoon sun is garish in the living room. There have been some touches of the soft, gold light autumn brings, but this is pure, harsh summer-white light. A wave of heat presses in when I open the door.

"Hello, you must be Jed's parents."

"Sure are. I'm Lou and this is Dorothy."

I shake hands with the white-haired man holding the screen door and then reach for his wife's hand, but she just pushes ahead and wraps her arms around my neck. Her hair is red and her face is round. Her pale skin is covered in freckles and when she smiles her bright blue eyes disappear into the crinkles on her face.

"You are so sweet to open early for us." Dorothy comes into the house speaking in a soft, powdery voice with a slight English accent. She's short and round, Lou stands behind her holding their suitcase and a lavender shopping bag.

"Darling, hand me that bag, please."

"Of course." He hands her the bag and she places it on the coffee table.

"Here is something to show how much we appreciate being your first guests." She pulls out a box wrapped in light green and white with an elegant lavender ribbon.

"Oh, you didn't need to bring anything."

Dorothy smiles and nods once. She's so queenly and it's not merely her accent.

She holds out the box for me to open. Inside layers of cream tissue paper lies a leather guest book. Soft, buttery mahogany leather encases pages of ivory linen. I cradle it to my face and draw in the rich scent. "Thank you so much."

Dorothy takes my elbow in her hand and pats my arm with her other hand. "No, thank you, for opening your lovely home to us."

"Well, let me show you to your room. Your sons are already here."

"Hey, everybody." Laney sticks her head in the front door. "Vase delivery."

"Laney, darling." Dorothy holds her arms open.

"Mrs. T! This weekend was my idea because it would bring you back to town." Laney swooshes in and sets her laundry basket stacked with vases onto the couch. She then bends down to hug Dorothy.

"Darling, look how beautiful she is. Didn't I always say she would be something special?" Dorothy maintains her hold onto Laney's arm, even as Laney hugs Mr. Taylor.

Laney's exotic today. Her tropical print sun dress with a halter top, isn't too low-cut, but mashes everything together just right. The tight waist and bodice flair out to a full skirt. The dress is beautiful, but the wedge heels and the way her hair is swooped to the side in a jeweled comb say that she took extra time with her appearance.

"Mother, Father, you're here." Gideon comes around the corner from the kitchen.

Dorothy steps toward her oldest son and with her hand still

on Laney's arm, pulls Laney with her. "Gideon, look who's here."

Laney looks up through lowered lashes at Gideon, "Hi, Gid."

Oh, now I see who she was dressing up for.

Gideon hugs his mother, hugs Laney no differently and then shakes his father's hand. "Good to see everyone. Vanessa just called and she'll be here later. Apparently Lenox Mall is open later tonight."

"Oh, that's right." Laney interjects, "It's a special event for the weekend. I guess there are a lot of folks in town for the first college football game of the season. Alabama and Clemson play tomorrow night downtown. What else is there to do in Atlanta on a Friday night with the Braves tanking, but shop."

It sounds like the premier shopping mall staying open late was her idea, and maybe it was. A way to get Gideon's wife out of the picture?

Jed had followed his brother into the room, but hovers in the background. He speaks up, "Betty made reservations over in Dalton for dinner tonight."

Dorothy leans over to Laney and whispers, "Like Vanessa would eat in Dalton."

"Okay," I interrupt. "Let's get Mr. and Mrs. Taylor settled. You're in the Orange Blossom Special room." My scowl at Laney tries to convey the idea of behaving.

Laney widens her smile and drops Dorothy's arm as I steer the senior Taylors to the kitchen door.

Laney swirls toward Jed. "Jed, honey, could you take these vases into the kitchen for me? I'll arrange those roses for Betty."

"Oh, no. The roses are for Vanessa."

The frown is loud and clear in Jed's voice as he lumbers to pick up the basket of vases.

Gideon clears his throat and excuses himself. The front screen door bangs and he strides across the porch.

As the Jackson and the older Taylors file ahead of me down the hall, Laney whispers to Jed, "Remember all those walks your brother and I use to take you on? Do you think we should join him now?"

Jed's "no" was emphatic and quick and no need to see his

face to know it's suffused with red. *What is Laney up to?*

Dorothy exclaims over the Florida quilt on the bed in the Orange Blossom Special room. It's as light in feel as the Southern Crescent room is dark, but both rooms embrace you with comfort. Added touches here include orange blossom potpourri in tiny china bowls and in the background the fiddle tune which made the train famous plays softly.

"My grandfather worked on the railroad in Eastern Pennsylvania," Lou says to Jackson. "He used to tell us stories about his days as a hostler. I bet no one knows what a hostler is."

"Yes, sir." Jackson's eyes light up, "Your grandfather took care of the engines when they were in the yard, didn't he?"

"Well, yes, he did. So, you know about railroads?"

My rolling eyes can't be helped. "He loves trains. Why do you think we've got this whole thing going?"

Jackson grins, "Guilty. I also work for CSX, and if the ladies will excuse us, I believe I hear a whistle. If we hurry we can be sitting on the front porch as it passes."

They're gone before we can excuse them.

Dorothy hefts her short self onto the bed and then in a rather unqueenly way, flops back. "I'm exhausted. We took every back road between Raleigh and here looking at train tracks. We got on the road early because Lou wanted to find a place to watch the hump at the yard in Hamlet, North Carolina. There is a merciful God because Hamlet's historic depot and museum is only open on Saturday afternoons."

"No way." I grin. "You've been sitting watching a hump yard? We used to do that with the kids. One time in Illinois or Indiana we actually took a blanket out and had a picnic watching the humping."

"Okay, what are y'all talking about? Sounds like a risqué conversation down here, but knowing you two, I have my doubts." Laney leans against the door frame with her arms crossed.

Dorothy laughs and pushes herself up to sit on the edge of the bed. However, her feet come nowhere near the floor. "You have a dirty mind, Laney girl. It's a train thing. A little hill, or hump, in a rail yard that they drive the trains over real slow. And then as a train car comes over the little hill they disconnect it. Once over the hump it gains speed and they switch tracks it's on and send it to the right train."

"Why isn't it already on the right train?"

With a shrug, I explain. "It might've come from Florida but while some cars on the train are going to New York that car might need to go to, I don't know, New Orleans or California. So the train has to be split up and the cars put in the right place."

"Fascinating, I'm sure." Laney puts her hands on her hips and sways over to look at the pictures on top of the book case in the corner. The pictures are ones I got off the internet of the Orange Blossom Special. "And so you and Mr. T sat and watched these trains do this humping thing all morning?"

Dorothy looks at me and grins, "She makes us sound rather voyeuristic."

"If Dorothy is like me, she sits and reads and inputs the correct exclamation to fit her husband's running commentary."

"Well, I crochet."

Laney turns around and lifts an eyebrow, "Y'all are saints."

"Yes, we are." We agree in unison.

"Come look at the roses. I've got them sort of arranged and just need to know where to put them."

Dorothy waddles off the bed trying to keep her burgundy linen skirt pulled down. Once she reaches the floor, she kicks off her short-heeled shoes. She has on panty hose, hose in Georgia in August. Maybe she is royalty. I'll have to keep an eye open for the white gloves. She huffs, "My word, did he bring roses for *her*?"

Laney and I meet eyes on the poison in the word "her."

Dorothy tilts her head, "Laney, who did you marry?"

"Shaw Conner. Do you remember him?"

Dorothy stops in the hall to think. "I'm not sure. Was he in school with you and Gideon?"

"Yeah, he was the pitcher on the baseball team when we won state."

"Tall and blonde? Mother taught in the middle school?"

"That's him."

Still standing in the hall Dorothy peers at Laney through squinted eyes, bright and hard as Blue Willow china. Her round face wads up around her pinched mouth. Speaking through tight lips she asks, "Is he still good looking?"

Laney pauses, but her wheels are also turning and her eyebrows tense. She whispers, "You think Vanessa needs a little friendly competition?"

Dorothy pats the back of her hair and her eyes travel to examine the ceiling. "She needs to be reminded what she's got. And that's not just because I'm his mother." Dorothy's eyes bore into Laney. "You and Shaw will join us for dinner tonight. You and Jackson too, Carolina."

My answer comes out like a squeak, "Okay".

The two stare at each other. Watching the two women in front of me mind meld makes my throat dry.

I am *so* out of my league here.

# Chapter 9

The birds began waking a short time ago. Here and there, they pop out, sing a few bars, and then flit away into the woods. Silhouettes of the trees got darker as the sky grew lighter but now leaves and branches come into definition as the air turns peach-colored. My coffee is cold, but I keep sipping it anyway. Having hot coffee means leaving my Adirondack chair Jackson and the kids bought for my birthday last year. An afghan from the couch is tucked around me to keep the morning chill from seeping in. My muscles have liquefied—along with my brain.

Was it eating so late, all the scheming, or having a house full of guests that kept me sleepless last night? Finally around six a.m., I gave up trying, put on my sweats, a West Georgia hoodie, and came out to watch the sunrise. Hope everyone else slept better.

Vanessa showed up last night just as we were leaving for dinner. Betty and Jed had gone on to the restaurant to make sure everything was perfect. Jackson and I drove with Dorothy and Lou, the men in the front seats talking about trains. Shaw and Laney stuck around to drive up with Vanessa and Gideon.

The drive up was a history lesson on the Taylor family. Lou and Dorothy moved to Chancey from Columbia, South Carolina during Gideon's senior year. Lou had been hired as the principal for Chancey High, leaving behind his teaching position at the University of South Carolina. Moving from the state's largest city, the capital, and the environs of a major college campus, Gideon didn't enjoy Chancey; which thirty years ago was even more cut-off from the outside world.

The bright spot in his short time in Georgia was Laney Troutman. "Heavens, she went after Gideon like he was the last loaf of bread at the Piggly Wiggly before a snow storm," Dorothy exclaimed. "At the time, Lou and I hoped Laney would tie him to Chancey." Her eyebrows lifted, "That was before I realized how confining a small town can be. But he never looked back. I lost him and Laney. She was the only breath of fresh air in this town. We lived here another twelve years, until Jed graduated. He and Betty got married graduation weekend and never left." She'd shuddered as she said it and then laid her hand on my arm. "Lou and Jed always loved this town. But once Gideon left, I couldn't wait to get out. We moved right after Jed's graduation and we've been in Raleigh ever since. Of course, I hoped Jed and Betty would move also, but..." Her squinted eyes moved to watch the darkening hills out her window.

Another sip of cold coffee doesn't help me figure out if Laney and Vanessa really hit it off or if they're playing the two queen bit like Savannah and Jenna. The two queens, Laney in a blue-green silk dress and Vanessa in a white knit skirt and sweater, held court together at one end of the table acting like a couple sorority sisters. I found out later they actually were in the same sorority, just at two different schools. Jackson and Lou huddled at the other end of the table talking trains. Betty and Jed spent the evening catching Dorothy up on town gossip, which also helped me get the lay of the land. Shaw and Gideon popped in and out of all the conversations as they continuously left the table to conduct business on their cell phones.

Is cell phone usage the new way of declaring male superiority?

We'd been told it was casual, but some people apparently don't understand casual. Shaw and Gideon both wore suits, more male preening probably. Dorothy, Betty and I wore khaki or cotton while Lou, Jackson, and Jed wore golf shirts and casual dress pants. I'd met Jed several times as we got closer to opening the B&B, but Betty I'd only met in passing. The mayor and his wife have six kids, all in middle school and elementary. I like Betty, she's not in competition with anyone, even her sister-in-law. Betty acts as if producing six healthy children out-queens all the tanning and big hair in town. Plus I like her because she outweighs me by at least twenty pounds.

Anyway, it was a full evening leading to a sleepless night for me.

The sky is bright now, with a little blue tinting. The birds are fully awake and making a racket as they gather breakfast. A jade green hummingbird darts here and there around the Rose of Sharon bush at the end of the deck and at the pot of petunias near my feet.

"Good morning." Gideon steps out of the kitchen behind me. "I was going to have a cup of coffee? Would you like a refill?"

"Sure."

He takes my cup and brings it back full. "You drink it black, right?"

"Yes. How did you know?"

"Last night after dinner when we got coffee with dessert that's how you drank it." He hands me my full cup. "I'm in politics, I remember things about people." He pulls out the nearest chair and eases into it.

"So what exactly do you do in politics?"

"I've managed a few campaigns, but I'm thinking about running in the near future." He shrugged and smiled. "Hence the visit to Atlanta."

"Would you run in Georgia?"

"No, but some of the movers and shakers of the party were here this week so I wanted to be where they couldn't ignore me." He sips his coffee. "Vanessa's dad is leaving his state senate seat next year and that is where I'd run. We've lived in his district since we got out of college and moved back to Florida for us to go to law school."

"Vanessa's a lawyer, too?" Funny I hadn't seen that in the

way they all tip-toe around her and treat her like a queen.

"Well, she's a judge, now."

Okay, a judge. I can't make that work either with the honey-haired woman in the tight knit outfit last night.

"This was a great idea for Jed to invite us out here. We needed to get away."

"Not sure we can compete with Lenox Square and Atlanta though."

"Oh, don't think that way, you sound like Mother and Jed. Vanessa loves our room and thinks Laney is a hoot." He leans forward, "She always wanted to see this old girlfriend of mine mother can't stop talking about. You probably noticed last night that Mother and Vanessa don't get along."

With a lift of my eyebrows and shoulders, hopefully he'll get the message this is a conversation I don't want to be in. "Well, I better start getting breakfast together."

Gideon stands also. "I'm going to take a walk out on the bridge. What a great use of the old trestle. Dad and I use to come up here and watch the trains." He pauses with his hand on the stair railing and a grin stretches across his unshaven face. "Hmm, now that I think about it, Laney and I also use to come up here to watch the trains," he winks at me and jogs down the steps.

Tuesday morning after Labor Day, Susan and I huddle next to each other at one of Ruby's tables. Only one corner of the table separates us so we can talk in private—as private as possible in Ruby's.

My mind still swirls around the past weekend. Our first guests left deep impressions and questions. They also left promising steady business for the B&B. "So Laney knew all this?" I just can't get my head around that. "She flits around flinging hair, straining blouse buttons, and dragging vowels through syrup and yet, she knew?"

Susan taps the side of her head, "Yep. Not fair is it? She got looks and brains. Not much gets by Laney, especially if it can help someone in her circle. You're in her circle." She picks up her coffee, "And even more important, she has the brains to hide her brains."

"Lou has booked a full week in October for his rail club and Vanessa's dad made one call to Railfan & Railroad and they're going to come interview us for an article, with pictures and everything. I thought the PR Laney talked about was having the Mayor." I grin and relax into the chairs Susan and I have occupied for the past hour. We put in two volunteer hours at the middle school helping with eighth grade class pictures but made it here by 10 a.m.

"So, all that's great, but what about...you know?" Susan leans closer to me.

"What?"

"You know. The ghost."

"It's not a ghost. Seriously, it's just her imagination."

"Vanessa seems pretty sure of it."

"Oh no. You don't think she told her dad, do you? He wouldn't believe her, would he? What if he told the magazine?"

"Jed and Betty believed her. She's a judge."

"It must've been a shadow or something." I fall back in my chair and screw my eyes shut tight.

I can still hear Vanessa's scream Saturday night. I practically fell down the stairs right on top of Jackson who had suddenly stopped his descent and was standing at the bottom of the staircase gaping at Gideon and Vanessa. The judge and senator-wanna-be stood in our foyer wrapped together in a sheet. One king-size sheet. That's all. We could tell because of the way they kept tugging on the sheet trying to cover all that tan, Florida skin.

"She thinks she saw a ghost," Gideon explained. "I didn't see anything. I was, uh, well..." He grinned, "I didn't see anything."

"I did see a ghost. He walked right across the tracks and sat on your front porch. Right out there in the rocker, then he disappeared. Just disappeared!" Vanessa's bare arm kept waving. The sheet kept slipping. Jackson and I kept staring.

"Cool, a ghost!" Bryan rushed around us to stand in front of the toga-draped couple. A thirteen-year-old on the scene sent everyone scurrying to their rooms.

I pry open my eyes and smile at Susan, "Maybe they were confused."

"I hear they were naked."

Oops. "Hoped Bryan hadn't noticed."

"Oh, it's not Bryan that's telling everybody. It's Missus. She called Gideon and Vanessa for all the details and even set up an interview for Charlie. Should all be in this week's paper."

My eyes forget to blink and my mouth is glued shut.

So now it's official. We have a ghost.

# Chapter 10

"No one is even discussing whether or not it's a ghost. The only argument is whether he's a vagrant from the depression-era that just fell off the train he was hitching a ride on or a soldier from the Civil War." I toss the oven mitts onto the patio table to express my disgust. I pull out my chair to join Jackson and the kids seated already and waiting for dinner.

"If only Vanessa had been able to see the hat he was wearing a little clearer."

"Jackson! For crying out loud, she didn't see anything. There is no ghost. There is no hat," I shout across the dinner table.

Bryan is studying his broccoli and Savannah is studying her lap.

"Savannah. Stop texting."

"So, what about my dress for the pageant?"

Maybe I should just let her text. "What kind of dress do you need? Aren't those pageant dresses expensive?"

"Everything is expensive to you. Missus Bedwell wants to take me shopping but I'm afraid she'll want me to get some old fashioned thing if she pays."

Jackson lights up like Dollywood at Christmas, "Hey, this is Missus' idea anyway. I'm sure her tastes are fine."

They could probably hear Savannah's eyes rolling on the Gulf Coast.

My mouth is full of chicken casserole, so they have to settle for a shrug from me.

We love eating outside. The humidity has broken and a

breeze stirs the air. The sun is behind the house turning the sky pink and purple. Lightening bugs dot the darkening trees where the grass fades into the underbrush, while cicadas and katydids call good night to each other. Scanning the edge of the woods, I look for a ghost. Maybe there's something, and then it's gone.

I keep insisting there isn't a ghost, because I can't decide what I'll do if there is.

All those people on *The Travel Channel* who calmly lead folks on tours of their homes showing off their own personal ghost mystify me. Can I do that? Can I live here explaining every creepy noise or hazy figure passing the window is just our ghost? Will I sniff for that minty tobacco smell as proof our "visitor" is in the vicinity and chuckle? Can I calmly work in the kitchen when I feel someone watching me, even though no one is home?

My steadfast argument remains that Vanessa is delusional— but I believe her. Completely. I've seen the ghost, but no one knows. They can't know until I decide how to act. Bryan's seen it and I think Savannah has too, but, like me, she's still deciding how to handle living with a ghost.

"Haunted bridge, haunted hotel, haunted wood. Is there no synonym for the word haunted?" I ask in disgust and wave the *Vedette* at Laney. The paper came out this morning and our ghost is the lead story.

Laney is hosting the B&B committee for the historical society. She's bent over at her oven taking out trays of tiny biscuits. She turns and sets the trays on the island where I'm seated complaining.

"Take those off and put them in this basket." She leans on the counter with one hand and puts the other on her hip. "Its publicity, go with it. We all know there's not a ghost, but if folks want to believe there's a ghost then what's the harm."

"But what if there *is* a ghost?"

Laney had turned away from me, but she stops and twists back toward the island where I am now concentrating on the biscuits. "These are adorable. I bet they taste delicious." I pop one in my mouth, but quickly pop it back out and into my hand. "Wow, they're hot."

Laney stares at me. "What do you mean? *If* there's a ghost?" Uh oh.

I blow on the biscuit and try to keep my eyes down. But I can't help it and I look up into Laney's blue eyes. When our eyes meet it only takes seconds for her eyes to widen to match her gaping mouth. "You've seen it!"

"Seen what?" Susan and Missus come into the kitchen.

"The ghost! Carolina's seen the ghost!"

"Hush, maybe it wasn't. Maybe it's..."

Missus sets down her brown purse and pulls out her cell phone. "Charlie has to know about this. He'll want to put this in next week's article."

"Don't you dare call him. I'll deny everything."

Missus hesitates, and then snaps her phone closed. "Well, I suppose we do need to see if you have a legitimate story. Folks will think you just want to add to the excitement since you do have a monetary investment in Colonel Lawford Thomas Cogdill."

Susan settles onto the stool next to me, "Tell. What did you see?"

"Wait," I cock my head at Missus, "who is this Colonel guy?"

"My great, great uncle Colonel Lawford Thomas Cogdill." Missus lifts her hand to her throat and her eyes glaze with tears. "The dear boy was wounded at the battle in Tunnel Hill, but he wouldn't stay in the hospital there. He wanted to see his mother and died trying to get to his home there on the riverbank. He loved that view of the river and it is completely understandable why he just cannot leave."

"Really? That's who it is?" This makes me feel better. Knowing who our ghost is and that he just wants to look at the river, well, maybe I *can* live with him.

"Baloney. Missus. You've been going through those old records at the museum all week trying to find some dead relative to be the ghost." Laney bats a dish towel at Susan, "There's the doorbell, go answer it and take them to the family room." She hands me the basket of biscuits, "Take this to the buffet and we'll talk about this ghost thing after the meeting."

There are ten of us on the B&B committee. We fit easily in Laney's family room. The old farmhouse Shaw's grandparents lived in had been gutted and restored. Only last year they'd updated that original restoration with new floors, fresh white paint through-out, and a new family room. In the addition, walls of windows look out over the pecan grove on one side and on the other side, the sparkling pool.

Susan's greetings to those at the front door can be heard as I fix my plate. The biscuit basket sits beside a platter of fried ham and an assortment of jams. My plate fills quickly with the doll-sized biscuits and their different fillings. I take my freshened mug of coffee and sit down in the padded rocking chair.

Missus precedes the women in to the room. She bypasses the food and sits on the end of the sectional couch with only a glass of water, no ice. "I was hoping we could hold the meeting before everyone ate."

"But the biscuits are hot. Besides, you're the only one that's going to talk so the rest of us might as well be eating, right?" Laney hands plates to anyone thinking of by passing the food.

My strategically held coffee cup hides my smile and stuffed mouth. But Missus catches me. "You might want to finish that so you can give us a full report on your opening weekend."

Her stern words wipe my smile away and cause me to pop my last bite in my mouth. The tender, hot biscuit with the cold strawberry preserves makes me want to moan. However, Missus is staring at me. I'll save the one with ham until she's not watching.

"Let's get started. We have a lot to do," Missus decrees.

"Oh, I left my newspaper in the kitchen." I remember as I brush the crumbs off my fingertips.

"I'll get it," Laney says from the doorway.

"Has everyone seen the paper?" Missus asks. Nods all around assure her that everyone is up-to-date. "I asked Charlie Spoon from the *Vedette* to join us, but he says he's got to be at the Laundromat this morning. Something about an electronic paying system they're installing today and he needs pictures for the front page. So I will inform him of the details of our work. Carolina, if you're through with your breakfast, you can have the floor."

The way she said breakfast, you'd think I'd sat here and eaten a pound of bacon and a dozen eggs. "Thank you, Missus." I take a deep sigh, "Well, things went great this weekend. I can't think of anything we really need to talk about." I realize I have some jam on my finger and lick it. That's enough of a pause for the torrent of questions.

"Was there a ghost?"

"Were they really naked?"

"Is Gideon running for Governor of Florida?"

"Did Jed and Betty have a fight? I heard Betty was crying yesterday at the China Buffett."

Missus holds up her hands, "One question at a time. Maybe I should say, one *appropriate* question at a time."

Susan runs a hand through her hair like she's trying to think of an appropriate question. She blurts, "What about the muffins? Did getting them from Ruby's work out?"

Silence echoed by stares meets her question, but Missus leans toward me. "Yes, how were the muffins?"

"The muffins were great. Jackson ran down and got them Saturday and Sunday mornings. Ruby sent honey butter, preserves and apple butter. On Monday morning all the guests were going to Cracker Barrel so we didn't get fresh muffins. I stopped by Ruby's on Monday and paid the bill. Not having to cook was nice, but we may want to change that later. And the cookies you all provided were really appreciated in the afternoons and later at night."

"Which were the favorite cookies?" Janice Wenton asks innocently. However, I'd already told her Sunday at church her snickerdoodles caused a fight over milk late Saturday after the ghost incident. (We obviously couldn't go to back to bed after all that excitement.)

"Your snickerdoodles were wonderful, but all the cookies were gone by Sunday night. Jackson and the Troutman boys spent Labor Day building a fire pit in the back yard so this weekend we're going to do a bonfire and hot dogs. We're charging extra for anything like that but that way they don't have to travel into Dalton for dinner both nights. This weekend the guests are some men Jackson knows from Atlanta and they've said they want to cook hotdogs on Friday night."

"But what about the ballgame? How will you do that *and* be at the game?" Laney asks.

"Honestly, Laney Troutman Connor," Missus' use of the maiden name causes us all to sit up straight. "This is business and important to our town. Football comes second."

"Football never comes second," Cathy Stone explains, shaking her head. "Especially when your daughter is cheering."

"Oh, that's right. Savannah is cheering and FM and I told her we'd be there." Missus actually loses her train of thought and I reach for my ham biscuit.

"It's not a problem." I explain before I take a bite, "Jackson says the men won't be here until nine and so they'll eat something earlier. They just want to hang out at the fire and have a hot dog or two around ten, so we should be home. Saturday night they're going to the VFW fish fry but want to do a fire later that night too."

Veering back to the game, Cathy's eyes light up. "Is Savannah excited about her first game?"

After our first committee meeting Susan had explained Cathy's obsession with Chancey cheerleading due to her glory days in her own black and gold, short-skirted uniform. Glory days that ended with pregnancy and then a wedding during Christmas break of her senior year. Cathy is petite and cute, but behind the cuteness, tiredness peeks out.

Cathy leans toward me with a dreamy look on her face, "The first game is just the best. I can't wait 'til tomorrow. I bet

Savannah is just beside herself!"

Looks of pity shoot around the room, but Cathy's eyes are focused on me. "Yes, she's thrilled." I look at my lap and add a quiet, "I guess."

Savannah and Parker broke up and he's already dating one of her friends back home. She's like an early blooming cherry tree that gets hit by a late frost. The blossoms are still there, but everything is droopy and the bright pink is tinged with brown. And then I met her in the kitchen one night last week when I was getting a snack. She darted in from the back deck. Her red, swollen eyes testimony to a good cry under the stars, but they were stretched wide in disbelief.

"Mom, I..." she gasped and then she just stood there. She struggled with what to say, but the topic was clear to me. She had seen the ghost. Of course a good mother would try to help their scared daughter, I know. But, I couldn't. So, I walked past her to the cupboard and grabbed an unopened bag of Oreos from the cabinet. I tore them open and gave her a handful. Then, I poured her a mug of milk and told her good night. Call me a bad mom, but I felt pretty good that at least I had real Oreos instead of store brand.

Cathy says my name and I realize she's still talking to me. "What uniform are they wearing tomorrow? You know, I helped pick out the new ones this year."

"I think the yellow top with the black skirt, right?"

Cathy nods, "That will look great with Savannah's hair, what about her pageant dresses? I think blue would really bring out her eyes."

Laney's dark head jerks up from where she is bent over the table consolidating platters of food. "Savannah's in the pageant?"

"Absolutely," Missus states. "And as for the color of her dress, that is for all to find out when she steps onto the stage."

Laney has one hand on her hip and the other at her throat. I look at her and smile, "Yeah, I haven't seen it. I wasn't sure this was even going to happen."

"Of course it will happen," Missus declares. "Savannah is the next Miss Whitten County. Sit down Laney; we've got business to do. Now, Janice, fill us in on the advertising you've arranged for the re-enactment days this weekend at Tunnel Hill."

"I believe I'll have a biscuit or two," Missus says as she gathers her papers. The room has finally cleared out. Everyone but me stood around wanting to talk. But, before I could exit, Laney made it clear I was to stay go over some "boring" accounting stuff.

From the kitchen, Laney sticks her head into the family room, "Let's go sit on the front porch, it's so breezy and shaded out there."

Wrapped around the Conner farmhouse is a deep porch. Baskets of hot pink and deep purple petunias hang along the edges. Facing the old, black-top road, cushioned wicker furniture looks out on the shaded lawn. Like most old houses, the front lawn is small. Tall forsythia bushes, with long waving branches, form a fence at the edge of the road.

"I needed a diet Coke after all that coffee this morning. Did you all get what you wanted?" Laney settles into one end of the settee and Susan takes the other end. Missus sits on the edge of her chair, her plate on the edge of her knees. How does she do that? I take the other chair and brace for Laney's reaction to the pageant news.

"So, let's hear it." Our hostess dives right in.

After a deep breath, I plunge in. "Well, she's never even mentioned being in a pageant or anything like this..."

Laney laughs, "No, about the ghost. Of course, Savannah wants to be in the pageant. Every girl wants to be a beauty queen."

Susan and I exchange raised eyebrows.

"And Missus may be right, Savannah might just win. The last two winners have been long-haired blondes and I've told

Jenna that's going to go against her."

"My thoughts exactly," Missus agreed. "And I must say Laney, that Angie girl of yours is quite delightful. I don't appreciate all the piercing and the overly dramatic choice of lip color. And, of course, the hair dye is atrocious. But she has a nice spirit and she's quite polite."

Laney lifts up and curls her legs on the seat beside her. "Why, thanks. But enough kid talk, I want to hear about the ghost."

Relief floods over me that Laney's not mad about the pageant. Now the ghost stuff seems like nothing. "Back in the summer I saw something like a small cloud moving right at the edge of the woods a couple times. First I thought it was smoke, but we checked it out and nothing was on fire. And we never smelled a fire. One time the cloud seemed more like a figure than a cloud, but it faded away before I got a good look." I take a deep breath, "And then I saw him on the front porch."

"Like Vanessa!" Susan exclaimed.

"Yeah. I was coming home one night and when the headlights hit the front porch there was a guy, he was all pale, even his clothes, and he was sitting in one of the rockers. The car bounced over the tracks and when the headlights hit the chair again, he was gone and there was no one around the porch or the front yard. A person couldn't have disappeared that fast, right?"

"What was he wearing?" Missus demands.

"Like Vanessa said, he looked old fashioned, but I don't know what he had on exactly. But he had a beard and a hat, a cap really."

"Bryan's seen him late at night out walking on the tracks, right?" Susan grins. "That's why the boys always want to stay at your house. They stay up all night looking out Bryan's window."

"Grant hasn't seen him." Missus states and then seeing our questioning looks, adds, "Has he?"

"No and he is so disappointed because he planned on spending last Saturday night with Bryan, but I wouldn't let him because it was your first weekend with guests. He just knows if he'd been there he would've seen it finally."

"Those boys might've seen something a whole lot more

interesting than a ghost if they'd been looking out at the tracks last Saturday night." Laney laughed. "The senator-to-be likes watching trains right out in the open. If I recall correctly."

"Okay give," Susan demands. "How much of this did you anticipate with Gideon and Vanessa?"

Laney lowers her lashes and then flashes her blue eyes at her sister, "No woman likes to think her man is contemplating going back to a high school sweetheart. And no man can resist being chased by a high school sweetheart. I just laid down some good dry tender and handed them lit matches. Of course, I also remembered how much Gid enjoyed watching trains." She tilts her head and stares at the ceiling. "I might've reminded him once or twice how much he enjoyed it all those...."

Susan shuts her eyes, "Okay, we get the picture."

"Now, I had no idea they'd be interrupted by a ghost. I thought they'd have a great time, go home and talk it up. They're important people, you know."

"Enough of them," Missus says as she sets her empty plate on the side table. "We've gotten what we needed out of the promotional weekend. Now about the re-enactment over at Tunnel Hill this weekend. FM and I will be attending as always. Who else is going?"

Susan shakes her head, "I can't go. We're taking the youth group to Six Flags."

"I'd rather die," is Laney's air-tight excuse.

"Jackson and I are planning on going with his friends. There's a railroad tunnel or something?"

Missus' patience is wearing thin as she stands and informs me, "It *is* called Tunnel Hill. FM and I will look for you near the sutler tents, okay? We have friends that come from Ohio each year so we will be with them."

"What is a sutler tent?" Susan asks.

"They provide the accoutrements to those engaged in the re-enactment. The term is authentic as sutlers have always existed to supply troops. For the re-enactors they provide the same service with period uniforms, blankets, eating utensils, lanterns." Missus waves her unfolded napkin in our general direction, "Everything you need."

"Really?" I stand up. "I'm kind of looking forward to seeing all this. Jackson and I have never been to a re-enactment. But I've got to get to the grocery store before schools out. I hate shopping once all the teenagers are on duty." I nod to Laney, "Nothing against Angie, but the rest of them are such a pain. The way they look at you and whine. 'Do you want some help to your car with that?' And you know if you say, 'Yes,' your eggs are going on the bottom."

Susan laughs, "Okay, I'll send Grant over this afternoon with some cookies for the weekend. Let me know if you need anything else."

As I step off the porch, I notice the maple tree near the driveway has a faint touch of red and the sky is that deep blue that only comes in September. Today's the day. The day a pitcherful of golden light is tipped over and autumn is officially in the air. The thermometer says eighty-eight, but the light has thickened and the air has thinned. Summer is getting ready for bed.

# Chapter 11

No-bake cookies lay in little piles on wax paper spread over the dining room table. The chocolate and oatmeal cookies won't harden if there is too much humidity in the air so I always associate them with the beginning of school and fall. Butter, sugar, and cocoa stirred into velvet and then thickened with oatmeal, the house smells like a candy store. Sweetness even permeates the air outside where I'm sitting.

From the back deck, I hear Savannah come in the front door. I yell, "Hi there, I'm out back." Hopefully, she'll wander this way and I won't have to ask her to come out. She is so much easier to talk to if it's her idea.

"You made those cookies." She lays her books and purse on the edge of the deck and sits down. "They're not hard yet, are they?"

"No, shouldn't be too long."

"You used to make those on the first day of school when we were little."

"Really?"

"Yeah. Did you get my cheerleading skirt hemmed?"

"Uh huh. You have a rally or something tonight?"

"It sounds so stupid, but I have to go. The kids here get excited over nothing."

"But you loved the pep rallies back home, didn't you?"

"I guess." She lays her head back against the dark green cushion and closes her eyes. "Parker and Hannah are official. It's on Facebook."

"That stinks. Sorry it turned out like this."

"I knew it probably wouldn't last long with me living way out here, but I didn't think he'd date my friend. I'd started not liking him so much this summer." She sighs as she tries to put everything in perspective. "There is this guy here."

"Who?"

She grins and even with her eyes still closed I see the blossoms perking back up, "Ricky Troutman. And he's the quarterback so that would be kinda cool. Plus, Jenna can't date him because he's her cousin."

"Well, I wanted to ask you about something else."

She opens her eyes and leans forward.

"This ghost thing. What do you think?" I pause to see if she'll start talking, but in teen vernacular, she freaks out.

She jumps up, "I will not be the new kid in school *and* the freak living in a haunted mansion. Like I told everyone at school today after that stupid newspaper article, there is no ghost. Period."

"You're sure you've never seen it?"

She looks me straight in the eye, "Seen what?"

"Okay, I get it. But I'm a little afraid I might've seen something. No, I'm pretty sure I've seen something."

"Well, keep it to yourself. It's bad enough Bryan is going around telling everyone he's seen the ghost man. Missus wants me to do an interview with the paper and even wants me to work up telling a ghost story for my talent in the pageant. Everyone is crazy." She walks over to lean on the railing and looks down toward the woods.

"Well, what are you going to do for your talent?"

After a long pause, she sighs, "Probably the story. I don't have a talent, but I am good at dramatic readings. Remember those couple debate club meetings I went to freshman year? The coach said I was really good."

"You never told us that."

"I also never told you the coach had a crush on me. That's why I quit."

A shudder travels down my body. "Okay. Well, don't let

Missus push you around. You'll be fine."

She doesn't answer, just stands looking down the hill.

"So you're doing okay here?"

The pause stretches on until she finally nods, "I think so. I miss having places to go all the time, like Starbucks or Taco Bell or any place to shop, but then I'm liking being outside so much. We hang out in the school parking lot or the church parking lot and it seems more relaxed. And Angie. You know I could never be friends with someone like Angie at home. But here, they all know Angie's cool and they kinda ignore the piercings and stuff. And Ricky is this stud quarterback, but they all remember him from kindergarten so there's not this star thing going on."

She turns and leans against the railing, "Cheerleading is fun, and that couldn't have happened at home. It's not so bad. I thought I'd die out here, but it's kinda peaceful." She shakes her silky dark hair and smiles, "Also, I'm really smart here. There's not all those AP kids who'd rather get herpes than a 'B'."

Her analogy makes me cringe, but knowing those AP kids' parents, she's right. They'd prefer their child bring home an STD because there's medicine for that, while there is no remedy for a substandard grade.

"Think the cookies are hard enough?" She lifts her books and steps toward the door.

"Probably. Do you have much homework? What time is your rally?"

"I've got a little homework and I have to be back at school by 6:30."

"Okay, I'll make you a hamburger in thirty minutes or so, okay?"

"Sure." As she crosses the threshold of the open door she leans back out. "Did you notice how blue the sky is today? Kinda feels like fall."

My heart melts. Maybe the princess is not a forever curse. I'm sure she'll make many more royal appearances, but no dragons will have to be fought or frogs kissed or dwarfs housed to eventually banish her to a hidden tower in a magical forest. Nope, apparently the curse is broken by love and discipline and

discarded calendar pages.

"Carolina!" Jackson shouts across the field turned parking lot. "Meet me at that side gate."

I pick my way across the stubble, glad I wore tennis shoes and not sandals. After parking, Jackson went back to get a schedule of the re-enactment events. I reach the end of the field and meet him on the gravel road.

Jackson reaches for my hand, "Wasn't the game fun last night? I don't think I've been to a high school football game since my own senior year." He grins and asks, "You know my favorite part? When Bryan and Grant and the younger kids played football down in the end zone during halftime."

"My favorite part was seeing Savannah the Cheerleader look cheerful for over an hour. No sulking, no rolling eyes. I often thought she must be more fun with her friends than she is at home, and now I have proof. I don't expect her to be different at home, it just gives me faith that she won't turn into a lonely old lady living with a bunch of cats."

The sun darts in and out of the clouds so even though the temperature is near ninety we're comfortable as we walk up the gravel road toward the abandoned tunnel.

Little boys run by in blue Union or gray Confederate pants, suspenders and caps. The girls dash by wearing full dresses in light, breezy calico.

Women in long dresses and shawls mix with the assortment of folks in Georgia Bulldog and Tennessee Volunteer t-shirts. The men in period dress are on the field preparing for the re-enactment battle which begins in about an hour. We hear the drummers and occasional bursts of a bugle, and then shouts as the men go through their drills.

We veer to the left, away from the battlefield and see the tunnel opening. A man in denim overalls talks to a group of visitors. "This here tunnel is full of ghosts: Soldiers who crept here for some shade and coolness after a hot battle, a decapitated passenger of a long ago circus train, or the driver and horses of a buggy that wasn't quite fast enough to beat a train.

We enter the tunnel with a few others and the big bear of a man in the overalls. He fills us in on the history as we walk. "This was part of the first railroad across the Appalachians. The Western & Atlantic Railroad opened the tunnel on Halloween, 1849 and it became a lifeline to the new town down south, Atlanta. Then on April 7, 1862, Union soldiers stole The General, a locomotive stopped for breakfast in Marietta, Georgia. The plan to destroy bridges and track sbetween Atlanta and Chattanooga didn't work due to them being chased by two locomotives going backwards. Yep, folks, I said backwards." He stops talking and spits off to his left side. "The Confederates didn't even have time to turn them engines around, I tell you. Shortly after flying through this very tunnel, The General came to a stop and the The Great Locomotive Chase was over. The Union men that stole the engine scattered to the woods, but were all found and some of 'em hanged."

"There's been several movies made about it and to think the chase went through here," Jackson lays a palm on the cool red bricks lining the area of the tunnel we're passing through. "Amazing. . ."

Asphalt pathway now lies where the tracks once traveled. Flood lights placed ever so often help us see what our guide in overalls points to. "See those gouges where the bricks are torn right off? That's from when the trains and cars just got too big for this tunnel. The new tunnel was built and this one closed in 1928.

"I played here as a boy in the sixties," a man in the group says. "We climbed over the banks of kudzu and just slipped down in here. No gates or nothing. We'd play soldiers or cowboys and it was so dark you couldn't see anything to be afraid of."

I shiver, not from the chill of the dark tunnel, but from the thought of being in here in total darkness. It's creepy enough with the spotlights and sure footing.

We walk the length of the tunnel, 1477 feet, and at the other end hear a train on the CSX line which sits next to the tunnel. Jackson's rail fan buddies, our guests for the weekend, are ahead of us and they head to an opening in the flood of kudzu where the active rail line can be seen.

"Go on with them. I'll start back through the tunnel and wait for y'all on one of the benches." My encouragement is met with a quick kiss and Jackson dashes off as he gets his camera ready. How he can be so fascinated when every train looks the same? Then I get a mental flash of our closet. But seriously, black shoes are *not* all the same. Right?

Back in the tunnel the overalls guy is talking again. He's telling the story of how a buggy driver turned into the tunnel thinking another train wouldn't be coming soon. And then how he heard the whistle behind him. The chilly air settles inside me.

The story floats through the darkened passage. "In the dark of the tunnel the engineer couldn't see the buggy. The terrified horse is running for his life as the rumble of the train fills the space behind him and they get to right here when the engine overtakes the buggy." I look at the small group gathered about fifty yards from me. A little boy backs into his mother's legs and a teenage girl tightens her grasp on her boyfriend's arm.

"We've had visitors from all over the world report glowing green lights coming at them but the lights go out right at this spot. Some believe those lights are the eyes of the panicked horse running for his life, which ended where the lights always go out."

"Hey."

I yelp and jump up just as Jackson sits beside me.

His grin is huge, "Sit back down. Did you think a ghost got you? Shoot, we live with a ghost. Takes more than a story to scare us, right?"

"Have you seen it?" I plunge right in. Maybe it's my racing heart or maybe it's just that I'm sick and tired of jumping at the word "ghost".

He looks back to his friends who are still outside comparing pictures on their digital cameras, and then turns to gaze at me. "I can't say I've seen the actual ghost, but I have felt like something is around at times. I haven't said anything to you 'cause I figured you'd be on the first mule leaving town if you really thought there was a ghost or whatever."

"I've seen it and I've even talked to it." My blurted confession causes my throat to constrict.

"What? Where? Did it talk back? Are you kidding?"

I try to relax my throat by clearing it, but all that does is build more pressure in my chest. I stand up and start walking. The tour group has gone on and their conversations are only a faint murmur.

"Wait, tell me." Jackson leaps up and walks beside me, but staring at me instead of the pathway.

Taking a deep breath loosens my lungs and vocal cords. "I've seen him on the front porch. I've talked to him down at the willow tree and no," I shoot a scornful look at my stunned husband, "he didn't talk back. I just go down there to sit..."

"...and hide." He tilts his head and lifts an eyebrow at me.

"Yes, sit—and hide. At first, I felt like maybe I was actually breaking through on this God thing like they keep talking about at church. But then I realized it must be the ghost. I just feel so heard and un-lonely. I'm used to feeling lonely if you're not around and now with you traveling so much...," I shrug and weave my hand between his body and arm. "I'm crazy aren't I?"

He shakes his head, but I see doubt in his eyes.

I've got to explain this, "I keep watching those haunted shows on TV, you know, where the people get accustomed to living with a ghost? I mean, if they can do it, why can't we?"

"Are you messing with me?" Jackson stops walking and tightens his hold on my arm so I stop too. "You know there are no such thing as ghosts, right?"

We're standing in a dark spot of the tunnel and I turn my head to the side. Why is this haunting me? I laugh at my choice of words and Jackson's grip on my arm loosens.

"Okay, so you are joking. Good, cause this is getting out of hand." He untangles our arms and takes a step away from me.

"You had me worried there for a minute." As he looks back over his shoulder, he waves at the guys who are headed our way.

"No, I'm not joking. I believe there is a ghost and I'm glad to have him around." I whip around to keep walking and I know Jackson is confused. Heck, I'm confused. But for the first time since I saw the ghost I can breathe. So I breathe in and out until I get to the end of the tunnel. For the first time I care about something enough not to change my mind just to maintain harmony. Great, I finally take a stand and it's about someone who died a hundred years ago.

They guys at the tables selling rebel flags probably think I'm laughing at them.

# Chapter 12

"I told Jackson, that's my husband, about you. I think he's decided to pretend we never had that conversation today." I lean my head back against the bark of the old willow tree. "But I think I'm okay with that."

Jackson is up the hill building a fire for our guests. We got back from Tunnel Hill about an hour ago. The car ride home was pretty quiet except when we talked about the re-enactment.

"Hey, yeah, you were in the Civil War. Did you really fight that close to each other? I can't imagine being able to see the people that are going to shoot at you and just keep marching towards them. And all the smoke and the cannons were so loud. I bet it was scary, wasn't it, Tommy?" I like thinking of our ghost as Missus' relative, but I have trouble picturing him as a colonel or as Lawford Thomas Cogdill. I prefer to think of him as a scared boy about Will's age. Tommy.

Sunlight shoots across the tree tops as the sun begins its descent. With the yellowing and dropping of the willow leaves and the slight breeze I now get glimpses of the sky when I look up. Willows don't have a lot of little branches, just big main ones hung with curtains of leaves, like those beaded, door curtains from the sixties. Some of the leaf curtains hang in mid air while others pool on the ground around me like designer draperies. Since the bank slopes off pretty steeply I see the river flowing past. Grass doesn't grow in this shade, so I leave an old picnic tablecloth folded up down here. That way I don't have to sit in the dirt.

"Anyway, I think Jackson isn't sure how to take me saying I believe in you. I even told him I talk to you. I don't think Jackson and I have ever disagreed about something. You might find that hard to believe but we haven't and it's not because I'm a wimp or Jackson is some kind of ogre. It's just that we're pretty content with things most of the time. All that stuff people fight about just doesn't mean that much to either of us. Does that make sense? Plus, I guess, neither one of us likes confrontation."

I grin and stretch my legs out in front of me, "But I gotta admit I felt pretty good being so forceful about believing in you. I kind of liked the idea of pushing back. And since we moved here, with having friends and being on committees and running the B&B, I just don't have time to read as much as I used to. I think I lived through all those people in the books and I didn't miss having drama or excitement in my own life."

"You know, I've now told Laney and Susan and Missus and Savannah and Jackson that I've seen you. Mother and Daddy would be so proud of me, wouldn't they? Wouldn't Daddy have loved a ghost to brag about? He'd have sold tickets. The Haunted Houseboat." I grin. "I guess that's what Missus is saying, that our ghost will bring in customers." I mentally chalk one up for Missus.

"Now several times a day I want to stuff all this back into the bottle, screw the lid on tight, throw it in the river and go back to my books. I don't feel like the world knows what it's doing giving me this life with a cheerleader-beauty pageant contestant daughter, a full-fledged business in my home, friends inviting me to pool parties, and all these big plans. I think this life was meant for someone else, don't you?"

"Oh, yeah, Tommy. You have to understand I can ask you all these questions, but you can't answer me, okay? There's only so much I can take in a ghost and I've decided talking is not on the table."

With a roll forward onto my knees, I stand up. "Well, friend, I need to go make sure everything is defrosted and ready to cook. You're welcome to join us at the fire, you know." A breeze blows the willow arms slightly as if they are accepting my invitation.

"Talk to you later, Tommy."

Savannah and Ricky are at the movies, supposedly. Bryan is with the youth group at Six Flags and will spend the night at Grant's. The fire is a nice bank of embers with a hot flame so cooking the hot dogs and sausages didn't take long. Carrying the condiments back into the kitchen, I chuckle. It's funny to think it was just a week ago tonight when Gideon and Vanessa saw the ghost. Or Tommy, I guess I should say. It's kinda nice that everyone knows about him now. Jackson and Savannah will come around, or not. Just thinking about not being on the same page as Jackson makes my heart skip.

With the refrigerator open the light illuminates the dark kitchen while I put the ketchup, mustard, and onions away. Into the emptied picnic basket go the marshmallows, Hershey bars, and graham crackers for s'mores at the fire. Hooking my arm through the basket handle, I walk back out onto the deck.

"Hey there," Jackson is waiting on the deck when I come out of the kitchen. He reaches for the basket. "Here, sit down for a minute. I came up to replenish the cooler but the guys can wait a few minutes."

I set the basket on the table, pull a chair out and sit down.

"You were down at the willow earlier."

"Yeah, it's beautiful down there at dusk. Your fire sure turned out nice."

"Yeah, it did. Hey, you know I don't have a problem with you talking to this ghost, right?"

"Really? But you don't believe he exists."

"So? We don't always have to agree. Just because we're married it doesn't mean we're always going to agree on everything."

"But I like it when we agree on everything."

"I know you do, but that doesn't mean that's how it should

be. We can agree to disagree."

"Okay," I smile at my husband who is obviously the best guy in the world, "let's go have some s'mores." I stand up and reach my hand to him. He takes my hand between both of his.

"Carolina, you know I love you, right?"

I pull and he lifts up to stand beside me, "Of course I know that. I love you, too."

"So, if you feel like you need to talk to someone about all this ..." he pauses and just dips his head to stare into my eyes.

Pulling my hand from his, I reach around his shoulders and lay my head on his chest. "I know, I can always talk to you, Sweetie."

"Sure, but you know, if you want to talk to a *professional* our insurance will cover it."

"What?"

"Yeah, I checked earlier and it kicked in sixty days after I started working for the railroad so we're fully covered now."

I squeeze him tighter, not as tight as I want because that burst of adrenaline I've heard about getting during moments of extreme stress didn't show up. I was hoping for cartoon hulk strength where I squeeze so hard his head turns into a red balloon and explodes.

He pats me on my back, "Okay, honey, I know you're emotional, but I guess we should get on down to the fire. I'll fill up the cooler and be there in a minute." He gives me another affirming squeeze then steps out of my arms, lifts the cooler and walks into the kitchen.

And what do I do? Just what do *I* do?

I pick up the basket, go to the fire and eat s'mores. After all, maybe he's right. Maybe I am crazy. But I'm not crazy enough to pass up melted chocolate and gooey marshmallows on my worst day.

# Chapter 13

Jackson left at around 5:00 this morning for South Georgia and he's going to be gone all week. The tension began melting from my shoulders the moment he closed the door behind him. When the kids were little, I hated when he had to travel. Now, well, it's kind of relaxing not having to get up to fix his lunch or cook a sit-down dinner. The kids and I are fine living on Spaghetti-O's, corn dogs, and frozen pizza. Although, I have discovered that after three days of eating in front of the TV, they start asking for "real food in the dining room."

Family dinners are a great idea in abstract. In reality, they're a lot of work.

This time, however, reduction in stress isn't coming from the reduction in work. Yesterday was awful. I'm so mad at Jackson and he hasn't a clue. That's the worst part. He feels all noble and helpful. I just wanted him to leave.

Going back to sleep after I heard him leave was the plan, but my tight shoulder and neck muscles wouldn't let me get comfortable. Finally, I gave up and stumbled down to the guest rooms and stripped the beds. It's now only 7:30 am and I've done two loads of laundry.

I pile the comforters into a basket and take them out to the line to air for a few hours. It's an overcast day, with rain expected tonight so I'm hoping to get everything dry and off the line early.

Having a clothesline is a dream come true for me. My old neighborhood association, The Nazis Neighbors, determined that clotheslines are the first step in the degradation of society. A clothesline on Monday means a junked washer on the porch by Wednesday, and by Friday a Chevelle on blocks in the front yard with naked toddlers running around it. They've obviously done studies on this phenomenon and determined clotheslines must not be given a foothold.

There was a little secret one I pulled out in a corner of my backyard between two tall camellias. I'd sneak around hanging clothes outside after everyone left for work and then broke all traffic laws getting home before the evening dog walking-yard examining-I-can-wear-a-sports-bra-without-a-shirt parade began.

Now my clothesline is awesome. A permanent, three-line affair in the side yard. The sheets I put out about an hour ago are already dry. I take them down after I throw the white comforters over the lines on the other end. All is quiet this morning as the buzz of summer has hushed. My flowers look weary. We won't have a frost for a while, but the zinnias and begonias look ready for the show to end.

Bryan and Savannah are rummaging in the cabinets when I come back into the kitchen.

"Where are the moon pies? You know that's what I eat for breakfast," Savannah scolds me.

"No, I didn't know and I don't want to know that. I bought all those nature bars or whatever you asked for, there's three boxes right there."

"Gross. I thought I liked them, but they're really gross."

"Well, have some cereal." Apparently cereal is gross too, as she rolls her eyes at me. "How about you, Bryan? Want some toast or a bagel?"

"I had a bagel already; I'm just getting a fruit snack for break."

"Oh, yeah, I'm not driving today. Ricky is picking me up."

"What about your brother?"

She shrugs.

"No, you're supposed to give him a ride. That's the deal. He'll just have to ride with you and Ricky."

"Yeah, right," she laughs. "No way."

And I lose it. "I'm sick and tired of your selfish attitude. You think the world revolves around you, but—newsflash—it doesn't! So either you're driving your brother to school or he's riding with you and Ricky. That's it!"

"Whatever. Don't flip out."

Bryan hoists his back pack on one shoulder, "Yeah, Mom. It's okay. Grant's mom is picking me up anyway 'cause Grant left his shoes here yesterday."

They leave cabinet doors hanging open, something smoking in the toaster, and my teeth grinding. I follow as far as the kitchen door. Exiting the house, her highness holds the door for her brother and they exchange eye rolls.

In this circus, I'm the guy who cleans up behind the elephants.

Mid-afternoon and the house is getting darker. I grab an apple and head outside to get the comforters off the line. The tart granny smith tastes like fall and the gathering clouds and blustery gusts push summer farther south. I wander around the back yard watching the racing, pushing, changing sky. My hair whips around my face and my spirit lifts. To live here on the side of this hill, watching over the river and the bridges, feels like an extraordinary blessing at this moment. A plop of rain hits my uplifted cheek. I rear back and throw my apple core toward the woods and then hurry for the clothesline. Wind-swept, fresh cotton billows around me as I try to pull together the comforters and other bedding. I shove them in the basket and lift it as I race for the deck and back door as the drops fall faster. Just ahead of the sheets of rain, I toss the basket into the kitchen then turn and lean on the door jamb and look out across the wet decking and yard.

Rain hems in my house and me. Dirt, grass, and water scent

the damp air and it pushes me toward the shelter of my home. Yet, there is a beckoning also. Step out. Feel. Taste. Drink. I open my hand and reach out. Come play, it calls. The rain is warm and pools in my palm. It splatters on my wrist and bare forearm. I reach further, how long has it been since I walked or danced or even just stood in the rain.

Maybe...

No, the beds need to be made.

Two of the three rooms now have clean sheets and freshened comforters. In the Orange Blossom Special room, I've spread the kitschy map of Florida quilt and in the Southern Limited room, the creamy crocheted lace throw drapes across the bed. With my lighter load, I step into my favorite of the three rooms, the Chessie room.

Chessie, the cuddly kitten tucked in fast asleep on snow-white linens, became the mascot of the Chesapeake & Ohio Railroad after appearing in an advertisement for the railroad in 1933. "Sleep Like a Kitten and Wake Up Fresh as a Daisy in Air-Conditioned Comfort" was the slogan. Chessie the kitten not only became a popular symbol for the railroad, but she even starred in two children's books. Chessie acquired two kittens in 1935, Nip and Tuck. During World War II, her mate Peake went overseas in a war bonds campaign using Chessie's image. Chessie stayed here and did her part encouraging home support of the troops.

Even now, Chessie calendars are popular and I found several on eBay cheap. So I ordered them, then cut out and framed the cutest pictures to cover the walls. A current calendar hangs beside the small secretary desk near the door. We painted the room dusky blue and Ronnie painted the furniture antique white. He then distressed the white wood to make it look loved and worn. I firmly forbid him to do that to the furniture, of course he did it anyway—and it's perfect.

The curtains are yards and yards of unironed, unbleached muslin. Angie hemmed the bottoms but left the edges frayed, again for that well-loved look. They frame the side and front windows and let in a soft gray light today that matches the room perfectly.

On the bed, the white comforter is coupled with a light gray, cashmere-like throw. It lies in puddles across the bottom of the bed. At the top are pillows appliquéd with Chessie, Nip, Tuck and Peake. I found several Chessie scarves on Ebay and Susan figured out a way to put them on the pillows Angie sewed.

The bed calls to me for an afternoon nap most days, and on such a rainy, quiet day the temptation is powerful. But I really have things to do before the kids get home. Besides, I just got everything perfect. The pillows are plumped, the comforter straight and the thick, silky throw is puddling perfectly. First the rain and now the bed—why is everything trying to get me off task today?

I switch off the light and pick up the basket, happy that the guest area is done.

But only three steps from the Chessie Room, I stop, drop the basket and go back. The room is perfect—perfect for a nap. But...

Unload the dishwasher or lay down on that bed? Take another couple ibuprofen to relax my shoulders or sink into that gray softness and close my eyes? Stand here and keep thinking or kick off my shoes and stop thinking completely?

Why, thank you. I believe I will.

# CHAPTER 14

"We're having the Pageant Tea and an open house for the B&B on Saturday. Do you have any reservations for this weekend?" Missus asks.

Of course I shouldn't have gotten up from my nap to answer the phone.

"Carolina? Are you there? Were you asleep? You sounded groggy when you answered the phone."

"Of course not. I'm just confused." (Who takes naps in the middle of the day?) "When was all this decided? We didn't talk about it at the meeting, did we?"

"Not the B&B committee meeting, but the Fair committee met this morning and the venue for the Pageant Tea had to be changed. Chammy Phillips over in Collinswood has hosted the last four years. However, Chammy's husband, Randolph, has inherited the family affection for Jack Daniels and someone subtly recalled a recent jaunt around Collinswood Square Randolph took in a golf cart borrowed from Manor Country Club. In itself, a funny tidbit of Phillips family drinking and driving lore, however he appeared to be wearing only his Auburn tie and his golf shoes. I believe it was also subtly hinted that there may exist pictures of this little venture that might somehow be released to members of the press."

"Let me guess, you're joined on this committee by our own editor, Charles Spoon, right?"

"Why, Carolina! You're getting right devious in your thinking. But now that you mention it, I do believe Charles is on the committee. And, yes, he did happen to attend the meeting."

"You used blackmail without even checking if having this tea thing is okay with me?"

"Are you busy? What could possibly be the problem?"

Missus waits while I try to think of something. "I guess there's no problem, but I don't know anything about having a tea."

"Of course you don't. I will take care of everything. Now, if you will please answer my original question, do you have reservations for this weekend?"

"Not that I know of. Laney would know for sure."

"Wonderful! I've already talked to her. Good-bye."

One thing about talking on the phone with Missus, there's never any long drawn out good-byes. I hang up the phone and remember what I told Tommy this weekend about sometimes wanting to throw all this in the river. This is most definitely one of those times. Missus is cooking up something for this weekend for my house and I'm on a need-to-know basis. Six months ago, I didn't even know these people existed and now they run my life.

Susan answers her phone like she's in a hurry. Of course she does everything in a hurry. "Hey!"

"Susan, its Carolina. Have you heard about this Pageant Tea thing?"

"A little, why?"

"I'm just wondering what's going on. You know how it is trying to get answers out of Missus or Laney."

"Really, it's like talking to the squirrels about leaving your bird feeders alone. I'm about to get a gun and start shooting these rascals in my back yard. I'm going through a ten-pound bag of sunflower seeds every week."

"Well, I'm not to the point of shooting Missus or Laney—yet."

Susan laughs, "Be sure and let me know when it gets to that point, you know Missus would want it in the paper. Hey, why don't you all come to dinner tonight? It's just stuff from the garden."

"Jackson's out of town so it's just me, Savannah and Bryan. That okay?"

"Sure, Griffin has to eat and run since he's got a City Council meeting at seven. We're eating at six, is that good for you?"

"Perfect."

That phone call ended much better than the last one. Susan could have her own show on *The Food Network*. When she says "just stuff from the garden" she means fried squash, corn pudding, fresh green beans cooked with ham, sliced tomatoes still warm from the sun and home-grown watermelon. We ate Sunday dinner there a couple weeks ago and my kids almost overdosed on fresh vegetables. I thought they'd turn their noses up but they said working in the garden and actually picking their own food was "cool."

I tried letting them pick their own vegetables from our freezer but they said it wasn't the same. Garden snobs.

"The sleepover was kinda Angie's and my idea." Savannah is spearing lima beans on her fork while she talks. She shrugs and pushes the fork into her mouth.

"Hey, I was there too." Susie Mae speaks up. Susie Mae is petite and reminds me of a pixie. She even has the same pixie haircut I used to have, only I was in elementary school, not high school. With that haircut, I looked like a little boy, but with her big blue eyes, the wispy dark hair around her tiny face is adorable. She's named after her grandmother's favorite cousin and it fits her. I often wonder about naming your kids something cute like that. What if they turn out to be this hulky Amazonian thing and their name is all wrong.

But Susie Mae fits her name perfectly. She's a sophomore, a year behind Jenna, Angie, and Savannah. She's two years younger than her sister Leslie, who is at work tonight. Leslie plans to be a veterinarian and works at the vet out on the highway. Between her studies, college applications, and working almost full-time, we only see Leslie when she's cheering at the football games.

"You're hanging out at Missus' now, too?" Susie Mae's dad stares at her. Griffin shakes his head and then looks down to scoop another forkful of squash casserole onto his fork. "You girls being best friends with that old lady is strange. She's whacked out, I tell you. Some of the stuff she's come up with at the council meetings just leaves your mouth hanging open. Her and Angie? That just don't fit in my head."

"So this is new? The girls hanging out with Missus?" I'd been wondering about that.

"She's fun. She's kinda mean," Susie Mae adds quickly, "but not to us. She's funny mean."

"And funny mean is what?" Susan leans forward toward her daughter.

Susie Mae is trying to look past her mother at Savannah, and I realize that's why Susan is leaning. She's blocking the girls from looking at each other. So I clear my throat to get Savannah's attention.

Savannah shoots me a quick look and realizes she's been found out, so she sits back, picks up her cornbread from her plate and acts completely disinterested in the conversation.

"She just knows stuff about everybody," her eyes widen. "And I mean everybody in town."

"Can you pass the corn on the cob?" Savannah asks. "What is that white corn? I've never seen any like that."

"It's called Silver Queen, isn't it good?" Griffin takes a piece from the bowl before he hands it off to pass down the table.

Susan ignores the corn decoy, "Like who does she know about, and what does she say?"

Susie Mae has finally gotten the shut-up vibes from Savannah and her eyes grow even bigger. "Oh, nothing, really.

She's just a nice old lady that we're trying to help."

"Help her do what?" Susan asks.

"Clean her attic and stuff?" Grant asks. "I want to get up in her attic. I bet it's full of cool stuff. Can we help?"

Bryan nods but he can't speak because his mouth is stuffed with watermelon.

"What a great idea. We'll ask Missus." Savannah smiles at the boys and then turns her innocent eyes on me, "But I thought you wanted to know about the sleepover."

Griffin lifts his head from his ear of corn and licks the butter and salt off his lips, "Is that this weekend? Some kind of sleepover pageant thing was added to our agenda for tonight's meeting. It was e-mailed to me with the changes this afternoon. Grant, go get the sheet of paper off the desk in the kitchen. It's an extra copy I printed by mistake." Susan's husband reminds me of a wrestler. He's short, but compact with muscular arms and legs. He reaches out for the paper when Grant gets back to the table.

"Yeah, here it is. The Pageant Tea has been moved to Chancey and will be Saturday afternoon at the B&B. Saturday night there will be a bonfire to which the council is invited. Then the six contestants will be spending the night at the B&B."

"There are only six contestants? I thought this was a big deal."

Susan shrugs, "It is, but it's never had many contestants. Our fair is pretty small compared to the bigger counties."

"Plus the entrance fee keeps out those who want to be in a pageant just for the fun of it but don't really belong," Susie Mae pipes up.

"What?" I ask looking at Savannah. She's shooting angry shut-up arrows at Susie Mae.

Pixie eyes wider than ever, she nods. "That's what Missus says."

"How much is this fee?"

"Five hundred dollars."

"It cost five hundred dollars for you to be in this pageant? Missus paid that for you?" I guess I should've asked more questions.

"Well, it really began as a fundraiser for the fair," Griffin explains. "The girls and their families are supposed to get sponsorships from local businesses. But it slowly turned into the parents just paying the fee. Maybe that's something the council should talk about. Not allowing the money to come from only one source. Put the community involvement back into it."

Susan puffs out, "Have you forgotten you have a niece in this thing? Laney will come down on you like a rabid bulldog if you mess around with it."

"True, I believe I will heed the honored tradition of keeping my mouth shut."

Bryan nods, "Good idea, Mr. Lyles. That's what works best for me."

We all laugh at Bryan's junior high wisdom and Griffin pushes away from the table. "I shouldn't be too late. What time you all gonna have dessert? I'll see if I can make it back in time to fill you in on all the details."

"Around 8:30?" Susan looks at me, "Can y'all stay that long?"

"Sure, my kids got their homework done earlier, or so they say."

Griffin comes around the table to give Susan a quick goodbye kiss and then leaves.

"Do you want to hear about the sleepover or not? We've got a show to watch," Savannah asks.

Grant rakes a pile of macaroni and cheese into his mouth, chews quickly, and swallows, "Can we be exused?"

Susan nods and the boys jump up, grab their dishes, and take them in the kitchen. "Thanks guys, we'll get the rest of it later."

"Okay, the men folk are all gone. Let's hear about the sleep-over."

Savannah pushes her plate back and crosses her arms on the table. "Angie and I..."

"I was there too," Susie Mae reminds her.

"Okay, Susie Mae, Angie, and I were talking about how two of the six contestants come from Chancey and so why shouldn't there be something here for us. I really wasn't thinking of our house, more like Missus' house or the Pendle mansion, but you know Missus is set on getting that money from the grant."

Susie Mae shivers, "And she hopes they see the ghost. That's why she wants them to spend the night there."

"And the bonfire? Who thought of that?"

Susie Mae grins at Savannah, "That was Mr. FM's idea and boy did they have a fight about it. Didn't they, Savannah?"

Savannah's face lights up, "Man, they were shouting and Missus threw a pillow at Mr. FM. He said that he wanted to get in on the big shindig weekend and she told him he was to keep his big ol' stinkin, cigar-smellin' nose out of it!"

Susie Mae giggles, "And then Missus told him he just wanted to see the ghost and he said she was right. When he said she was right, Missus stopped just as she was going to throw another pillow at him. She laid down the pillow and said that was a good idea."

"And that was it." Savannah waved her hand. "Not another word."

I can't help laughing, "And you girls were right there for it all?"

"Yep, sitting on the couch, right between them. They were standing over us at each end." Susie May nods at Savannah, "Remember how Mr. FM was standing over Angie's end and she actually got some spit on her when he was yelling?"

We all groan and Savannah shrugs, "So that's how it all came around. Missus is real excited about this ghost thing you know."

"How about you?" Susan asks my daughter. "Your mom told us about seeing it? Have you seen it?"

Savannah looks at her lap and shakes her head, "No. I don't really believe in ghosts."

Susie Mae studies Savannah and tilts her head, "But you said..."

Savannah lifts her eyes and hisses, "I said I don't believe in ghosts." She stares at Susie Mae, daring her to argue.

Susie Mae drops her eyes. She raises her cloth napkin to wipe her mouth and then pulls it back and forth in her hands several times. Susan and I watch the girls and under her mother's eyes

Susie May abruptly lays her napkin beside her plate then places her hands in her lap.

Seeing that both girls are finished talking, Susan picks up her plate. "Well, I guess we should get the table cleaned off before Griffin is back ready for dessert." Susan starts stacking plates and Savannah is the first to leap to her aid.

Something is going on with my daughter and this ghost thing. I watch Susie Mae try to catch Savannah's eye as they clear the dishes but nothing works. Savannah has cut her out. Savannah and Angie are both so secretive and Susie Mae is quite a talker. I bet her secrets' privilege will soon be revoked.

# CHAPTER 15

These people think it's nothing to invite half-a-dozen people over for coffee.

"We're meeting at your house at 10 a.m. to discuss the tea and sleepover. We need to decide how to lay everything out. Tomorrow is fine with you, right?" That was all Missus said last night before she abruptly hung up.

Lying on the sofa, full of Susan's peach cobbler, I planned on watching reruns of "Friends" for a couple hours. But Missus' call threw my evening agenda under the train. I cleaned until one a.m. and now at eight a.m. I'm making a coffee cake from a recipe on the back of the Bisquick box, except I can't find cinnamon or vanilla. I'd probably be better off just cutting up and serving pieces of the box.

My coffee mugs not only don't match, they have things like "Bank of Marietta" or "Coffee or Die" written on them. Cloth napkins? I don't think so. Mine are paper—discount, generic paper. To buy cloth napkins or matching cups would mean I anticipated inviting people over. The coffee cups seemed fine for B&B folks. Hey, if they want to spend the night in someone's home then they get what they deserve. I feel expectation for the gathering today calls for something more. Something I don't have and thought I'd never want.

Whose life have I stumbled into, and don't they want it back?

Did I say coffee for half-a-dozen? Try a couple dozen. Missus called in the entire Historical Society. Luckily, the B&B committee members—who know me—all brought food. Laney showed up early with her forty-cup coffee maker. People own things like that? And did they stop to buy Danish and donuts? No, everything is homemade. Sticky orange-cinnamon swirls, cherry bites with drizzled icing, oatmeal-raisin bars, and fresh-cut fruit grace my counter. Cloth napkins wait patiently in Janice's Loganberry basket and Cathy's mom sent her full-set of Blue Ridge Crabapple coffee cups, saucers and dessert plates.

"And Mama said to just leave them here to be used this weekend unless Missus wants something fancier," Cathy tells me for the seven hundredth time. "Mama has to work during the day when we have our meetings, you know, but she wants to be a part."

Laney leans against the counter at my back and murmurs, "If Cathy'd get off her lazy, ex-cheerleader behind and get a job her mom could quit waiting tables at Ruby's. And I guarantee Missus will want china cups and saucer for the tea. Not this tacky dishware sold at roadside junk stores."

I turn to face her and change the subject before Cathy overhears Laney's catty comments. "What's Jenna think about the slumber party?"

Laney frowns, "She thinks Missus and her little girl group, Savannah, Angie, and now Susie Mae, have something up their sleeves. She's like me and suspicious by nature, but I've got to say this does seem strange." Laney hesitates and then leans closer to me, "Susan, Shaw and Mama all say I need to put a stop to this thing Angie and the girls have going with Missus. What do you think?"

"I, uh, I'm not sure. Savannah is so headstrong and I kinda, well, I kinda try to hmm, I don't know. What do you think?"

"That the girls are fine. They're smart. They know what

they're doing." After setting her coffee cup in the sink, she runs her hands down her hips, smoothing her taupe linen dress. Her gold jewelry flashes as she pushes her hair behind her shoulders. She shimmies her chest so it peeks out of the sedate, business dress then arranges her gold coin necklace to lie like buried treasure along top of her cleavage. "I hear Missus and Charles coming in the front, let's go see what they've got planned." She puts her hands on her hips and pushes her shoulders back. "Me and my new dress are hoping for a ribbon cutting ceremony Saturday."

Missus walks straight through the living room to the back yard. "We need to set the tables up outside so traffic for the open house will not be impeded. The weather is to be perfect this weekend."

From the deck, I watch her examine the back yard and deck. The men and women crowded around her keep their eyes on the tree line. Missus breaks off to walk around the yard, but the others huddle closer to the house. Their palpable fear strikes me. I don't feel any fear now around Tommy. I know he's out there, but I'm not afraid.

Charles scuttles across the yard, leaving Laney with the Mayor and another council member, both male. "Hey there, Carolina. You know, I need to get an interview with you for this week's paper, you know. Can we talk after this meeting?"

"Okay. I guess. What do you want to talk about?" But he's already cutting across the lawn back to Laney.

After today, I'm feeling better about this weekend. Everyone put this together in a couple hours. Laney and Susan keep telling me to let Missus handle everything, but I'm not great at, well, trusting people. My closed-off life meant less people to trust; so much simpler. I'm not sure if I'm actually learning to trust, or if I don't have a choice but to cling to them. Like a drowning man grabbing anything that floats.

"So, you know, I've heard you've seen this ghost. Right?" Charles sits on the edge of the couch with a notepad and pen in his hands, his elbows resting on his thighs. His head is pushed toward me, his jaw leading the way.

Is this supposed to make me comfortable and ready to talk? I grimace for a moment, but everyone's left, so might as well get this last thing over.

I take a deep breath and pretend I'm on the *Travel Channel* ghost show. My chin lifts and my eyes smile, "I've seen something, but..."

"I hear you talk to him."

Wait, who knows that? "Talk to him? Well, maybe just when, well... I don't know."

"Does he talk back?"

"No, no he doesn't talk back."

"So you do all the talking. Is he young or old? You know our research shows that a young man was killed by a train on the old bridge back in the 20's. Could that be him?"

"I thought he was a Civil War soldier."

"Did he tell you that? Is he wearing a uniform?"

"He's wearing a cap and a short jacket and long pants. I'm sure of that because everyone else had on shorts."

"You seem pretty comfortable with this ghost, you know. Aren't you afraid?"

"What's to be afraid of? He just wanders around, right? I find him to be company sometimes."

"This weekend you're hosting the young women participating in the pageant; do you think the ghost will make an appearance?"

"I don't know. Some of our guests have seen him."

"Okay, that'll do it." Charles slaps his notebook closed and stands up.

"Really? That's all?"

"I got everything I need for this week. I'll be here for the Open House on Saturday. See ya." He turns and leaves.

He'd hit the porch before I even thought about getting up, so I relax into the chair. The house is clean; the committee washed every dish and packed it all away. There are leftover goodies for when the kids get home later. The windows are open and crows call to each other. I lay my head back and close my eyes, but the conversation with Laney slams into my mind. What are the girls doing with Missus?

Sighing, I slide my feet into my shoes and stand. I need to talk to Tommy.

Sunlight peaks through high clouds and blue sky shows up in patches. A cool breeze greets me as I step off the deck. From this distance the willow is more yellow than green and enough leaves have fallen that when the breeze blows I can see the river sparkling through the willow curtain. More red and gold edge the full, green boughs. In the winter we'll probably be able to see the entire bend of the river. And snow? This hill in white and ice crystals coating the bare limbs—we'll need sleds, even if we only get a couple snowfalls a year, this hill is too perfect not to have sleds. I push aside the leaf drapes and step under the willow.

"Tommy, this place is so beautiful. I know why you just can't leave it." I shake out the old picnic tablecloth and then fold it into a square just big enough to sit on. "Did you see all those people here today? They were so scared you were going to jump out and say 'Boo!'" I laugh. "But you're not like that, are you?" I settle down with my back against the trunk of the tree.

"I was just thinking about how all this must look in winter. How many winters have you seen come and go here? I feel like you're part of this place. You belong here." I pick up a slender, yellow leaf and twirl it. I release it and watch the dry leaf drift to the ground.

"Do I? At times, I feel at home and then other times, well... I don't even recognize the person living in my own body. Like this morning, I'm standing next to gorgeous, confident Laney and she's whispering gossip to me about the people all around us. I felt like one of the popular girls at school. And everyone telling me how they enjoyed being here, in *my* home. It's wild."

"Sitting here though, watching the river, talking to you. This feels real. Were you lonely before I came? Were you on this riverbank waiting for me?" I chuckle. "I hope that doesn't creep you out."

Everything is so still now, the last breeze fades into nothing. I see something in the river coming closer. A log bounces past riding the current. "Wow, Tommy, look at that branch, how fast it's going, yet I didn't realize the water was moving at all." I watch the branch until it's out of sight.

"That's kinda like my life. Clipping right along, me never thinking about where I'm going or how fast." I shake my head and sigh, "Now, I can't stop thinking." My eyes tear up and I take a deep breath. "You know, I think Savannah and Parker had sex and that makes me so sad, but... honestly, Tommy, I don't really want to know. I just want her to grow up before she makes more and even bigger mistakes."

"It's hard, Tommy, knowing what to do, what to say. And this thing with Missus. Susan says we should get to the bottom of it; Susan wants to know. Laney says leave it alone; Laney doesn't want to know. And I don't want to make a decision either way. Can't it all just go away?" I screw my eyes shut tight. "I'm just a big ol' chicken. And Jackson comes home tomorrow. I don't want to deal with him either."

With my head back and eyelids relaxed, my thoughts wander for a few moments. My chest lifts and falls slowly.

Wow, a nap on the riverbank, how refreshed I feel. And Tommy must've been whispering in my ear while I slept, because I wake with one thought pulsing in my mind. "This is *your* life."

The thought pounds and makes me smile, strengthens me. But why should it? Of course, this is my life. I know that and I'm trying to make the best of the mess. But maybe it's not a mess? Maybe it *is* just my life?

I stand and stretch, "Thanks, Tommy, but I really don't come down here to get more questions." Through the branches, I see my house and behind it a train is flying past. Clouds filter the sunlight and the maple trees beside the house are dappled with shady spots. I pull the branches aside and gaze at the house and train and trees. *This* is my life. *My* life.

Okay, maybe I can work with that.

# Chapter 16

"So, Susan, what should we do about this thing with the girls and Missus?"

"Whoa, what's gotten into you? We've not even had any coffee. Give me a minute." Susan pours a stream of cream from the small metal pitcher on our table into her coffee. "I'm glad you called, I needed to get away from the church and the school. This time of year, I am at one or the other constantly. And Leslie is driving us all crazy at night with college applications."

"Where does she want to go?"

"University of Georgia is number one. If she goes out of state, she has to get lots of financial aid. We'll see. When Griffin and I went to UGA you just applied and went, no worries. Now it's crazy trying to get in."

She lifts her cup and takes a sip. Morning sunlight pours in the front of Ruby's, a rich, golden yellow and the air is brisk. I examine my arms, or really the sweater covering my arms. My mother sent it to me last year from a trip they took to Colorado. It's hand knit in shades of lime green and hydrangea blue. It comes to my knees and has a hood with a tassel and that hangs down my back. It is beautiful and luxurious—so not me. I laughed at the note my mother sent with it saying the sweater reminded her of me. Obviously, she's never met me. I never wear anything so brightly colored or extravagant. But today, well, today I'm wearing it. I know everyone is staring at me, but *this* is *my* life, Tommy says. My life.

"Isn't this wonderful? The warmth, a cup of coffee, a good

friend, people talking, nobody in a hurry." Susan takes a deep breath and I follow her example.

"This *is* nice—" I hesitate but the words jump out. "I've got to tell you something. Today is the first day since I was in college that I've called someone and asked to meet for coffee."

"Really?" Susan grins and shakes her head at me, "Why?"

"Why did I call you or why didn't I ever do it?"

She smiles wide, straight, white teeth in her tan face and shrugs. With her hair in a simply ponytail and her dark blue, zippered hoodie she looks like she's in elementary school. "I guess both."

"Not sure." I wave at Ruby to let her know to send over some muffins, "Maybe it's that the kids are older and I'm not working."

"And maybe it's because people in Chancey don't let you breathe," Susan laughs.

"That could be some of it. A lot of it."

From behind the counter, a lady I've seen at church comes toward our table.

"Here you go, ladies."

"Libby, have you met Carolina yet?" Susan asks. Then she looks at me, "This is Libby Stone, Cathy's mom."

"Hey, nice to meet you. Cathy enjoys getting together with ya'll . She loves the B&B."

"Oh, you lent me the apple dishes for yesterday's meeting. Thank you. They are beautiful. I don't have anything that nice."

Libby's light complexion reddens, "They are nice, aren't they? I get a new piece every birthday and Christmas. I always wanted beautiful dishes when I was growing up. I like for them to get used, no sense in having something so pretty sit around collecting dust."

"I've seen you at church, you sing in the choir don't you?" I ask.

"Why, yes, I do. You ought to come join us. We have a lot of fun and you don't actually have to be able to sing. We truly take to heart that God says he loves a 'joyful noise.' Y'all need coffee? I best get to making a round with the pot. Nice to meet you, Carolina."

"You, too." I turn to Susan. "She seems awful nice. Cathy and her son live with her folks?"

"Yeah, it's a heartbreaker. Cathy got pregnant during football season senior year. She's a born cheerleader and she's so enthusiastic about everything—even her quickie Christmas wedding. Poor Libby and Bill, they'd been determined for years Cathy was going to college. Libby even had a tip jar here labeled "Cathy's College Fund" and for years, she immediately put all her tips in it. Anyway, Cathy and Stephen got married but divorced that summer around their six-month anniversary. Stephen went away that fall to college and graduated this past May. He moved back here this summer."

"For Cathy and the baby?"

Susan shakes her head and waits as Libby walks near our table. "No, he's teaching at the high school and engaged to be married this Christmas. The baby, Forrest, is almost five now and Stephen's only seen him once since he's been back."

"Oh, that is a heartbreaker. I don't know what I'd do if Savannah got pregnant."

Susan nods, "I know. Leslie is so focused I really never worry about her, but Susie Mae, well, no. Everyone knows Susie Mae would never do something like that, right?" Susan's ponytail sways side to side. "No way."

"So what do you think is going on with Missus and the girls?"

Susan lifts her cup to get Libby's attention, "I'm not sure. I'm not scared of them getting in trouble. Missus is the soul of propriety and I'm sure she makes them toe the line, but a blip is growing on my mama radar. Griffin's beside himself. He says, well, you heard him the other night, he says Missus is crazy. That she's obsessive about building Chancey into some kind of tourist Mecca, like Helen or Dahlonega. And then..." Susan twists her mouth as she pauses.

"What?"

"Really, I think Griffin is more scared of Susie Mae being with Angie than her being with Missus."

"Yep, I can sure see that. What is the deal with her and the black stuff and the piercings? To be honest, I was shocked when Savannah started hanging out with her."

"Laney says it's just who she is and we've all kinda accepted that. She is a sweet, sweet girl, but my daughter wouldn't be allowed to run around like that. Shaw's gone so much and he never could put his foot down with Laney or the girls."

The front door flies open and Missus dashes toward our booth.

"Scoot over, let me in. Scoot," she hisses at Susan. She doesn't wait for Susan to move over, she drops beside her and pushes. "There."

Mouths hang open all over the café, especially at the table Missus has joined.

"What is going on?" Susan asks.

"Nothing."

"Nothing, my eye. Tell us what is going on right this minute," Susan demands.

Before Missus answers, the door flings open.

"I saw you come in here. You think I won't say anything in front of all these people? You got another think coming, Shermania Cogdill Bedwell." FM stands in the door with hands on hips.

Missus picks up the muffin Susan had eaten half of and shoves it in her own mouth.

FM marches to our table and turns to face his wife. "Well?"

She lifts her hands, shrugs and mumbles, "Wait a minute. My mouth is full."

FM scowls at the people in the booths next to us and then sits down beside me. "Scoot over, lady. I need to sit here for a minute."

Susan leans over the table and whispers, "What in the world is going on? You two are going to have Ruby calling the police if you don't stop this."

"Missus, FM, do you want me to call the police?" Ruby has on a black and gold Chancey High t-shirt over a red turtleneck and black nylon jogging pants. In her hand, she brandishes a cordless phone over our table. "I've threatened to call the police many times over the shenanigans in this place, but I've never actually gotten to dial 911 and my dialin' finger is itchy."

I clamp my lips to keep my burst of laughter inside. Ruby is Dirty Harry.

"Sure, call 'em." FM hollers. "There's been a robbery."

Missus picks up the cream pitcher and calmly speaks to her husband, while crumbs blow out with each word. "If you don't shut-up, I'm going to throw this on you." She turns to Ruby, "Good morning, Ruby. I believe we would like some muffins, those cheesy bacon ones, if you have them. And please bring two more cups of coffee. That's all."

Ruby likes being dismissed by Missus about as much as she liked getting dismissed by Laney my first time in here. She weaves back and forth like her itchy dialing finger is getting the best of her, then leans over Missus. "I'll have you know you ain't nothing I ain't seen before, Shermy."

Missus ignores her and finally, with an upward tip of her chin, Ruby leaves our table.

"Carolina, how are things progressing with the weekend plans?" Missus directs her question to me, but never takes her eyes off FM.

"Fine."

"Really, that's all you have to say? Everything is so fine you're sitting here having a little chat session with Mrs. Lyles?"

"You're crazier than a yellow jacket in a Coke can," Susan spits at Missus. "You're going to rag on her? Now what in the Sam Hill is going on?"

FM bursts, "She stole it. It was my great-granddaddy's from the Civil War. It always hung above the mantle. Daddy himself hung that there when Great Grandma Lavonia passed on. She gave it to him as the oldest son and then on his death-bed, Daddy made me promise it would hang there for as long as I live. Dadburn you, Missus, I promised my daddy on his death bed, you was even there. You heard me promise."

Ruby sashays to our table with our muffins. I'm glad Laney's not here to point out that Ruby has again came out from behind the counter twice to deal with my table. "Here you go, FM.

Have a muffin and you'll feel better. Libby, put their cups right there." Ruby waggles a corner of her behind on the seat next to FM and then puts an arm around his shoulders. "You know she's probably just messed up her medicines, FM. It'll be okay."

Missus moves her eyes off her husband and digs two holes into Ruby. "You must have lost your mind, Ruby Jean Harden. Get your nylon covered rear end off that seat and put it back behind that counter where it belongs. If you ever touch my husband again, no one will need to call 911, the police will hear you screaming."

"Libby, pour their coffee so they can get out of here quicker," Ruby says as she stands up. "I have work to do."

During the commotion, I noticed the bell on the front door ringing, but not until now do I realize an audience formed. All the chairs, booths, and stools are taken, when only fifteen minutes earlier there were plenty of empty spots. Libby is racing from table to table, taking as many orders as possible before the crowd disperses.

Susan rolls her eyes, "Now look. You've attracted a crowd. Okay, so about this, whatever it is you say she stole. What exactly are we talking about?"

Little crumbs blow out of Missus' mouth, "Shhh, not so loud." Then she adds another big bite to the full mouth she already has.

FM shakes his head, "Missus, I'm warning you. If that shows up on eBay I'm, I'm... I don't know what I'll do."

She mumbles, "Do not be so silly. Eat."

FM looks around at the folks openly watching our table, picks up a muffin, and then dips his knife in the bowl of creamy butter. He takes his time buttering the muffin before taking a bite.

Susan and I stare at each other, then I pick up my muffin I'd been eating before the excitement. "So Susan, we were discussing why our daughters are spending so much time with Missus these days."

"Yes, we were. I think when we finish our breakfast we'll be taking a walk around the corner to the Bedwell home for a little talk, won't we?" Susan turns to Missus who nods as she thrusts another hunk of golden, cheesy muffin into her mouth

FM pulls his head back and looks over at me. "Oh yeah, Mrs. Jessup, I'm coming to that bonfire Saturday night. Do you want some homemade beer? I make a great brew."

I freeze, picturing a hillside of drunk council members looking for the ghost with a gaggle of beauty contestants squealing in the background. "Uh, I don't think so, Mr. FM, but thanks for asking."

"Okay, just want to help." He lifts his perfectly buttered muffin half, stares at it, then snorts. "Missus said you didn't want any beer, but who believes a thief?"

Missus leads us onto her front porch. "Let's stay out here. I don't have all day to sit and visit."

Like we interrupted *her* morning.

Susan takes a seat in the porch swing and I sit in a white wicker rocker with purplish-blue cushions. FM sits on the top step, a little removed from the conversation. Missus spreads her celery green skirt out as she sits on the wicker loveseat. Her hands are ungloved and she appears at a loss for what to do with her hands for a moment. I stand back up to take off my sweater, the little walk and higher sun warmed me up.

"I must say, Carolina, that sweater becomes you," Missus notes.

"Thank you. My mother sent it to me last year."

"Did she make it? It looks like it was made for you."

I fold the sweater over my arm, "She didn't make it, but it does fit well."

"The colors are what fit you," Susan adds.

"Really?"

"Absolutely. Good strong vibrant colors." Missus lifts her chin. "Now, what do you ladies want to talk about?"

I sit back down, the sweater folded across my lap. I stroke

it and wonder about their comments. Susan gets my attention back on our mission.

"What is going on with you and our daughters?"

"Why do you want to know?"

"Excuse me?" Susan is as thrown by this answer as I am. "We're their mothers."

Missus shakes her head gently and smiles, "You have nothing to worry about. They are helping me with some research for the museum. I found Angie and Savannah in the museum one day and we became interested in some, uh, some undiscovered aspects of the war."

"Savannah and Angie were in the museum?" Susan and I ask at the same time.

"Yes, yes they were," Missus says confidently.

Okay, she's lying. There is no way Savannah walked into that museum on her own two legs. No way in the world, but really, would Missus just lie?

"And then I suggested to Savannah she enter the pageant. First, she was reticent but under my gentle persuasion, she realized her potential. I know you'll agree, these girls need someone to teach them how to become graceful, Southern young ladies. I've thought for years we need a cotillion class like when I was a young woman." Missus smoothes her skirt and waits for us to agree.

"You're teaching them manners? First you say they're hanging out in the museum and now you're saying they willingly spend so much time here because you're teaching them cotillion etiquette?" Susan set the swing in motion with a kick of her feet. "I don't think so."

"Now wait a minute here, I thought we were going to talk about my sword!" FM has left his perch on the steps and is standing over his wife. "What did you do with my great-granddaddy's sword?"

"You stole his great-grandpa's sword?" I sputter. We just keep going further down the rabbit hole.

"I did not steal his great-granddaddy's sword and I want this conversation to cease right now. FM, you have a whole bed of irises that needs to be divided and replanted. You have my word that your sword will be back above the mantle one week from today. That's all I'm going to say on the subject. As for the girls," she turns ice-gray eyes on us, "I am appalled at the questioning of my judgment and honesty."

Her gaze chills the morning air and the questions freeze on our tongues.

FM rubs the back of his neck for a minute and bobs his head a couple times. "Okay. Good enough for me. One week from today." He shoves his hands in his pants pockets and stabs his head at me and Susan. "You ladies want any irises? I'm going to have a couple bagfuls of tubers to get rid of."

Susan looks at me and I stare at her. Cotillions, swords, and irises—somehow we lost control of this conversation.

Susan sighs, "Sure, I'd love some irises."

I shrug and lift my palms in acquiescence, "Me, too."

Missus stands, stiffens her back and bestows a queenly nod, "I thought so."

# Chapter 17

"No. You can't be here. This doesn't work at all."

"Mom, it'll be fine," Will assures me as he hugs me again. "We didn't even bring home laundry because we knew you'd be busy this weekend."

"So if you knew I'd be busy, why are you here?"

My tall, blond son grins and shrugs, while his friend T.J. peeks around him, "Isn't there going to be like these beauty queens here or something?"

Will elbows him, "Shut up. But, yeah, Savannah was talking on Facebook about your guests this weekend and I thought we could come help you out."

Oh no, they're here for the girls. "There's no room. You can't stay."

"But I checked with Savannah and her room is empty so we're going to crash there. You won't even know we're here."

Jackson pulls open the screen door and wades through the Friday evening, standing-room only crowd in the living room. He drops his suitcase when he sees Will. "Hey, what are you doing here?" After he hugs his son, he gives me a hug and kiss.

"They heard about the girls being here this weekend."

"Really?" He gazes at me to get a read on what he's suppose to say, but I see in his eyes a desire to high five his son.

"This isn't a good idea, is it?" he asks, reading the teleprompter in my eyes.

"No, it's not a good idea."

He nods and looks back at Will. "Really, son. You should've

called and talked to us about it."

Will hangs his head, wheat-colored hair falls in his eyes as he looks back at us. "But we're here now and what if we really do try and help?"

Jackson shrugs, "Okay. Well, as long as you help and don't cause any problems, I think it'll work, right honey?" Jackson nods at me but doesn't meet my eyes. "So where y'all going to sleep?"

"Savannah's room."

"But she's sleeping there tonight," I interject. How did this go from "no" to "go"?

Will starts herding his friends toward the stairs, "She said she'd stay on the couch or something. She's been talking to me and T.J. about it on Facebook."

Of course she did. I don't really know much about this Facebook thing, but I hate it.

"C'mon, Mom. It'll be fine, really."

"Is this all of you?"

"Yep, just us five: Me, T.J., Arthur, Brett, and Lon."

"I think it'll be fine, honey." Jackson gives me another hug. "The boys can help out with the bonfire tomorrow. Hey, d'ya hear that whistle?"

All six boys (including my husband who has been out working with trains all week) mash out the front door to watch the oncoming train.

Standing in the living room door, I know that the three-engine, seventy-car Norfolk Southern train bearing down on the bridge out front is nothing compared to what's headed my way this weekend.

Sunflowers, big heads with velvety brown centers crowned with glorious golden-yellow petals fill pitchers and vases inside and outside my home. Fresh flowers have occasionally shown up at my house for anniversaries or birthdays, but never like this.

At 11 a.m. flowers and dishes and food, started showing up for the 2 p.m. tea. Jackson, Will, and the rest of the boys were situated around the TV in the living room eating bagels and watching ESPN's *College GameDay*.

Laney stepped into the center of them (I swear she licked her lips but I'm not going to think about that) and announced that they were to go to her house where Shaw has a big screen TV and five pounds of lunch meat. They stood, stretched, and left. All their unasked questions answered.

My daughter opened her mouth to object but Laney stopped her with a raised hand, "No, Jenna is not at my house. She's at Susan's getting ready."

Savannah smiled and acknowledged Laney's girl savvy with a nod. "Okay, 'cause T.J.'s mine."

"I thought you and Ricky were going out?" I asked.

"After the way he played last night, not hardly. I'm getting in the shower."

My shudder couldn't be helped. "She's so cold."

Laney pushed her UGA sweatshirt sleeves up to her elbows, "Well, Ricky's my nephew and I love him, but he had me rethinking his Christmas gift last night. He was bad, real bad. Now let's get this place ready."

And now, the train affectionately known as *The Pageant Tea* is leaving the station. A huge bouquet of sunflowers welcomes the tea guests into the living room. The tea is in full swing in the back yard and everything in the house awaits the open house. Red and white enamel ware pitchers in each guest room brim over with more bright sunflowers. In the kitchen and dining room, emerald green glass vases and serving dishes sparkle in the afternoon sun. Tiny sandwiches and fruit fill the borrowed dishes and wait for the open house to begin at three o'clock.

The transformation of our backyard amazes me, it looks like a spread in Southern Living. The table where the contestants sit is covered in white lace and old linen. The sunflowers try to compete, but don't stand a chance against the glossy hair, bright eyes, and vivid sun-dresses. The girls chatter and laugh. Their beauty and youth causes me to catch my breath. Those of us at tables around them know how the sunflowers feel.

Cathy Stone brings a pitcher of lemonade to the table of mothers and offers refills. Laney lifts an eyebrow, "So, Cathy, are the girls behaving over there or telling any stories we mothers should know about?"

"They're looking forward to tonight, the bonfire and the special guests."

"Oh, who are the special guests?" the mother to my right asks.

"The town council has been invited," Laney interjects. "I'm sure that's who the girls are talking about."

"Why would they be excited about them?" a suspicious mother at the end inquires.

"Oh, you know," Laney waves her hand in the air, "Just to be treated like royalty, and of course the press will be here also."

"That's right," an enthusiastic brunette to my left says. "I do hope April doesn't hide in the back like usual. She's so shy and worried about being too tall and she hates it when people notice her for her hair. It is completely natural, my mother had the same shade of red." Just over April's mother's shoulder, I see Laney rolling her eyes. Earlier today, Laney filled me in on the other girls. She knows all four and their mothers. I must remember Laney might not be the most generous, or even truthful, commentator.

"Well, Carolina, what about this ghost we've heard about? You've talked to him and everything?" The mother of Natalie, the shortest and least beauty queen looking entry, asks from across the table. "I saw your interview in the newspaper."

Suddenly, I'd rather confess there are five college guys sleeping on the premises tonight and have that conversation. However, Missus threatened my life if I let anyone know about the boys.

"You know, Charles spent maybe five minutes interviewing me. I don't know where he got all that information. Like, him saying the ghost is a man killed while hopping a ride back in the depression. I don't think anyone knows who the ghost is."

"Didn't you say you thought he was a Civil War soldier?" Laney asks. "Some relative of Missus'?"

"And you all sit right there on your front porch talking?" Natalie's mother squeals, "Look I have goose-bumps just thinking about it."

"No, not on the porch. We meet down at the willow tree."

Silence and hanging mouths create a chasm between me and the rest of my table. I think I said too much.

"I'm joking, it's just a feeling I have when he's around and when ..." involuntarily my eyes dart to the willow tree and every head turns to it.

"That tree?"

The breeze picks that moment to dance through the hanging leaves and everyone at my table shivers. Laney turns, slowly shakes her head and whispers, "I thought you were joking but I feel like something's out there."

A hush settles on the other two tables and all eyes watch the swaying curtain of yellow and green leaves. Was that a shadow of someone walking underneath the tree?

"Time for dessert," Cathy announces from the deck and scared shrieks jump back at her.

"You scared me to death!" April's mom yelps. With a hand to her chest she leans toward me, "I swear I thought I saw something. Are you sure it's safe for the girls to stay here tonight?"

Hey, there's a thought. I pull my face into a mask of sorrow, "Maybe we should cancel." Could Tommy be my salvation? "If you're not comfortable...?"

"Like I could get Pace away from here now," her mother exclaims. "Look at them, they can't wait to sleep in a haunted house."

Sure enough, the girls' table practically levitates from the circling buzz.

"Oh, they'll be fine. My daughter, Angie, has stayed here many nights and nothing's ever happened." Laney dismisses any concern and lifts her fork, ready for the slice of peach pie Cathy is setting in front of her.

The homemade pie calms everyone down, but still it's obvious the willow tree is under scrutiny. Quick glances in that direction and intense stares when possible are hard to miss.

Natalie's mother finishes her pie, wipes her mouth with the white, cut-work napkin and then reaches out to pat my hand as she loudly opines, "I guess we may never know if the ghost is just a homeless ne'er do well or Civil War soldier. Really, does it matter?"

"Of course it matters!" Missus stands at her table. "We don't need some mangy bum too stupid to get off the tracks wandering around our town. That's just ridiculous. Everyone knows these mountains are full of our brave boys just trying to finally get home and have some peace."

"Now, Missus," Chammy Phillips, whose last run-in with Missus involved being blackmailed and losing the Pageant Tea, wades into the conversation. "You just think a soldier from the War will give you a heads-up on the grant application. Although, everyone knows your ghost is just some hobo who fell off a train back during the depression—hardly anything to build a tourist attraction around."

"At least he's not naked and running around in his school tie, right Carolina?" Missus spits as she drags me into her battle with Chammy.

"Ah, no. We don't allow naked ghosts."

Chammy Phillips throws her napkin down on her empty plate at the committee's table. "You listen to me, Shermy Bedwell. You leave Randolph out of this or I'm going to..."

"Thank you to all the committee members," Laney announces. She stands up and starts applauding.

I clear my throat and speak up over the weak clapping, "Girls, make sure you have your cases and whatever you need before your mothers' start home." I leave my table and walk over to the girls to start them moving. While doing so, I steal glances at the woods. Did Chammy's comment make Tommy mad?

An orange extension cord lies across the deck, snakes around the s'mores table, crosses between tubs of soda and ends at a small TV situated near the bonfire.

"What's with this?" I ask Jackson, pointing at the cord.

"For the game. Georgia-Alabama starts at 8 pm." If you want anyone to stay for this bonfire, you gotta have a TV out here."

"You tell Missus that. I'm not getting involved."

"I'll just have Will tell her," Jackson grins as he shoves his hands in his jean pockets and walks toward me and the deck. "She's deeply infatuated with our son, you know. He took her for a ride in T.J.'s truck and is 'yes ma'aming' and 'aw shucking' her up one side and down the other."

"Yeah I know. I'd be embarrassed to death if it wasn't working so well."

The girls tumble out the kitchen door in cut-offs and tank tops. The moms left flinging out instructions for behavior and apparel but when the last car crossed the tracks, the sun dresses were history.

In the lull between afternoon and evening games, and in the absence of mothers and committee members, the college men descended on the house.

Will had come home earlier to schmooze Missus and run errands. However, with errands done and the shadows stretching across the trees, the kids have a jaunt on the walking bridge planned. Savannah jogs down the deck steps and grabs T.J.'s hand. She pulls him toward the driveway side of the house and the crowd follows.

Their chatter and laughing fades and I sit down on the top step. Jackson joins me. He puts his arm around me and I lay my head on his shoulder. We've had no time to talk since he got home yesterday. The house being full of people and activity makes the distance between us acceptable. We've yet to talk about the ghost, or his suggestion I'm crazy. When he travels, I feel like we never complete a conversation or know what's on each other's mind.

For the first time, ever, this doesn't bother me.

"Hey, I'm going to Grant's now, okay?" Bryan opens the door

and sticks his head out.

"Okay, behave yourself and we'll see you at church in the morning." I pull away from Jackson and turn to look at the youngest Jessup. "And you better not be wearing that same shirt, you hear?"

He rolls his eyes. "'kay." The door slams behind him.

"Hey, we actually got rid of a kid." Jackson says as I lay my head back on his shoulder. He then adds, "Of course we gained ten in his place. It sure is crazy here, isn't it?"

"You've noticed? I feel like I've been dropped in some made-for-TV movie."

"Well, the kids seem happy, and I do love my job. I don't like being gone, but I don't hate Monday mornings now." He squeezes my shoulders, "But what about you? How are you doing?"

"I guess I'm fine. Chancey takes some getting used to and the B&B thing doesn't seem real. Laney and Susan are great. But it doesn't feel like home, yet."

"You miss Marietta and your job?" He drops his arm from me and leans back.

Laughter comes from the river side of the house where the kids are on the bridge. A squirrel darts around the stacked wood waiting on the fire tonight. Orange and violet clouds sail over the mountain ridge across the river. Sitting on my old deck gave me a view of at least half dozen other houses, nothing like the beauty here. This hill, our home here brings such solitude, such aloneness. And yet, I almost feel swallowed in people and drama and decisions.

"I don't know. I don't actually miss it ... ."

Jackson waits, but I can't finish my thought. I don't know what I'm feeling or thinking. Would I go back if I could? Do I wish this move had never happened?

Answers just don't come.

# CHAPTER 18

The clouds skated across the sunset and dusk brought an empty, darkening sky, which fills, one-by-one, with stars. Sparks leap from the fire to join the show in the heavens and as they lift, up and up, it seems they might break free. But they only disappear in the darkness or tumble back to earth. A strange mix of people circle the fire. The youthful freshness of the girls, the strong faces of Will and his friends, and then the weary but content countenances of council members all stare into the fire.

Will and his friends being here works out great. They pull us together because they are comfortable with adults and teenagers. They bridge the gap that would've existed. Jackson pokes the fire with his stirring stick. He looks up at me, winks and then nods across from me. I follow his nod and see Missus seated between Will and Savannah on one of the benches we set up. What is it with her and my kids? Also, Savannah and T.J. are holding hands.

FM, Griffin, and two other council members are huddled in a corner they've made out of two picnic benches. The TV is at the apex of their corner and they huddle to hear the sound that is turned down low. The boys can see the TV but they say they don't need to hear the announcers as long as UGA is winning.

Seated behind our rickety card table, I'm elbow-deep in chocolate bar wrappers, graham cracker crumbs and marshmallow goo. I'm s'more central. Why is this a mom job? There are at least 15 men (Will and crew included) here who have in their lifetime each eaten their weight in s'mores, but can't quite figure out the complicated recipe. And the girls might as well be putting worms on hooks as spearing marshmallows on sticks.

Okay, I'll give that I did buy cheap marshmallows, the costs being saved in the powdered-sugar coating that keeps them from sticking together. So instead of a bag of fluffy, white, treats, I have a mass of gooey, gummy, sticky sweetness which I am pulling lumps off. I then mold the lumps around the end of the sticks so they can be melted, possibly browned and/or blackened, lumps.

Then in between molding marshmallows to be roasted, I'm scraping the toasted gunk off the sticks with two graham cracker squares—one of which has a section of chocolate bar placed in its center. I hand the mess to the roaster, who oohs and aahs over their amazing culinary creation. Emeril Lagasse would be "bamming" their heads together if he had to cook under these conditions.

"Jenna! You're going to poke me in the eye! Quit flirting and watch what you're doing." I yelp as I grab the stick headed for my face. Molten marshmallow threatens only inches from my nose.

"Sorry, Ms. Carolina," she giggles, looking at me for maybe a second. "April, get up! I'm sitting next to Arthur."

I scrape her s'more together, hand it to her with my right hand while my left hand grips the stick still threatening to leave goo in my hair. "Here. Take your s'more and sit down."

"Thanks!" She sashays over to claim her spot by Arthur, the tall, thin UGA tennis player. If the way he's gazing at Jenna is any clue, we'll be seeing more of him around Chancey. He and Will were roommates at orientation last summer and are still good friends. He's from Massachusetts and Jenna's southern belle lessons, learned at her mother's knee, are magic. April didn't move so Jenna wiggles a seat next to him and the way she's licking the goo off her fingers has Arthur watching like she's playing at Wimbledon.

"Will, please hand me another Diet Coke," I shout across the fire. I'm going to need all the caffeine I can get to stay awake on my guard couch tonight. There will be no fraternizing on my watch. And my watch is all night.

"Can I have one of those?" Charles Spoon sidles up to my table as he sticks his reporter notebook in the back pocket of his baggy jeans.

"A stick? Sure. I guess you want a marshmallow too." I hand him a stick to hold and then mash a lump of marshmallow onto the stick. "You getting some good pictures?"

"Sure, you know. This is a great idea. I haven't been to a bonfire since I was back in school. Don't know why, cause I sure do like it, you know." He sways back and forth as I take my time.

"Your article about me and the ghost, why did you ask me about talking to him? How did you, I mean, why did you think that?" I grip the stick so he can't walk away.

"Don't know. You do, don't you? Talk to him? You said so in the interview, right?"

"Yes," I take a breath, "But why did you even ask me that in the first place?"

He shifts his weight around on his feet and then stares at me. "What are you asking me? I don't understand what you're talking about. You talk to the ghost. You told me that."

"But who told you first?"

"You? I don't know. If you don't want people knowing you talk to a ghost then don't tell a newspaper reporter." He growls as he jerks his roasting stick from my grasp. "You sure are strange. Telling me stuff and then wanting to know who told me."

He marches off to the fire and I try to remember. *He did mention it first, didn't he?*

"Here's your Diet Coke." Will pops the top for me and sets it on the table then he squats down beside my chair. "You think we're done with the s'mores? Me and the guys thought it'd be cool if we all took a walk across the bridge. It's so awesome being out above the river when it's so still and dark."

"And when there are so many young, pretty girls?"

"Doesn't hurt, but we were thinking of everyone going. What

do you think?"

"Sounds good to me. You're right about it being great out there at night. Why don't you get Griffin or Missus or FM to announce it."

Will explains his thoughts to Griffin who stands and stretches. He nods at Will so it must meet with his approval.

"Folks, Will Jessup has a great idea. Since it's half-time of the game a little walk out on the bridge might be called for. Especially since many of you are the council members that made that bridge happen."

I shove all the wrappers and empty marshmallow bags into the empty graham cracker box and then try to stand without touching anything with my sticky fingers.

Jackson walks over and pulls out my chair I'm trying to scoot back with my legs. "Here, let me get that." He lifts the chair and moves it away. "Think the fire would be okay if I went too?"

The simmering fire is clearly within the stone-edged circle. "Yeah, I think it'll be fine. We can keep an eye on it from there and we won't be long."

"Wow, you're a mess," he comments when he steps forward and can see me in the firelight.

"Thanks for noticing. I think the s'mores were a hit. You go on with the others, I'm going through the house so I can wash up."

As I step up on the deck, the last of the group hooks around the driveway side of the house. Back towards the fire, Jackson lays his stirring stick down. He then tucks his hands in his pockets and walks around the river side of the house to meet up with the group. Between the hill slanting to the river and the house is only a small path through the brush and woods, which is why Will led the group around the other way.

Inside the kitchen, I set the left over chocolate bars on the counter and throw the extra bag of cheap marshmallows in the garbage. I take a sip of my Diet Coke and turn toward the hall to the bathroom in the guest area, but realize there is part of a chocolate bar stuck to my sleeve. I must've laid my arm on it when it was soft and melted. Now it's attached for life. Roughly,

I pry it off and circle back to the kitchen garbage can.

Now my shirt needs to be changed, so I dash up the stairs. In our bedroom I take off my shirt without turning on the light. That way the blinds don't have to be closed. Light from the hall lets me see in our bathroom, where I wet a wash cloth and run it over my face and arms. Goo-free, I grab my red West Georgia University hoodie hanging on a hook behind the door and throw it on. Shoot! I hear a train, and I'm going to miss it. Standing on the walking bridge as a massive train barrels across the river only yards away takes your breath away. At night it's even more impressive.

I run down the stairs and grab the front door-knob just as the train roars across the bridge. A quick look out the front window, reveals the yard illuminated by the engine light. Someone stands by the tracks, waving a stick or something at the train. I step away from the door and push my face between the curtain and the window sash to see the front yard. The train, and its light, is gone, but the person with the stick runs toward the house. The man, or woman, hurries up the porch steps, right toward me. I drop the curtain, pull open the door, and race onto the porch. But no one's there. The end of the train moves past and shouts come from the direction of the bridge.

"Did you see it? Was it him? Where did he go?"

The boys are first to the porch. "Mom, it was the ghost! Did you see it? Where did it go?" Will paces at the side of the house. "Looked like he came right here."

"Yeah, I saw him and then he got right about there and disappeared. I saw him through the living room window."

"I want to go home. I'm not staying here with a ghost." April is crying and peeking out from behind Arthur. She has a wad of his shirt clutched in her hand so he can't move more than six inches from her.

"You said you wanted to see the ghost this afternoon," Jenna spits with a toss of her blonde ponytail. But she's got her arm wrapped tight around her Uncle Griffin's arm.

Charles Spoon scurries up, he not only runs crab-like, he's weighted down by his camera. "Is he still here? Which way did he go?"

Will and the boys had darted around the side of the house as they sprint back toward us they shout, "No one around there. He's gone."

T.J. steps up to Charles, "Did you get any pictures?"

The newspaper editor rubs his forehead, then pitches his head back. "No. Just you dang fool kids running towards him. He took off as soon as you started running. So someone who got closer tell me what you saw. He had something in his hand, didn't he?"

"Yeah, it was like a stick or a hoe and he was waving it at the train. I thought he was going to step right out in front of the train, didn't you?" Arthur is prying April off him as he talks.

Jenna releases her grip on her uncle's arm, "Can we go back to the fire and talk. I want to sit down." She takes a step towards Arthur, who puts his arm around her and starts around the house.

"I don't want to go back to any old fire. I want to go home," April demands. Her face is shiny with tears and Natalie puts an arm around her.

"I'm sure we're fine. He's gone now, isn't that right, Ms. Carolina?"

My mouth doesn't seem to work, probably because my brain is shuttling information back and forth trying to put together what just happened. Jackson steps up on the porch and guides me to sit down in a rocker, but I shake him off. "No. Jenna's right. Let's go out back." I push Jackson towards the steps and start towards him when I'm grabbed from behind.

"Hey, whoa!" Pace Jacobs, the contestant from neighboring Collinswood had ran up on the porch when the group came looking for the ghost. As she turned to follow us down the steps she slipped and grabbed the hood of my sweatshirt.

Grace and youth kept her from falling, but I land right on my unyouthful, ungraceful behind and roll backwards so that my legs lift into the air.

Jackson and Pace grab my arms to help right me.

"Stop. Wait." I close my eyes, bite my tongue, and think

about the pain. Is it real pain? Or just a stinger, like they say in football? Can I walk it off? Or am I in real trouble? I take a deep breath and relax my back. "Okay, I think I'm good. Just help me up, slow."

"I'm so sorry, Mrs. Jessup. I guess my sandals are slippery, my feet went right out from under me. I grabbed and didn't even think about making you fall." Pace's brown hair cups around her concerned face as she moves the rocking chair back. Griffin and Will help Jackson get me righted.

"I know, honey. I'm fine, I just need to rest a minute." Standing straight, I take another deep breath. Nothing feels too bad. "However, I think I just want to go inside. You all go on back to the fire."

"Are you sure?" Jackson asks as he opens the screen door.

"Yeah."

Will herds the group around the side of the porch.

I turn and plant one foot in the living room when I remember something. "And Charles, I saw all those flashes as I was hitting the deck and rolling around. Those pictures better not show up with some caption like "Haunting Hits Hotel-keeper Hard, you hear me?"

Charles grins and lifts his camera in salute, "Dang, Car'lina, you might have a knack for this newspaper thing, you know. That sounded pretty good."

# CHAPTER 19

Part of the deal with letting Will and his friends stay the weekend was that they would go to church Sunday morning. I thought that might make them rethink staying, but it didn't.

I give myself the morning off. A night of sitting/sleeping in the easy chair with my sore back makes sitting in a pew unappealing. Also, it may take several days for the water heater to catch up after all the showers taken to get rid of the smoky smell from the fire. I shooed Jackson out with the young people and now have the house to myself. I hid some leftovers from the tea yesterday in a cooler on the deck and when the coffee is done I'm having breakfast out there. The young adult Sunday School class is supplying muffins and coffee for everyone to meet the pageant contestants this morning, so we didn't have to feed them again.

My gray sweat pants and navy sweatshirt ward off the chilly air seeping in through the front screen door. Shadows still sleep on the front porch and after the noise from the leave-taking the house seems to be settling down for a little snooze before really starting the day. I lay my head back on the couch and close my eyes. The guests finally left last night a bit after midnight. Jackson watched over the boys and girls at the fire until nearly two am while I nodded off and on in the living room.

When they all came in, I got a second wind and dismissed all thoughts of any late-night rendezvous with my invitation for them to stay up with me and watch my set of five *Anne of Green Gables* dvd's. The boys shuffled up to the top floor and the girls closed themselves off in the guest rooms. The house was quiet until the cell phone alarms started announcing shower times at 6:30 am.

With a smile, I snuggle into my covers while the coffee drips into the pot; I survived the pageant tea and sleepover. After church the girls are heading home. I'm meeting Jackson and the college guys at the Chinese Buffett next to the Piggly Wiggly after church and after that the boys will pack up and go back to Athens. My shoulders liquefy as I realize by this time tomorrow, Jackson will be on the road to somewhere and Bryan and Savannah will be in school. I love Monday mornings.

My head jerks and I struggle to open my eyes. Ten o'clock. I fell asleep but my growling stomach wakes me up. I stretch and yawn my way to the kitchen. I fill my coffee cup to the brim, grab a saucer from the cabinet, and walk out on the deck. My back feels pretty good. The morning is all blue sky and breezes. Leaves, drying and changing color, rustle with the wind. Now it even sounds like fall.

I sit my cup on the table. Coolers with those blue freezer blocks hold the leftovers from yesterday. The coolers are lined up behind the table to be out of the way, I maneuver through the chairs and open the first one and a burst of cold air pushes out. But that's all it holds, cold air. Why would Jackson have put in new ice blocks if it was empty? I close the lid and open the next cooler. Again, no food just cold air. Okay, the third, and last cooler, better be full and then I realize there is no third cooler. There was a third cooler last night. We were rotating the freezer blocks and I changed them out last night before the bonfire and then Jackson did it when he came in at two a.m. Yes, I distinctly remember him saying he took care of all three coolers last night as he headed upstairs to bed.

Wait, there's no third cooler. Great, We've lost someone's cooler. Susan's probably. But even worse, my breakfast's gone. I was looking forward to a couple of those little cream cheese and cucumber sandwiches. And the strawberry tarts? those are gone, too. My stomach growls to remind me I've been promising it homemade delights. "I guess I'll just have to pretend with a

Pop Tart," I mumble as I stomp back into the kitchen. "This isn't fair. The only reason to have a party is the leftovers."

"Is that what you wore to church?" I hate for my first comment up on seeing my children to be negative, but he has on a too-small, holey Spiderman tee-shirt. Bryan nods at me as he runs across the gravel parking lot. He spins up gravel when he comes to a stop in front of me. I'm leaning against the side of my van. Church must've gone long today.

"Yeah, see, "he pokes a finger through the hole in the side of one of Spiderman's' legs. "It's my Holy shirt—perfect for church—get it? Holey, Holy?"

"Yes, I get it."

Susan comes up behind him, "Sorry about that. I had to go early to set up the video for the high school class and didn't see him until after church."

Griffin lays his arm around his wife's shoulders, "I thought it was funny. I thought everyone would get a kick out of."

Susan rolls her eyes, "You're the one that should be kicked." She shrugs, "Oh well, what can I say? I left the comedian here in charge. But never mind that, what about last night? Griffin told me the ghost showed up."

"I can't believe I wasn't there, again!" Grant kicks a spray of gravel up as we all start walking towards the restaurant entrance.

"Hey, stop it!" Susie May yells at her brother. She's tailing behind Savannah, Angie, and Jenna who are walking with the guys.

Will turns around and makes a dash at Grant. "That gravel hit me, you rug rat." They chase around the parking lot, but make it to the canopy entrance in time to go in with the rest of us.

"Savannah, see if you can get the long table," Jackson yells up to the front.

When we get inside its obvious the long table isn't big enough and it's filled with the kids.

Griffin commandeers another table for the adults. "Laney and Shaw will be here later. Shaw has a supposedly quick trustee's meeting after church and Laney went to some other church this morning."

I turn to Susan and lower my voice, "What is with her going to different churches?"

"We'll find out when she gets here. She says she needs different things at different times and one church doesn't fit her all the time. Who knows? It's Laney. But I want to know about last night."

"The ghost showed up, but I fell and then went inside so I missed out on all the conversation. You probably know more from Griffin than I know."

Jackson nods, "Everyone had pretty much the same story. We were watching the train and right after it crossed the bridge the headlight hit on a figure standing next to the tracks. It was holding something up and waving it. It was a man and it was all white, but we were way down on the bridge, so that's all we could see."

"And then it moved toward the house," Griffin adds as he tosses a clump of Chinese fried noodles into his mouth. He chews and leans forward. "Everyone started running and of course the boys were in front. They said he got near the porch and then disappeared."

"Yep, I had my hand on the door just at that point. I saw him run toward the house and I think he actually came up on the porch, then he was gone." I shake my head. "Something was weird, and I was trying to figure it out when the guys came rushing on the porch. Then I fell and with all the confusion I can't remember what I was trying to figure out."

Jackson picks up his plate and stands, "If we let those kids get in the buffet line before us there won't be anything left but those little corn cobs and flat green beans." He tilts his head toward me, "You were kind of out of it when we got to the porch.

You were staring at the rocking chair and not saying anything. Remember? I thought you wanted to sit down, but then you said we should go out to the fire."

We all stand, pick up our plates, and move to the front of the restaurant. "That's when Pace stumbled, grabbed my hoodie, and I fell."

Susan gets in line behind me, "How are you feeling this morning?"

"Better. A little stiff and I'm pretty black and blue on one hip. I think that's where I hit the rocker." I catch Susan's eye and nod to the kids table, "Look at that. Arthur is smitten with Jenna."

Susan grins, "Laney will be thrilled if Jenna is smitten, too. Since last year, Jenna's had a thing for the Addison boy who is dumber than a bag of rocks."

Arthur stands and puts out a hand for Jenna to take. She grips his hand and rises. I look for Savannah and find her at the corner of the table texting. Angie stands over her, reading what she's writing. T.J. is in line with Will and Bryan. Wonder who the girls are texting?

I fill my plate and set it on our table, then I ease my bruised body into the chair. "Hon, what did Savannah have to say about the ghost last night?"

Jackson, takes a bite of eggroll and shakes his head, "Nothing, right?" he asks Griffin.

"Not that I remember. She was talking on her phone, well, not talking doing that texting thing, you know." Griffin points a fork at Jackson. "Didn't she get mad at someone and leave the fire for a little?"

"She left the fire?" Susan asks.

"Alone?" I gape at Jackson.

Both guys lift their eyebrows. I set my lips and Jackson starts backtracking, "No, I'm sure she was alone. I would've noticed if she'd gone off with a guy."

Griffin nods too, "Oh, yeah. She was alone and she wasn't gone long."

Male self-defense has kicked in and the truth is whatever gets them out of trouble. I groan, "Whatever. So who was she mad at? Do you know that?" I try to keep sarcasm out of my voice, but I'm tired.

They look at each other, but the answer doesn't come.

"I'll ask Susie Mae later." Susan says, "She might know, although I think she's no longer in the inner circle."

"You know who else was uncharacteristically quiet?" Griffin attempts to regain his good standing with more info. "FM, didn't say a word about the ghost. Just kept staring into the fire."

"True, that is true." Jackson jumps on the re-instatement wagon, "He was full of bluster earlier, but then he just sat and stared until he left. Of course he was watching the game and it was so ugly for Georgia he might've been depressed about that."

"Now, Charles Spoon? He wouldn't shut-up. You know, he told about every ghost sighting this side of the Mississippi. You know, I couldn't wait for him to leave—you know!" We all laugh at Griffin's imitation of the editor.

Susan waves at the waitress to get a refill of her water. "So he says it's now proven the ghost is the hobo train rider, right?"

The waitress also fills my lifted glass. "What? How?"

"The anger of the ghost waving that stick at the train." Jackson recites. "I couldn't forget that because Spoon said it about four dozen times."

"And FM didn't say anything? Missus has been so sure it was a soldier I would've thought FM would be taking her part." I shrug. "Although Missus and FM rarely see eye-to-eye on anything."

Susan nudges my shoulder with hers, "Except your daughter. They are in total agreement she'll win the pageant."

Greetings from the kids table directed to the front door tell us Laney has arrived. She is wearing a hot-pink straight dress in smooth fabric with a sheen. The jacket has three-quarter length sleeves and falls to her waist. The square neckline shows no cleavage, and overall the dress is sedate. It looks like something Jackie Kennedy would've worn, of course in a more subdued color—until you look down. The hem hits at her knees and then those long tan legs end in hooker shoes. Hot-pink, four-inch, high heel slides that heat up the dress to incendiary levels.

Griffin grins, "She sure does provide a show. Always has."

Susan laughs, "Look at those boys, they're use to TV showing so much bare skin that they probably don't have any idea why that is so sexy. Wonder which church she upset today?"

"Hey all," Laney says as she sails to our table. And she does sail.

If I were wearing those shoes I'd be crawling.

"So, Sis, who did you grace with your presence this morning?"

Laney shakes her head at the waitress, "No, thank you, I don't need a plate. I've already eaten. But I would love a Diet Coke." She takes a deep breath and stretches out her arms. "I went to that darling little church over off the highway. I just needed to let God know how happy I am. I needed to shout and sway and lift my hands." She pulls out a chair and sits down, "Our sweet, little, 125-year old Myrtle Ames ploddin' out hymns on our ancient organ just couldn't do justice to how I feel today." She squares her chin and folds her hands underneath it, "I needed to be able to say 'Amen' and 'Hallelujah' without scaring the preacher into forgetting his sermon."

Jackson's intrigue causes his brow to crinkle, "So you go to different churches?"

"Why not?" Laney grins, "We say God is in all these different churches, why should he have all the fun? Sometimes I need to go where everyone is calm and quiet, and majestic music stirs my heart, and sometimes I need to go where the old hymns are sung by only a handful of people from old, worn books. Then there are days when I need deep, sincere prayer full of requests and concerns and praise and sometimes I need to go where the little children outnumber the adults and the place buzzes. Some Sundays I want the Word shouted and declared from the rooftops and other days I need preaching that is quiet and still so I can think."

"But don't you miss your friends, isn't fellowship part of church?" Curiosity gets the better of me.

"In Chancey? I can't get rid of these people. I see them morning, noon and night. Any more fellowship and I'm liable to get a gun. Thank you, darlin'" she says as the waitress hands over her Diet Coke. She takes a long sip through her straw. "So, what's this I hear about Savannah breaking Ricky's heart with that T.J. boy, and Ricky and her having a big fight right down on Main Street last night around midnight?"

Susan and I look at each other and then turn to our husbands. "What?"

"Yep, police picked them both up. Dropped Ricky off at Joe's, and took Savannah to her car parked out at the high school so she could drive home. Of course they followed her to make sure that's where she went."

"Why didn't they come in and say something?"

"She just waved and told them she'd go on back to the bonfire. They could see folks back there, so they just let her go. One of the officers was David Gutten." She leaned toward Susan and flicked her hand, "You know him. He took Leslie to prom her sophomore year and he graduated two years ago." Laney sits back and laughs, aware she has an attentive audience. "Savannah was throwing rocks from beside the tracks near the park at Ricky and he was hiding behind the little monument. She was yelling something about him embarrassing her and he was saying something about he was going to tell."

I look over my shoulder at the kids table to see if they can hear Laney, but something very interesting is apparently going on there as elbows rest on the table and everyone leans forward. Bryan and Grant are back in-line filling a plate with those fried dough balls rolled in sugar. I'm sure they were sent on that mission by one of their older siblings. With a little maneuvering, I can see who's talking—Savannah. She's probably filling in everyone about her brush with the law last night.

I push my seat back and wince. I forgot about my back. "I'm going to get some of those sugar balls." Laney is still talking so my movement surprises my table companions.

"What? Where are you going?" Susan's thin neck stretches to survey the scene. "What's going on?" But I'm already on my way to the buffet.

With the little tongs, I place a half dozen of the fried treats on my plate and walk to the kids' table. They immediately sit up and conversation stops. I pick up one of the light-brown, sugar-coated spheres between my fore-finger and thumb and hold it up. "Hmmm, Savannah, what do you think? If this were a rock, how far do you think you could throw it?" I meet her eyes leaving no doubt that I know the whole story.

Laughter spurts from Jenna. Will leans back and blows out a long breath. "Busted."

I turn for my table and hear behind me a flurry of whispers, "How does she know?" "Who told?"

Before I get to my chair, Savannah catches up with me. "How did you find out?"

"It sure wasn't from you, was it?" I dismiss her and sit down.

"Good job," Susan says quietly. "Keep'em wondering how you know and what you know."

"Yeah, good job," Jackson says as he reaches for a sugared treat from my plate.

I swat his hand, "Get you own, Mr. Bonfire watcher."

He raises a hand in surrender then stands up with his plate. "Good idea."

Laney takes one of the balls off my plate. "Wonder if dear brother Joe knows what Ricky is up to? And you know, I've not seen Ronnie around lately. Maybe I need to stop in and make a sisterly visit to Joe this afternoon. Wanna come?" she asks Susan.

Susan wipes her hands on her napkin, "Nope. I've got vegetables and flowers to get ready for the fair. They have to be there tomorrow by noon. I think I'll win several blue ribbons this year. Mom is working on a cake and pie and cookies, not to mention her canned goods." She turns to me, "I was going to ask if you wanted to come tomorrow with me to help me get everything there for judging?"

"Really? That would be fun. I haven't been to a fair in forever. I don't think my kids have ever been to a county fair."

"You know that's why there's early release Tuesday, right? So all the kids can go to the fair. Most of them are showing something—animals, artwork, vegetables."

Laney nods, "And the girls have a rehearsal tomorrow night.

You've seen the schedule, haven't you?"

With a shake of my head, I say, "No, Savannah and Missus say they've got it all under control."

Jackson and Griffin get up, "Guess we'll leave the pageant stuff to you ladies. We're going to get the check from the kids' table and see y'all outside, okay?"

"I absolutely *love* the fair and plan on being there every night. My only exhibit is Jenna, and we have hair issues to deal with this afternoon." Laney stands and smoothes the wrinkles across her lap, but tips her head towards the young people. "Who's that guy starring at my daughter like she's a hot Krispy Kreme doughnut?"

"That's Arthur, a good friend of Will's and on the tennis team at Georgia." I stuff my purse under my arm, "Let me tell you, Jenna has him wrapped."

"Good, she needs to work on her grades if she wants to go to UGA, maybe he'll be incentive." Laney winks, "You think he might want to come hang out at the pool today and she can practice for the swimsuit competition?"

My feet turn to rock, "There's a swimsuit competition in this pageant?" I screech. But I know the answer. *Of course* there's a swimsuit competition. My heart stops and my mouth dries, but I manage to announce, "No way is my daughter getting up there and prancing around in a bathing suit in front of a crowd."

Puzzlement jumps to Laney and Susan's faces and out of the corner of my eye, I see Savannah weaving around the other kids to get out the front door. I turn just in time to see her push past a couple coming in the door and dart onto the sunshine filled sidewalk.

"I can't believe there is a bathing suit competition. I just can't believe it."

Laney puts her hand on my arm and speaks softly, "Does she have a birthmark or something? Bless her heart, does she have some kind of physical problem?" Concern is overtaken by confusion on Laney's face, "Although, I've seen her in a bathing suit at the pool and she looked fine. I don't understand what's wrong."

"Really?" I just shake my head and laugh at my foolishness. The big-haired woman wearing four-inch, hot-pink, patent-leather heels doesn't understand?

Jackson leans over my well-padded, front-porch rocker. "There you go. Is it working?" He holds the temperature control for the heating pad. "I've got it on High."

"Umm, yeah. It's working." I close my eyes and lay my head against the thin pillow Jackson fashioned from a towel for me. The hard booth at the Chinese restaurant stiffened my sore back.

"Told you I'd make it okay for you to sit out here." He arranges a table at my side so my ice tea is within reach. "Just plugged the long extension cord into the socket by the front door." He sits down and then pulls his chair forward so he can prop his feet on the railing. "Perfect."

Orange-tinted maples and the porch roof shades us from the mid-afternoon sun. We face the road and the tracks, but he turned our chairs to look toward the river—and the railroad bridge, of course. Heat seeping across my back feels good. Occasionally, we hear whoops from Bryan and his friends along the riverbank or a bird calls from the forest. But the day is hushed, calm. Quiet, like you only find Sunday afternoon on a front porch.

We don't rock or move. Our eyes drift close and my mind floats like dandelion fluff. Before Jackson dozes off and while I can still corral a thought, I ask, "So what do you think is going on with Savannah and Ricky?"

"She made him jealous with T.J., I guess."

"Yeah, maybe that's all. I always feel like I don't know the whole story with her."

Jackson sighs and then mumbles, "She sure makes me appreciate how easy you are to get along with."

Tears leap to my eyes and I lift my head to look at my husband. The collar of his flannel shirt is worn on the edges, his cheeks fall slack and his hairline is more ebb, than flow. His eyes are still shut and he doesn't know he's made me cry.

He thinks I'm easy to get along with. I think I'm a pain.

The heating pad, my ice tea on a little table pulled alongside my rocker, making sure I can see the river—he takes such good care of me.

"Jackson?"

"Hmmm?"

"You know I love you, right?"

He smiles without opening his eyes, "Yes, I know."

"Ronnie has moved in with some girl over in Collinswood and dropped out of school," Laney whispers through the phone. "I can't believe I didn't know about this. He's my nephew, for cryin' outloud."

"So do you know his girlfriend?" I stretch and smile. My nap on the front porch fixed me up better than a trip to the doctor.

"Nobody, including his dad knew he even had a girlfriend. That's one reason Joe's so concerned. Ronnie met this girl who manages a gas station out at the interstate only a couple weeks ago. He got a job there and then moved in with her last week. Joe's been trying to keep him in school, but apparently he was flunking out anyway."

"Why are you whispering?"

"The kids are out at the pool and I don't want to go too far from the back windows. How did you keep all them apart at your place? Jenna has that Arthur kid drooling. And I don't know what you're worried about. Savannah looks like she's perfectly comfortable in her swimming suit. And if T.J. were a judge she'd be crowned Miss Universe."

"So that's where she's hiding out. She's not taking my calls, but I didn't really want to talk to her until I find out what you got from Joe and Ricky."

"Shoot. I forgot to ask once he told me about Ronnie."

"Laney! I'm pacing the floor wanting to know what happened. I'm just not use to my kids being involved with the police."

"Like I am? Okay, I'll call him when I get rid of these boys. Will said they had to leave in a half-hour."

"What are the ones *not* in heat doing?"

"Will, Brett, and what's the short kid's name, Lawn?"

"Lon, like that old actor Lon Chaney."

"Oh, well, Lon, Brett and Will are playing keep away with the younger boys and Angie.

"You called her 'Angie'."

"I've quit fighting it. Now watch, she'll go back to Janie because I've given in."

# Chapter 20

"Just back up on the grass there." Susan hollers and waves toward the side of her driveway. Her van is parked in the driveway with the back door lifted.

"Wow, is all that for the fair?" I exclaim when I walk around to the back of her van. The back seats have been removed and milk crates are stack two high. Susan is checking her list but stops to take a sip from her mug of coffee. "Yep, I had a great year and the kids have entries, too."

"What do you want me to do?"

"Let's put the flowers in your van. Those cardboard boxes have dividers so the containers sit snuggly in them. Let's get the boxes secured in the van and then we'll start putting the flowers in the containers."

"So tell me, what was the deal with Savannah and Ricky Saturday night? What did Laney find out?" Susan asks, as we stride through the garden, her with clippers and I with a vase of water.

"I fell asleep last night at seven after being up so late the night before. I missed Laney's call and didn't see Savannah at all. She had a final fitting and run-through at Missus' after she spent the afternoon at the pool." Susan hands me a bright red, multi-petal zinnia and I twirl it. The red is so true, so deep. I wish life was so easy, plant red zinnia seeds and get red zinnias. What in the world did I plant to get Savannah?

I sigh and stick the flower stem into the water. "Did you get anything out of Susie Mae?"

Susan stops and puts a hand on her hip, but doesn't turn toward me. "Susie Mae is taking a cue from Savannah and her cousins. I am no longer a person she talks to." Susan bends over again and clips some stems from a large clump of golden and orange swirled zinnias. She hands them back to me.

"Wow, these are beautiful. I bet you plant these every year."

Susan's voice is sharp as she strides down the path toward the van. "Nope, never had them before. They just popped up."

The caps of yellow petals streaked with orange are as large as my palm. The stalks are sturdy and as I place the flowers in the vase they stand above the heads of solid red, pink, and gold.

This flower is a winner, planned or not.

With everything buckled in, we are on the road a little before ten a.m. My van carries zinnias, marigolds, roses and other flowers I can't even name. They are placed in little vases which are held in place by the box dividers, but Susan says they'll all be put in soda bottles for judging. I'm guessing Susan will win a lot because, really, there can't be that many people spending their time doing this, right?

We wind through Chancey and then head out east on the highway. Orange and black monarch butterflies dance along the roadsides, and in the ditches tiny birds dart here and there. Goldenrod and purple asters trim the tree lines bordering harvested fields. Back in the suburbs, the pumpkins on doorsteps and silent air conditioners announce Fall's arrival. Here the land declares Summer's end, putting everything in order before tucking in for a Winter's sleep.

My van swoops along the asphalt curves following Susan's van-load of bounty. In her garden this morning the plants looked tired. Yellowed leaves no longer hid cucumbers and squash. The zinnias, with browning leaves, didn't hold as many buds and blossoms as last week. As they gave up their best to

Susan's clippers, the air filled with the pride of a season well spent, a job well done.

A large, wooden green and white sign announces we've arrived at the County Fairgrounds. Buildings and pole barns lay to our left and there are cars everywhere. Okay, so Susan might have some competition. Are all these cars, trucks, and vans full of garden stuff? Susan pulls into a waiting line of traffic and I pull in behind her. We inch toward a man with a clipboard. He talks to Susan, makes some marks on his papers, and then waves me on to follow her. We drive along dirt and gravel alleys past barns and sheds full of activity. Livestock trucks line the roads and back up to every door. Smells and sounds rolling in my open window remind me the blue ribbon hopes riding in those trucks are cows, sheep, goats, and horses. Oh, yes, and pigs. This is right out of *Charlotte's Web* and the smile stretching across my face is one of disbelief. Who knew all this was still going on? Although I guess someone knew, because there are cars and people as far as I can see and today is only for people entering exhibits.

We finally pull around the last of the barns and turn to the right, away from the midway where cranes, trucks, and men assemble rides and booths. We pull into a field, which is being used as a parking lot today. I park beside Susan and get out.

"This is amazing! I had no idea it would be so big."

Susan is still in her seat, thumbing through papers. "Yeah, it's a pretty big fair. It's the oldest in this part of the state so the facilities have grown over the years." She pauses rifling her papers and nods at the building in front of us. "This building, the Atrium, is really old and so cool. Leave me your keys and you can take a walk around. I've got to get inside and see where I need to put everything."

"Sure you don't need my help?"

She doesn't look up, just holds out her hand. "Nope. I'm good."

I lay my keys in her open palm and set off towards the nearest open entrance. The building appears round, and as I get closer, I see it's all wood coated for many years with white paint. The roof is green and the second story is smaller and all window panes. The panes are about six inches wide and a little taller, maybe eight inches, and they are set in groupings of about thirty panes with a strip of white wood, only a couple inches wide, between each grouping. They aren't windows to open, just groupings of panes. I cross the red clay road and step into the cool, dark interior. The concrete floor spreads out and the building is indeed circular, but there is no second story. There's only one big room and all those panes of glass, up where a second story would be, let natural light flood in.

An intricate maze of tables, display boards and shelves spread in every direction. Poster boards designate what will be shown in particular areas. Earlier, I would've laughed at the delusional organizers thinking this room, these shelves, tables and boards could be filled. However, I now wonder if there will be enough room for all the treasures waiting in all those vehicles. Still feels like I've wandered on to a set for a corny, 1930's musical.

A powerful desire to wear gingham comes over me.

"Something else, isn't it?" Charles Spoon knocks my arm with his elbow. "Built in 1934, you know, and one of the oldest fair buildings in the state." We both look up as clouds pass overhead and block the sunshine pouring in the hundred little windows above us.

Charles lifts his camera and points at the play of light and glass and clouds. "You know, I got a bunch of pictures at your place Saturday night."

That's right, the kids talked about him snapping pictures in all the madness. I forget the fair, the building and close my eyes. That figure jumping up the porch stairs. Jumping. Something just isn't setting right about what I saw but I can't make the events stand still long enough for me to figure it out.

I lower my head and open my eyes to see Charles staring at me. His camera. "Did you, ah, did you get any of...?"

Charles feels his teeth with his tongue behind closed lips. He nods, "I got something, but I don't know. I guess it could be something."

"What did you get?"

"You know, I'm just not sure." He shakes his head and looks down at his worn brown shoes, "Naw, I'm not sure. Gave the pics to Missus. Let her decide."

"Decide what? She wasn't there. How will she know what to even look for? Besides, she's only interested so she can win some stupid grant."

Charles cocks his head and squints at me, "And why are you interested? Why do you care so much?"

My eyebrows lift, my breathing slows. Why am I so interested? Why is this ghost on my mind all the time? "I don't know. Maybe I just need to find a good mystery to read so I can quit making up mysteries in my own life." I step away from him, "I'm going to find Susan."

My words sound practical and strong, until I turn away from Charles and mumble, "I need to talk to Tommy about this. No, I mean Jackson. I need to talk to Jackson about this."

"Lunch?" I ask as I meet Susan at her van.

She sighs and rests both hands on her slim hips. Her hay colored hair hangs in twigs around her face and she reaches up and jerks out her pony-tail band. She smoothes the loose hair, ties it back, then drops her hands back to her hips. "I'm not in a real good mood. It might be best if we don't."

"Wait, are you mad at me?" I step toward her van so that I'm between her and her door handle.

Susan gnaws on her lips like she's keeping them from forming the words they need to form. She folds her slim, tan arms into a pretzel, presses them hard against her chest and her lips find release, "Susie Mae won't talk to me. She's clammed up and I know it's because she'd rather be a part of Savannah and Angie's little coven and, honestly, that scares me to death. Everybody knows you moved here because you caught

Savannah in bed with that boyfriend of hers."

Her lips empty of words now press into a thin line of judgment and all I can do is stare.

A tremor snakes up my back and I shake my head. "No. No I didn't find her in, in... I mean, I think I might... No." I take a deep breath. "I didn't find her in bed. I, uh, I found condoms in her purse, but she said they weren't hers."

"You didn't break up some sex party at your house in Marietta? Alcohol punch being served from your grandmother's silver punch bowl? Police arresting kids for drugs?"

"Are you kidding? I don't even have a punch bowl, from my grandmother, my aunt—no punch bowl. I just found the condoms and put the house on the market. It sold before I could change my mind."

"But, but you always act like Savannah is so bad and Retta, well, Retta was your realtor so we thought you'd told her... " Susan waves her limp arms. "... all that." Susan nods and plants her fists on non-existent hips. "And you never explained Retta's comments at that first council meeting about your family falling apart and your kids needing more supervision."

"Well, I don't know for sure she didn't have sex with Parker, I mean, c'mon should I believe she's holding condoms for a friend? Unless it's her boyfriend." I raise my eyebrows and shrug.

Susan let out a breath, "Right now with everything that's gone through my mind in the past twelve hours, I'd be really happy to find out that's all she's done."

My eyes stretch wide, "Well, it doesn't make me happy!"

"I just meant I thought she was, well, doing what I'd heard she did before. And I thought she was involving Susie Mae. I don't really care what she's doing or Jenna or Angie. But I will not have my daughter caught up in their... their *activities*."

I tilt my head. "Is this just Griffin getting all worked up? You've been fine with the girls hanging out."

Susan's lips purse out, her voice drops an octave, "I haven't mentioned it to him. That's part of what's killing me, not telling him. He trusts me to know what's going on with the kids. Leslie always talks to me. Susie Mae has to be involved in something awful to cut me out like this."

"But you were fine yesterday. When did you hear this?"

Susan steps back and puts her head down. "Ahm, I'd rather not say right now. I need to get home so we can get back here tonight for the opening." Her eyes meet mine, "But please, keep Savannah away from my daughter right now, okay?" She bumps against me to get to her door handle and opens her door slowly, pushing me out of the way.

After getting in and starting the engine, she sits for a minute but doesn't acknowledge me still standing there. Finally, she rolls down her window a couple inches.

"Thanks for helping me today." She pushes wisps of hair off her forehead, "You think you can get home or do you want to follow me?"

"I'll be fine."

She nods and pulls out.

I push my hair behind my ears, running my fingers through it several times trying to focus on the tugging so I don't cry. My nose burns on the inside and I feel the crush of heat releasing behind my eyes. I rush to my van and yank on the door handle, but I only get a broken nail as the door is locked. My keys. Susan has my keys. I draw in a jittery breath and the tears push forward. I look at the tracks she left in the grass, but her van is no longer in sight. Whether it's due to her turning off the tracks or to the flood in my eyes, I don't know. I lean my head against my window and try to calm down. I need to think.

Charles is here. That's right. I just need to find Charles. I dig in my purse for a napkin or Kleenex and I see my phone. I could just call Susan, but I can't. I can't call her now. I'd rather stay here until Savannah can come get me than face Susan.

However, I jerk out my phone. Charles' number is in my phone from when he kept calling to get invited to the bonfire. Forget Susan. I just need to get home.

"You know, those are some good lookin' pigs." Charles moseys, and I do mean moseys, down the last aisle in the last barn.

"Yep, Some Pig, right?" I grin and nod at him.

"Hmm?"

"Some Pig, like in Charlotte's Web?"

"Oh, yeah, yeah." He chuckles. That's about a country fair, isn't it? I'd forgot about that. You know, my youngest, Amber, loved that book."

"You have kids?"

"Oh, yeah. Four of 'em. Raised 'em up in Illinois around their mother's family. We divorced when the youngest was fifteen."

"I'm sorry. How long ago? How did you end up down here?"

"Oh, let's see, that was back in the late eighties. I came down here because Missus offered me a job. She wanted Chancey to have a paper, you know, so she started one. I have family here. Well, I *had* family here. My aunt passed away back in '93."

"Missus owns the paper?"

"Sure she does. You know she and FM only had one son and when he left for college, she needed something to do with her time. She bought a paper and a radio station. Radio station failed, you know."

"Where did her son go?"

"Hmmm?" Charles stops and starts scribbling in his notebook.

"Her son? Where did he go?" I stop beside him and wait while he writes down whatever suddenly struck him.

"Oh, don't know." He bustles out into the sunshine, "Now listen, where is it you need to go?"

"Just to my house."

"But what about your car? You can't get hold of Mrs. Lyles?"

"We're coming back tonight, I'll get it then. I don't want to bother Susan."

He cocks his head at me, "But you were doing her a favor, surely she wouldn't mind. You all fightin' or somethin'?"

"I'll tell you if you tell me about Missus' son."

Charles grins and his bushy gray mustache nearly touches

his wire-rimmed glasses. "Deal. I like people that don't treat information casually, treat it like it's a business." He points to my right. "My car's this way."

We walk through the field and I tell him about Susan's accusations.

"Here it is." His car is an old army jeep and there are no doors. Not even a roof. I climb up in the seat and realize there is nothing but straps and metal bars and a seat that belongs in a cheap theatre.

Charles shoves his camera and notepad into a knapsack lying behind his seat. "So, you didn't walk in on some teen-age sex party at your old house?"

"Charles! You heard that too? Does everyone think that?"

He pauses, then nods and climbs into his seat, "Pretty much. You know, that's what everyone figures is happening in them big suburban homes when the parents are all at work anyway. We have cable too, you know."

"Well it's not. At least not where I lived and not with my kids. And if everyone thought that, why did they let their kids hang out at my house all those weeks when we were fixing up the B&B?"

"Well, you know, Mrs. Lyles was always there. Everyone trusts Susan Lyles."

"But they don't trust me?"

"Best put your seat belt on, you know." Charles points at the measly lap belt.

"Is this thing even safe?" I ask as I tighten the belt and grab onto the metal side with my right hand.

"Absolutely. I'm gonna stop and get some lunch. That okay with you?"

"Sure." He pulls out, bouncing over the field. I hunt for something to hold onto with my left hand and finally just grab the bottom of my seat. The engine roars and when we hit the gravel drive the crunching of the tires is deafening. He spins onto the blacktop and accelerates. The wind whips in the open sides and I realize there will be no conversation on this ride.

The smell of fresh-cut hay fills my nose, the roar of the wheels fills my ears. If I relax my hands, I could reach out and touch the roadside butterflies. Pavement flows beneath me and wind pushes my hair, my clothes, my skin. Every sense is assaulted and overwhelmed. I'm exposed to the sky, the fields, the road and I hate it. I just hate it.

Eyes closed, breathing controlled. I bury my senses deep in thought. I'm raw from living in this place, from dealing with these people. Every day here is like this ride—too much, too much of everything. The kids are safe with Susan, but not with me. My daughter stars in everyone's nasty gossip. My house isn't a home; it's a tourist attraction full of strangers and ghosts. Tears whip off into the wind as soon as they escape my eyes. I hate this. I hate this.

A jerk to the right and suddenly we stop. My eyelids pop open, the only body part able to move.

"We're here. You ever eaten Bobby Jack's Barbeque? You'll love it." Charles swings down from his seat.

I take a deep breath and unhinge my fingers. I wipe my face and blow out a breath from the bottom of my lungs.

"Fun, wasn't it?" Charles stands by the hood, wiping his glasses with the tail of his shirt.

"Do you own another vehicle?" My numb fingers struggle with the seat belt.

"Nope, bought this back when I left Illinois and Joyce, you know. Great, isn't it?"

My legs are both shaky and heavy, but I manage to fall out of the seat and stand on them. I run fingers through my hair and then lean back into the jeep to untangle my purse from the base of the stick shift. I'd purposely looped it around so it wouldn't fly off onto the highway.

The small, one-story yellow house sits on a concrete slab at the edge of a dirt parking lot. Part of the concrete slab is the front porch and we step up onto it.

"It's early. We beat the lunch crowd," Charles says as he holds open the aluminum screen door for me.

The floor inside is still the undisguised concrete slab. We step right into the dining room packed with lines of common, brown banquet tables and plain old metal folding chairs. Across one end of the room is a counter and behind it a kitchen. A screen door in the kitchen filters in sunshine and smoke, from out back. As feeling rushes back to my fingers and legs, my nose starts working. The enticing aroma of roasted meat, sugar-laden spices, and hickory smoke fills the barebones room and I'm starving.

A quick look around the room doesn't show me what I'm looking for. "I need to use the restroom."

Charles points to a door in the corner, "You go on. I'll get our plates."

"But I don't know what to... "

"There ain't no menu," the woman behind the counter yells at me. "Charles'll get your plate. You can go on to the toilet."

My dining companion laughs. "That's just Eileen. Go on, like she said," and he turns to the counter.

The bathroom is barely big enough to turn around in. As I wash my hands, I look to see what the ride has done to my hair and what the tears have done to my mascara. Must be awful lighting, because my eyes are bright, my cheeks flushed and my hair is fine. I look good? Okay, whatever.

Charles is sitting about half way up the line of tables against the back wall and he has two plates. I pull out my chair and sit down, the metal cold through my cotton capris.

"I got you sweet tea. There's only that or water."

"Thanks." I take a sip from my large Styrofoam cup and the sweetness is intense. I can't stop with a small drink.

"Bobby Jack used to sell barbeque out of his momma's house, but she kicked him out when the noise got so loud she couldn't hear her soaps in the afternoon. He and Eileen built this place about ten years ago." Charles heaps his fork with another mouthful of the pulled pork, then scoops some coleslaw on top. "They still live with his momma, you know, but now they all get along good."

I try the pork and coleslaw. The spicy-sweet meat and the vinegary-sweet slaw work with the sweet tea. Boy, does it work. A whole dill pickle on the side harmonizes—sour and sweet. We eat like teen-age boys.

"I was thinking," Charles says between licks of the back of his fork. Then he props his elbows on either side of his near empty plate and points his cleaned utensil at me. "Mrs. Lyles is afraid your Savannah is pulling her Susie Mae to the dark side, right?"

I drop my full fork back onto my plate, *the dark side?* "I guess, something like that."

"But you say your Savannah doesn't really have a dark side?"

My mouth won't open so I can agree with him. What if Savannah is a bad influence on Susie Mae? For all my righteous anger, I don't know. I don't know if Susan should be afraid of Savannah or not. "Charles, I'll be honest with you. I guess I don't really know my daughter. I don't know if she has a dark side or not."

He drops his fork on his plate, "You got to decide if you want to know her or not, cause your days with her under your roof are running out. I do know that. My kids were there one day and gone the next. Joyce bugged me to death, you know, to spend time with them, talk to them and I just wanted them to grow up." He lifts his cup and looks over its rim out the window behind me. "And they did."

"But what if I find out she's bad. What if Susan is right?"

Charles shrugs. "There's the rub. But isn't it like that with everyone in your life, some good, some bad?"

I nod and tear open the little handi-wipe that came with our meal. I clean my hands and then remember, "Oh, yeah. What about Missus's son? I didn't know they had children."

Charles clears his throat and reaches for my dirty plate. "Well, I don't rightly know that much. He, uh, left the first time right out of high school. College, I guess. She wanted him to run her new venture, the newspaper, but he didn't stay here long when he came back. Lucky for me, 'cause that was when I needed to get out of Illinois." He pauses and looks down at the table for a quick minute. His head bounces up, "Ready to go?"

"That's it? That's all you know."

"Yep, 'bout it." Charles stands with all the garbage in his hands and turns towards the counter. "See you later Eileen, tell Bobby Jack I said, 'hey'."

Eileen waves from the kitchen and I realize the place is filling up. "Did you already pay?" I pick up my purse from the seat next to me. I pull my wallet out and unfold from my now warm seat.

"Put that away," Charles waves at me. "I've never gotten more free food than I have since you came to town, you know, and opened that B&B. Seems like there's a to-do to cover out there every weekend."

Maybe a little too forcefully, I shove my chair in, "Tell me about it."

# Chapter 21

Eventually, Charles drops me off at home. All in one piece and without throwing up Bobby Jack's barbeque all over the highway.

The message light is blinking so I take a quick listen to the voice-mail. Jackson, calling from LA (Lower Alabama) wants to know what night the pageant is. Like I haven't told him thirty-seven million times. Susan says my keys are hidden in the flower pot on the front porch. Good, I don't have to talk to her, just get a ride from Savannah back to the fairgrounds.

Head Librarian Ida Faye Newbern, as she announces herself on the message, wants me to call her back. Great, they call personally here about overdue books. I'm really beginning to miss those impersonal automated calls. Guilt from a machine I can deal with.

My purse gets tossed into a kitchen chair and I ignore the dishwasher full of clean dishes and the sink full of dirty dishes. Twisting the deadbolt on the door, I open the glass door onto the deck. The fall afternoon sun is warm as I jog down the hill to the willow. Trees are red or yellow or green and the grass has a light coating of pine needles and leaves. Not yet enough to crunch beneath my feet, but it won't be long until there is a blanket of leaves to kick through. With a swipe of my hands, I step between the yellow and brown streamers guarding my willow room. My breathing slows, and I pick up the old table-cloth to shake it out. Folded back into a square, I drop onto it and take a deep breath.

The river is deep green and blue, reflecting the depth of both water and sky. The bushes along the edge of the water have thinned and I can now see the water up and down the bank from my sitting position. My back against the trunk, I finally let the tears roll. All day—for one reason or another—I've held them back, denied them, until I could get here.

"Tommy, this isn't working. What am I supposed to do? What else am I supposed to do? Didn't I leave my home, quit my job, move to the boondocks? I stay at home with them every day, I'm here. I open my house to gobs of teenagers, even got to know Parker. We figured out a way to get Savannah a car. We go to church every Sunday and help with youth group."

My head drops forward, "But I still don't know Savannah. I probably don't know Bryan either. That will be Susan's next accusation. My thirteen year old is probably running a shop-lifting ring and getting sweet little Grant involved." A sob reaches up my throat for punctuation. "I'm not only flushing my family down the drain, I'm flushing Susan's, too." I remember how the anger on Susan's face couldn't hide her hurt. Her hurt over Susie Mae not talking to her, and yet, I don't even expect Savannah to talk to me.

"Did your mom know you, Tommy? When you went off to battle? Did she know if you were good or bad? Listen to me. You went off to battle, of course you were good. Good, unselfish and now you spend your time sitting under a willow tree listening to a spoiled woman who doesn't know if she even wants to know her own kids." I lean forward and wrap my arms around my knees.

"And it's probably too late anyway, right? Savannah is 16, she'll be gone to college soon. Like Will." My eyes blur. My mom kept saying when he was getting ready to leave two years ago that when he moved to Athens, my house would no longer be his home. It wouldn't be the same. "And it's not the same, Tommy, he just comes here to visit now. He can pretend to be whoever he thinks I want him to be when he's here just like I did when I went home from college. Just like I still do now."

A small breeze ruffles the willow limbs to my right, nothing else moves.

"Tommy? Is that you? Funny, but I know you're here. Oh yeah, Charles asked me about you today. Asked why I am so concerned about you. At first I wasn't sure, but then I realized it's because I count on you being here and I'm afraid someone, either Missus or FM with their fighting about you, are going to chase you off." I lay my head to my side to stare at the branches that moved. "Don't go, okay?"

"Now, do I talk to Savannah about Saturday night? Do I ask about Ricky?" I sit so long my legs go to sleep, but Tommy never answers. However, as I stand I realize I wasn't really listening for an answer.

But then I did tell Tommy he is not allowed to answer me back, so why listen anyway?

"Yeah, I wondered when you'd get around to asking about it." Savannah twirls and lands in the rocking chair next to me. Her school books land with a thud on the porch floor.

"So, what happened?"

She looks to the ceiling and I fight to stay in my seat. I will not leave this conversation until it's done.

"Ricky is just a redneck jerk and we had a fight because I told him he couldn't come to the bonfire." She kicks off black ballet flats and plants her bare feet on the rocking chair rung. She bobs her head forward to start the chair in motion.

"And... " I promised Tommy to try, really try.

"And, that's all."

"Okay." I start to stand because, obviously, she's said everything she has to say. But Tommy must be sitting in my lap, because I can't get up. Then a question pops in my head, "So why did you go find him? Why didn't you just stay here at the bonfire?"

Savannah shrugs and pulls a lock of hair toward her face to

look for split ends, "I don't know."

Good enough answer for me, but Tommy wants more and makes me blurt, "If you don't know, then who does?"

Her blue eyes shoot back at me, "I said, I don't know. What is your problem?"

"Because someone knows what's going on and I'm going to find out. Guess I'll just go talk to Ricky." This time Tommy allows me to stand, matter of fact, he almost pushes me out of my chair.

Her feet hit the porch, "You wouldn't, would you?"

"Unless you tell me, I have no choice."

Savannah tucks her feet back on their perch and she nods toward my chair. "Okay, sit down."

Finally my daughter is going to talk to me but everything in me wants to run the other way. I whisper, "Help me listen to her, Tommy," as I sit back down.

"Somehow Ricky got the idea I, well, that I'm a big partier and so we've been going out and having fun. But I, well, I don't like his friends and now I don't like Ricky. He, well, I told him something one night when I'd had a couple beers and now he's saying he's going to tell everyone."

*When you had a couple beers?* "What's he going to tell?"

"I really can't tell you, Mom. It's someone else's secret, not mine."

"Susie Mae?"

Her head jerks up and she stares at me. "What? Why do you think it involves Susie Mae?"

"She's gone out partying with you all?"

"Maybe, a little. But the secret isn't about her. It's something else completely."

"So what happened Saturday night?"

Savannah takes a deep breath, "Like I said, Ricky was mad about not being able to come to the bonfire, especially when he knew Will's friends would be here. So he invited Angie and Susie Mae to a party out at the river. We, Angie and me, had decided to not hang out with Ricky anymore, but Angie had to go because Susie Mae was determined to go and she really is a baby. All Saturday night Ricky texted me that Susie Mae was really drunk and making out with a bunch of guys and then Angie would text me that nothing was happening. Then Angie lost Susie Mae."

"Lost her?" My stomach boils up at the same time I can't get a breath. "How did she lose her?"

"They left the river and were going to someone's barn and they ended up in different cars." That's when Angie freaked out and texted me to meet her at the high school."

"And this was after the ghost thing and when I was inside?"

"Yeah, I just slipped around the house and left. When I got to the school, Angie wasn't there. She called me and said she had gotten Susie Mae and taken her home and everything was fine. Then Ricky showed up.

Savannah pulls her sleeves down over her hands and folds her arms against her body. "Do you know what everyone here thinks about me?"

All I can do is nod because my throat tightens hearing the fear in her little girl voice.

"Well, I've not really minded it because it made me seem so, I don't know, like I was older and more experienced. But when boys think that, they really expect you to, well, they expect things." She takes a deep breath, "So I got in Ricky's truck to tell him I was through with him and that I'm not like that, and he said he'd tell everyone that secret I told him if we didn't, uh, you know. We ended up down at the square and he wouldn't leave me alone. We kind of fought and I found a half-full bottle of Mountain Dew lying in the floorboard, so I dumped it on him. That was when we got out and I started throwing rocks at him."

My mouth hangs open, but I remember to close it before she looks at me.

"And so that's it. The cops came and since I hadn't been drinking they took me to my car and followed me home."

"Did Ricky get in trouble?"

Savannah shakes her head, "Naw, he was pretty sober by then and so the cops just dropped him off at his house. You know they live near the square, so he went and got his car

Sunday morning."

"Susie Mae and Angie?"

Black hair fell to cover her face and a heavy silence seeps over the porch and quiets the almost flippant confession.

I wait.

Her whispered story drifts to me, "Susie Mae was wasted and apparently the car ride over to the barn was an adventure... she's really upset, Mom. Angie and Jenna have been talking to her, but I can't, I just can't." Savannah's eyes are filled with tears as she swings around to me.

"She says she didn't do anything, but the boys in the car say she did."

My mouth is dry and my heart is sore. "What does Angie think happened?"

Savannah shrugs, "She thinks nothing and so we're calling the boys liars. We've pretty much shut them up. Besides..."

"Besides, what?"

"Susie Mae is so good and her family is so good, no one believed the boys anyway."

"Why can't you talk to her?"

"It's my fault. She thinks I'm so cool and she wanted to hang out with us all summer. And Angie is so quiet. If I'd been there I wouldn't have let it happen." Anger jumps into her voice, "I just wouldn't."

No words or questions come. Exhaustion pours over me. My daughter opened up to me. Now what? "Is there anything I can do to help?"

Silence stretches between us and it doesn't make me nervous like it use to.

Savannah finally stands and stretches, "Thanks, but I think it's over now. Susie Mae was fine at school today. We were real proud of her. Plus, I told Ricky off yesterday afternoon and he feels awful about what happened to Susie Mae. I think he'll leave me alone now." She bends and lifts her school books into her arms. "And Angie and I aren't going out with any of that group anymore, so that's a good thing, right?"

"Right."

She reaches the screen door and then turns, "And, Mom, you can't tell any of this to Miss Susan, okay? Susie Mae doesn't want her parents to know because she says they'll completely freak out. She says she'll talk to her Aunt Laney if she needs to."

The screen door closes quietly behind her and I shiver in the early afternoon shadows. It's only Monday. Jackson will be in town for the pageant tomorrow night, but he'll head back out on the road early Wednesday morning. This is what I hate about his constant traveling; we never have time to talk.

And this conversation is definitely going to take some time.

Savannah and Bryan got out the door this morning with the minimum of words. My eyes burn and with them closed my mind looses focus. My breath slows and I drift towards sleep. Gravel crunching in the driveway causes me to leap from the couch. Burning eyes forgotten, a glance at the clock says that the kids are in class, so it can't be them back for something they forgot. I'm still in my robe, but that's not the reason I don't want company. The drapes hang at the side of the picture window and I pull them away from the wall and use them to shield me from sight of anyone coming up on the front porch. I'm not answering the door, but I do want to see who's carrying the pitchforks and tar.

I work a little crack between the curtain and the window frame but no one comes into view. My van is the only vehicle in the driveway and it is pulled way up on the side of the house. My visitor pulled their car up too far for me to see it.

A car door slams and my stomach clenches causing a shiver and flash of heat. No voices, but someone is walking around in the driveway, just taking their time. Now the steps stop. Where did they go? Maybe they're waiting on others to show up. Sweat from my flush of heat turns icy. On the end table curls of steam rise from my coffee cup. If I'd known this was going to be an extended stake out, I would've brought my coffee with me. But there's no way to move now without being seen.

However, that coffee is my salvation, last night precious sleeping hours were wasted beating myself up. I knew all along what happens in small towns. I walked right into this trap. They love luring you in with homegrown tomatoes and girly gossip, but in reality you're just fresh meat for their stew. They've torn each other up for years—decades, so when a new person shows up it's like you're the only barista working at a Starbucks crammed with time-crazed moms.

I try to turn and lean against the wall without being seen and then a face pops up on the other side of the glass and my heart stops. The eyes make contact with mine.

"Ma'am? Your electric meter is blocked by firewood stacked out back. I'll need to come back when you get that moved, okay?"

"Sure." I flutter the fabric between my fingers. "I'm just fixing the curtains." I bob my head at him, "Thanks for letting me know about the meter."

Okay, so no high school career survey ever mentioned me being a spy. But I am not paranoid. They're coming for me. I feel it. My hands-off parenting allowed precious Susie Mae to practically get raped. Angie is drinking. Ricky, the star quarterback becomes a stalker brought home by the police. Is it only a coincidence all this happened within months of us descending on Chancey?

I hate small towns.

After checking the front door lock, I hurry back to my coffee. But, you know, I've never had coffee in the Southern Crescent room. There's a nice high-back chair and a just polished table.

And, of course, heavy, dark blinds on the windows.

# CHAPTER 22

"How could you forget today is early release?" Savannah and Bryan push past me rolling eyes and flinging accusations in my direction. "We've been down here ringing the doorbell for like a million years."

"Where are your house keys?" Yes, I was hiding in my bedroom ignoring the doorbell, but seriously, they have keys. The pounding on the door almost caused cardiac arrest, then I heard my attackers yelling, "Mom."

My apologies follow them to the kitchen.

Savannah grabs a bottle of water from the refrigerator, "I have to be at Missus' in thirty minutes. She's loaded everything for tonight in her car and she's driving me to my hair appointment."

Bryan reaches to grab the refrigerator door before it closes. "When are we leaving? Grant doesn't need a ride anymore." He dumps fruit snacks from an open pouch into his mouth and snags a juice box from the bottom shelf of the refrigerator. "I'm ready whenever you are."

"I thought we'd just go later, for the pageant."

He stops, mouth hanging open so I can see jewel-toned, wet, rubbery bits of modern food science stuck on his teeth. "Mom, I have to go today. Everyone is going today. Duh, that's why we got out of school early."

"Did you say Grant doesn't need a ride anymore?"

His sister stops in the doorway.

Bryan shrugs and take a pull on the juice box straw, "He said his mom is freaked out about something and he has to go with her or his dad. But he said once they get there he can sneak off and meet up with the rest of us."

A moan escapes me, "Sneak off?" I can see my new rap sheet already.

Savannah starts moving again, so I throw a question in her direction, "Savannah, how was school today?"

"Good. I've got to get ready."

Okay, we'll talk upstairs. I cock my head at my son, "You got homework?"

"Nope. Teachers knew it was useless. Seriously, Mom, you said you'd take me. There's no admission for students today and we can get a pass to ride everything for only $20. We're going, right?" He opens another pack of fruit snacks.

How did I forget all this? I know. I was busy hiding and feeling sorry for myself. "Sure," I sigh. "We'll leave in 30 minutes. Okay?" Oh, the car. We'll drop Savannah off at Missus' and take her car.

As I leave the kitchen, I see the message light blinking. I haven't answered the phone all day. Caller ID told me the calls were from the library, one from Laney, and one Missus. Should I listen to them now? I know I have overdue books and I don't want to hear what Laney and Missus have to say. Forget the phone, it'll be here when I get back.

I tap on Savannah's door and open it. "So, how was Susie Mae today?"

My daughter is discriminately picking through clothing and make-up and hair things and placing the desired items in her cheerleading duffle bag.

Sitting on her bed, I clear my throat. "Savannah?"

She drops her shoulders, sighs, and then sits at her computer desk. "I guess good. Leslie came up to me at lunch and said I was not to come near her sister again."

"Oh no," I groan. "Are you okay?"

"Mom, everyone knows Leslie Lyles is a real pain. She thinks she's perfect. She's more of Susie Mae's problem than I am."

"I don't think their parents see it that way."

"Well, everyone at school does and that's all that matters to me. I gotta get ready. Dad will be there tonight, right?"

"Yep. Wouldn't miss it. Are you excited?"

Her smile lifts the room, "I really am. It's a big deal and Missus is so crazy. She's been texting me all day about stuff to remember and then at school I kept getting texts and notes and stuff from everybody. Jenna looks so worried. It's awesome."

"Wait, Missus texts you? At school?"

"Oh, Mom, it's fine. Nobody cares."

"I kinda feel out of the loop on all this pageant stuff."

"It's just not your kind of thing, I know that." My beauty queen daughter stands and starts stuffing more things in her bag. "I like it more than I thought I would and Missus is so into it."

Just another loop I'm out of. At the door to her room my thoughts spin on Missus and I turn back. "Did you know Missus and FM have a son?"

Bent over her bag, hair hanging so that I can't see her face, she freezes, but only for a moment. Then, without looking up, she says, "Really?"

"Did you know?" I ask again.

She stands and looks at me, eyes stretched wide, "Why would I know that? I really need to change." She takes a couple steps to the door and puts her hand on the knob, "I can't be late."

"Okay, okay." In the hall, I ease her door shut and realize she never answered. Now why did I think to ask her that and why did she avoid it?

Lines of cars on the highway. Lines of cars into the parking lots. Lines of people at the ticket windows. Then finally, I hand over $22.50, Bryan's ride bracelet is attached, my hand is stamped, and we're inside the fair. Vendor tents greet us and we pass by the latest technology in riding lawn mowers, retractable porch awnings, and swing sets. Sales people tempt us with lemonade or hot cider while handing us coupons for their products. Then we come to the gauntlet of politicians pressing calendars, stickers, and pamphlets. Anticipating high parent turn out, school board candidates are in heavy attendance.

Pushing past all that, the sounds and smells grow strong. Bryan rushes ahead and I grab the back of his shirt. "Wait. How will we find each other?"

"I could call you if I had a cell phone, right? But I don't. Mom, c'mon we'll find each other. Let me go."

Over his head, I see that it's mostly kids and parents. I also see four of his friends from school headed toward us. "It's three o'clock now. Your dad is meeting me here at the entrance around five. Then we'll look for you in the rides area, okay?"

"Okay, okay. Around five."

I drop my hold on his shirt before his friends can see and he's off.

Circling back to the sales tents, I accept a cup of hot cider from a man selling retractable awnings. I listen to his spiel, nod, and take a folder promising to show it to my husband. The rich cider relaxes me on my roundabout walk on the edge of the tents to avoid the politicians. Food vendors are gearing up for the busy night and grease pops in the first row of booths. Corn dogs, onion rings, funnel cakes, candy apples all make my little cup of cider seem unfestive and downright healthy.

Between the food area and the rides, there is a huge tent filled with picnic tables. A few people are scattered at the tables, mostly young moms with strollers. A seat along the edge provides a spot for people watching. The afternoon sun is warm, but the shade quickly cools me. I'd love to walk through the Atrium and see the displays and ribbons, but fear of running into Susan keeps me planted. Surely the fair is big enough so that I can hide out here almost as well as at home.

"Yoo-hoo, Carolina." Ida Faye Newbern from the library waves at me from the funnel cake line. She's one of the old, soft Southern women that say "yoo-hoo", dress in mauve, peach or seafoam-green, wear hose even in summer and smell like old Avon powder. The vendor takes her money through the little window as Ida Faye waves one more time at me. Then she holds up a finger telling me to stay put. "Carolina, I've been trying to get a hold of you," she admonishes as she enters the tent.

Okay, so home is a better hiding place.

"Really?" I say in all sincerity watching her advance with a paper plate laden with a hot, sugary funnel cake and bunches of napkins.

"Whoo, that's hot," she exclaims. A small cloud of powdered sugar pluffs up as the plate lands on the table. "I skipped lunch and only had a yogurt and oatmeal for breakfast because I knew *this* was my first stop when I got here today." She looks around before holding her polyester skirt and lifting one leg over the bench. She sits and pulls her other leg across the bench and under the table. "I've been calling and calling you."

"Yes, yes my overdue books." I flip my hair to the side and lift my chin. "I didn't realize they were *that* overdue. With such a small library, I guess you have to track down books so your shelves won't be empty." Remorseful does not describe my mood.

"No, I wasn't calling about *books*. We have a job opening and I want to know if you're interested." She pulls a piece of the funnel cake off and blows on it.

"A job?"

"Yes, Marney Jacobs is going back to nursing school so I need an assistant. It's a full-time position and I know you worked in a library for years back in Marietta, right? And I *see* how you feel about books when you're in the library." Ida Faye has the perfect librarian voice; she speaks in loud whispers and italics. She pushes the plate toward me, "Here have some."

Funnel cakes gets their name because the batter is funneled

into the grease in loops and swirls. After a quick flip in the oil, it's drained and then coated in powdered sugar. It's sweet, crisp, hot perfection on a paper plate. I take a piece and bite off an inch, which gives me a minute to think while I chew. A job? A job out of my house; surrounded by books. Put the stupid B&B back on the shelf and do something I know how to do?

"What do you think?"

"I think the funnel cake is wonderful and the job, too."

Ida Faye has gray eyes, she looks over the top of her brown rim glasses, "I need someone who's serious about books. Marney just isn't *involved* with books like *we* are." She breaks off another piece of the cake, "I want someone I can depend on to make the library a priority. Not look at it as *just* another job, like down at the grocery store or the school cafeteria."

"Oh, of course. I need to talk to Jackson to make sure... "

"What about your B&B?"

"That's what I'm not sure about. Jackson will be here tonight and we'll talk."

"Oh, that's right. Your daughter is in the pageant. She is *awfully* attractive and all the work she's been doing for her performance tonight is commendable. I was so happy to get the books she requested. Did they help her out?"

"Savannah requested books?"

"Yes, I figured you were working with her."

"Oh, yeah, I just didn't realize she, uh, had to request them."

"Well, they *were* rather specialized." Ida Faye no longer looks at me over her glasses, she's examining me through them.

"Ida Faye, I have to come clean on this. Savannah entered this pageant at Missus insistence and they are working together. I don't even know what she's doing for her talent."

"Missus? As in *Shermania Bedwell*?" Her back stiffens.

Great, I've opened yet another Chancey skeleton closet. "Yes." I don't know what else to say. I feel the job offer fading away.

She licks her lips and starts rolling up the paper plate with a good piece of funnel cake still on it. "Well, then. Tonight promises to be *entertaining*. Think about the job and talk with your husband. Let me know what you think *as soon as possible.*" She stands and begins wadding up the used napkins with the plate. "When I couldn't get in touch with you today *before* the classifieds deadline in the *Vedette*, I put in an ad for Thursday's paper. So the sooner, the *better.*"

"It sounds like just what I need. I'll get back to you."

As she turns to the garbage can, she stops and looks back. "Of course, I'd *need* to have you in for an interview, you *understand.*"

"Of course." I'm sure the interview got harder and more important after this little talk.

"See you at the pageant, Carolina."

"See you there." So I've run across another story line in the Chancey soap opera. Missus and Ida Faye. Well, who cares? I know I can't take the job, I'm stuck in the B&B.

My feet stretched out in front of me draw my attention. I tried to dress the part of a pageant mom today: Black shoes and slacks and a long emerald-green sweater with three-quarter length sleeves. Problem with all the black is the dust. My shoes are covered with a light film. I push at my hair, but it's just going to keep falling in my eyes because it's not been cut in months. And the five minutes I allow for styling isn't enough to keep it under control. Shoot, Ida Faye looked more like a pageant mom than me.

A job at the library. My eyes close and I lean against the table. The smell of the library. Paper, glue, books . Silence, respectful voices, whispers. I'm more comfortable dreaming about this job than I've been in real life since moving here.

"There you are!"

I squeeze my eyes tighter. Laney.

"What are you doing? Praying? Yeah, me too. I've been praying something fierce for Jenna today. She's driving us all crazy. Angie's practically moved into Susan's house because her sister is a diva on the brink. Open your eyes. What's wrong with you?"

I pry open my eyes and catch my breath. "Laney, you look... you look amazing." Her hair is huge. Big hair might not be popular elsewhere around the U S of A, but in the South it never goes out of style for beauty queens and televangelists' wives. Of course her hair has to be huge to match her eyes, which look like blueberry snow cones, bright blue, shiny and enormous. She has on a white, shirt waist dress with a navy belt. On most women the dress would be dull and secretarial, but on her it drapes like a toga. Her navy pumps don't have a speck of dust—how does she do that?

"Thanks. I'll be on stage tonight for the parade of queens since I was in the top five at the Mrs. Georgia pageant." She unties a pink sweater from her shoulders and lays it on the picnic bench to sit on.

I wipe my face to make sure there isn't sugar from the funnel cake. "Savannah's with Missus, why aren't you with Jenna? I didn't think of you being over here."

Settling on the bench, Laney holds up her tanned hand, "I can't let Jenna make me a wreck. I left her with her daddy. He'll just sit there and let her rave." She points a manicured fingernail at me, "And I know you didn't think you'd see me. That's why I'm here. You can hide all you want, but when I want to find you—I will." Her grin splits glossy pink lips over white dental-ad teeth.

"How often do you go to the library?"

"What?"

"Never mind. So, why are you looking for me?"

"You and Susan had words, I hear. What's the deal?"

"Ask her. She's your sister. You've not known me six months."

"Yeah, but I might like you better."

I hate that I'm thrilled by that. Might as well be in junior high. Tickled because the popular girl likes me best. "You don't like me better," I grump. "What do you want to know?"

"Did you walk into a teen-age orgy at your house in Marietta?"

"No! No drugs, no sex, no grandmother's punch bowl full of booze. No."

"And..." Laney rolls her hand in front of me like there's more to the story.

"And, nothing. I found condoms in Savannah's purse and I flipped out. I put the house on the market and it sold in three days. I felt like I wasn't keeping track of the kids so I decided to stay home with them. That's it. Oh, and Savannah says that the condoms weren't even hers."

"But you found out different, right?"

"No, as a matter of fact, I got to know Parker and he seems like a really nice guy." I shrug. "So... "

"So... what? That can't be it?" Laney's lascivious grin slips and she leans back. Her brow flattens and the light in her sparkly eyes goes out.

"What's your problem, now? You sat down here like we were best buddies and going to share all our secrets. So, I share and you get mad?"

"Yes, I'm mad." She purses her lips, but then they snap open. "That's it? The biggest crime you can pin on Savannah is she has condoms in her purse and you've let all of Chancey think she's a one-woman, virtue-slaying, alcohol-pushing, party-machine?"

"What? This is my fault? I only told one person, Retta. She's the one who spread it around."

"Nobody believes Retta. And that might be where it started, but then you constantly talk about not trusting Savannah and how she has to be watched. You're like a hawk with her. Then you didn't want the kids around this summer like you were afraid of what they'd do."

"I didn't want the kids there because we never had bunches of kids around back in Marietta. I don't like all the mess and noise. Believe me, if I was just afraid of kids losing control and behaving badly the first two I'd ban would be Angie with her piercings and Jenna with her 'ravish me, I'm a Southern belle routine'." I pause to take a breath, but then practically spit, "Wonder where she gets that?" My eyes travel down to the cleavage pushed against the wooden picnic table.

An outraged intake of breath causes the cleavage to rise. "You have lost your mind. We wanted to help you, and Savannah. Give her a fresh start here. But she didn't even need a second chance; she just needed a mother who had a clue. You don't like having kids around because you can't control everything they do and say. You find condoms, call your daughter a liar and move your whole family?" She pushes up from the table and steps over the bench. "I don't know what world you live in, but you can have it."

She swirls around and leaves. My mouth hangs open. Part of me wants to find those ugly words I said and push them back in. Another part of me is glad it's over.

I don't belong in the popular crowd.

"Yes, I'm eating my other corn dog. Go buy one if you want one."

Jackson lifts his hands in surrender, "Hey, just asking. So... sounds like with the way things are going around here, you don't need to ride the roller coaster for some ups and downs."

I shove the golden brown corn dog in mustard and then in my mouth. My grease quota was achieved with the funnel cake, onion rings and first corn dog. Now I'm going for the gold. Queen of grease. Now there's a blue ribbon I'd be willing to work for.

Despite my full mouth, I continue what I started as soon as I saw Jackson at the fair gate, "And she said I talked Savannah down, I don't do that. Do I?"

"Well, um," Jackson hesitates, looking around the table.

"You looking for something to put in your mouth, so you don't have to answer?" I press my lips shut and roll my eyes. My eyes settle on the half-eaten corn dog in my hand and I shudder, "Here finish this."

He takes it but just holds the stick, "Honey, all I know for sure is I don't like it when you're mad at me." He bites down and shrugs. "Besides, if Laney and Susan are your friends, why are they treating you so bad?"

"Yeah, exactly. I'm new here and they don't even give me chance. They practically pushed me into doing the Bed and Breakfast, and wouldn't leave us alone about church and getting together with their families. It was just fake, small-town pity. They were trying to help? Who needs that kind of help?"

Jackson shrugs and starts collecting the wrappings from dinner, "So, do we make Bryan go to the pageant?" he asks.

"Oh, I don't know." I rest my arms on the table and drop my shoulders. "I guess not. I sure wish I didn't have to go, I mean I want to see Savannah, but I don't want to see the rest of them. Laney up on stage may cause me to have a grease reaction right there in the audience."

We stand and walk to the garbage. Empty-handed we head through the carnival rides looking for Bryan to give him his good news.

"However, I may see Ida Faye at the pageant and maybe I can schedule an interview tomorrow. The sooner, the better she said."

"Wait a minute." Jackson grabs my arm. "If you take this job how does that affect the B&B?"

"It would go on the shelf where it belongs. Where we planned for it to be when we moved here."

"But the magazine interview? And we have bookings lined up."

I shake my arm to loosen his grip. "So? I'll cancel them. No big deal."

"Well, I think it is. We'll never get such good publicity again and some of those bookings are ones that came through the Rail Club back in Marietta. I don't want to let them down."

"Well then, don't let them down. *You* run the B&B. Jackson, I don't know what I want, but I can't take all this. I'm so exposed here and I just want my old life back."

Disappointment floods my husband's face. "But we can't."

"Look, I know you're disappointed in me, but you're not the one stuck here all the time." I bite my lower lip and walk away before the tears start. When I see Bryan in line at the Ferris wheel, I stride toward my son and reach out for his shoulder.

"Bryan. You don't have to come to the pageant." Sadness and anger mix into frustration, "Matter of fact, do whatever you want to do for the rest of your life."

I push through the line with his buddies saying "cool, whatever you want," behind me.

Past the Atrium is the auditorium where the girls will be. I checked it out earlier and so, without looking around, whip through the doors and take an immediate left down the hall to the bathroom. No need to look in the mirrors, I know what I look like and don't care. In the first empty stall, I sit and try to calm down. Things with Jackson couldn't have gone worse and I didn't even tell him about Savannah and Ricky and Saturday night. Or Susie Mae.

How did I get in the middle of so many messes? All my life I've just wanted not to be noticed and to be left alone with my books. But here I am, exposed. Exposed to the vultures who skulk around in lovely little hammocks and villages waiting for some unsuspecting suburbanite to stumble into their web. We can't move because we've wasted so much money on the B&B, but I want that job at the library. The desire to convince Ida Faye that she wants, no, needs me burns in my chest.

Finally calmed down, I smooth my clothes and leave the stall. No more confusion, I know what I want.

# Chapter 23

The auditorium lights go down and Jackson lays his arm behind me on the back of my metal folding chair. I wish I could push back and knock it off, but that's just not me.

Fantasizing about being mean, could I be any more of a wimp?

Jenna is stunning in rose pink with her mass of blond curls. April is cute, short and sweet. Natalie, Pace, and Laura look beautiful and happy. Savannah, though, takes my breath away. She's tall and her dark hair is shiny, her hydrangea-blue dress fits and flatters her. However my mouth hangs open because of her eyes, she is lost and scared. Her step is unsteady and her fingers, lifted to wave, shake. My little girl. Not the hard, demanding princess, just a scared, vulnerable girl.

The contestants walk past center stage. I watch Savannah scour the audience and I know, I know. She's looking for me. She wants to see me. She wants me to tell her everything is okay and so I lift my arm and wave and then next to me Jackson whistles his special call to the kids. Her eyes swing to us and she gulps. Our eyes lock and I say "I love you." A little nod from her and the pageant begins, but I'm in a fog.

I only watch Savannah and it's clear she's not going to win. During the question segment, she mumbles even though the emcee reminds her twice to speak up. She's struggling to even stay in the competition. I don't care. I just want to hold her and tell her I'm sorry. Take her home, fix hot chocolate, and snuggle on the couch. But I have to stay strong for her because she keeps finding my eyes and wanting me to cheer her on. So I do.

Her palpable fear during the swim suit routine causes Jackson to moan and put his head down with his hand across his forehead. All that leaves now is the talent portion; then the crowning and it will be over, all over. My legs itch at having to stay in my seat and not run to find her backstage.

Jenna sings a popular ballad and while it requires nothing special vocally, she performs well, is beautiful and the crowd pays her with long applause. Pace, with her lean dancer's body, executes a dance requiring athleticism and grace. The other performances are fine, but by time I realize Savannah will be last my throat is dry and my hands cramp from squeezing my fingers into my palms.

The stage goes completely dark and then a soft light falls on a stump sitting center stage. On it a girl waits with dark hair, bent shoulders and down cast face. Her long dress is bark-brown with a dirty white apron tied around it. She's skin and bones and a limp wrist hangs over her knee. She raises a weary arm to wipe her eyes and the face lifted to the pale light is my daughter's. Jackson and I are not the only ones that gasp at the transformation. Though she was scared and shaky earlier, this girl is broken, hungry. Despair fills her empty eyes and then she keens, "Tommy." Her wail stops my gasp and I'm struck by the raw power coming from this pitiful creature who is no longer my child, but a woman in anguish.

"Tommy, where are you? Why did you leave me?" Then a haunted whisper, "Are you dead? I don't feel you no more. I just don't know. I told them all you'd come back safe and sound and now, now I don't know. Are you dead? Does the dew wet your sweet blonde hair where you fell? My babies were going to have blonde hair and your... your brown eyes."

"Are you dead?" she shouts at the darkness. "Are your brown eyes closed forever?" Gripping her stomach with both arms, she rocks and whimpers, "Why did you have to fight? I hate this war, but I'd go fight today if I thought I could die, too."

The rocking stops and her vacant eyes well as her voice builds, "Buck Gentry says you're dead. He says he can protect me. You hear me, Tommy Cogdill! Buck Gentry wants to marry me and he's here, not off fightin' for some lost cause. I know you're true," she shakes her head, "but it's lost. Sherman broke me, honey. He broke my will for the cause and I... I think it's over."

"Buck says you picked the wrong side and I need to make clear whose side I'm on now that I don't have nobody." Nodding, she pulls on a hank of stringy black hair hanging against her wet cheek. "Nobody. Momma left for out west with Uncle Clyde and took the little kids. I stayed here to wait for you. Grandma says I gotta protect her and me 'cause the Home Guard is saying you deserted. Deserted!" Frantically her fingers work the piece of hair, "I know you just came to check on the farm but you put me in a bad place, a real bad place. Buck's in the Home Guard. He says he can protect me, Tommy."

Jerking up off the stump she paces, "Sarah Mantle is in jail 'cause Billy came home when he heard Sherman was here. Billy's gone now, and Buck says he ain't coming back. Ever. So Sarah's in jail and the baby is with her momma and daddy."

Haunted eyes in sallow, dark circles sweep side to side, "I'm waiting Tommy, right here where we use to meet but the leaves are falling and it's getting cold." She wraps her arms tight against her body and turns to her right. With a small smile, she closes her eyes. "The river, your river, is right here. It's quiet tonight but it's moving fast. Like the days. Everything just keeps moving." She stops and looks off to her left, "Hear that? A train's crossing the bridge. Remember the day we had to race off the bridge to beat that train? We jumped to the bank and you caught me, then we fell on the grass and lay there." Bright eyes stare into the light and flames jump to cheeks warmed with memory.

"Buck knows I still come here." With a shiver she drops to the stump, "He says it's time for me to stop roaming the riverbank looking for a ghost. He says I'm going to end up sleeping on a cot next to Sarah if the Home Guard thinks I'm trying to help you."

Thin, work-worn fingers pick at the soiled apron. "You're dead, ain't you? You're not coming home no matter how much time I spend here calling you. My babies ain't going to have blond hair or your brown eyes." Tears stream unchecked down pale cheeks. "I don't like Buck's mud-red hair, but if my little girl had it I'd like it, wouldn't I?"

A sob lifts her chest and her voice cracks, "You've killed me with all your talk and fightin' and... and if you are alive, don't come back here 'cause I won't be here. No more lying in the summer grass, no more touching my hair, no more watching the river flow past while we plan blond-haired babies." Sheer, raw will raises her arm to swipe away tears with her thin sleeve. She stands and lifts her chin. Cheek bones stand out in gaunt relief above her clenched teeth. "Tomorrow night is my wedding night and I'll belong forever to Buck Gentry and... " she swallows and ice fills her eyes. "And I'll hate you, Tommy, 'til the day I die."

Solid darkness hits me. I can't breathe. My throat is tight and dry. Suddenly, I inhale and tension in my hands, arms, and chest releases. Quick intakes of breath nearby, awaken me and I find myself in an auditorium at the fairgrounds, not on a cold, dark riverbank. The spot light reappears and shines on Savannah standing beside the stump. Applause erupts and a swell of emotion lifts us from our seats. My daughter's tears are gone, her smile is filled with gratitude and I can't clap fast enough. She bows, waves and walks off, blowing a kiss to her daddy and me.

Jackson and I turn to each other at the same time and our shock is mirrored. The emcee comes back out and as they give Savannah time to change into her evening gown, he explains the judging. I don't hear a word. My mind is stuffed with her words, her performance, the story, and my heart breaks for Tommy. I know now why he haunts my riverbank, but how did Savannah know all this? And does she know how good she is? She's never even been in a school play.

When the girls parade back onto the stage I search my daughter's face for that heart-broken girl in the brown dress. She's gone—her thin weary arms, stringy hair and gaunt eyes—all gone.

I feel as if I'm watching through thick, sound proof glass.

Lauren is draped with the Miss Congeniality sash and Pace walks to the emcee to accept her flowers as the 2nd runner-up. April lifts surprised hands to cover her mouth when she hears she's 1st runner-up. And then Jenna is crowned Miss Whitten County. I clap and cheer because Jenna *is* a beauty queen. Savannah's glowing eyes say she's fine with Jenna wearing the crown. Savannah is fine because of what she discovered tonight. She's not a beauty queen.

She's an actress.

# CHAPTER 24

"I was just so scared when the pageant started. The idea of getting to be Mettie and not me...Mettie is Tommy's fiancé name. Well, being her and not me was so awesome." Savannah turns as we walk to the cars to ask me again, "I was good? Really good?"

Bryan bounces around to walk in front of me, Jackson, and Savannah. He walks backwards, not worried about stumbling in the dark in the rutted field turned parking lot. "I thought you were great. Grant did too. Can we go back to the fair tomorrow night? The rides closed before we got to ride everything, that's why we were at the pageant."

"Well, lucky for you, or you would've missed your sister." My grin hasn't dimmed from the moment I finally got to hug her backstage. Nodding, I say again as I squeeze her shoulders, "You were amazing. Did you do that good during practice?"

Her daddy runs his hand through his hair, his smile as large as mine. "Honey, you blew me away. I had no idea you liked acting."

"Me either. I was supposed to tell the story and so that's what I practiced most." She pauses to gather her skirt away from the higher grass. "Then last week Missus suggested I try *being* Mettie. And, well, it just felt so great and Missus said I should do it that way, so we changed it."

"But where did you find the story?" I ask. "There's the van."

"It kinda came together from stuff Missus knew and all these books I got at the library and then the whole ghost thing. It all

215

fit together."

I laugh, "It sure did come together. I can't believe we've got three vehicles to get home, but I got left without keys this afternoon and had to drive your car." I hand Savannah's keys to her.

"I'm riding with Dad." Bryan interjects. "So, Mom, can we come back tomorrow?"

"Probably, but I can't think about it now, I'm exhausted. Boy, it'll be good to get home, won't it?" I open the van door and sit down. I'd parked Savannah's car next to the van earlier so she wouldn't have to walk out here alone. Jackson's car is only a couple rows farther.

The star pauses beside her car, "Well, Ruby's is open nights during fair week for pie and coffee. It's a tradition to go there." Savannah grins, "Earlier when I was bombing up on stage I would've rather died, but now I'd kinda like to go. Missus and FM will be there. Jenna too. Wasn't she beautiful?"

The past two days land like a bowling ball in my lap. Laney will be there, probably Susan, Ricky's dad, maybe. Jenna's whole family. "But what if Ricky's there?" I blurt.

I remember I didn't tell Jackson about Saturday night when he tilts his head at her and asks, "You and Ricky fighting? You can't fight with the quarterback during the season you know."

"No, we're not fighting." Savannah says and I catch a guilty look before she turns to put her key in the car door.

"Good, I'm up for Ruby's. How about it?" Jackson stands between the van and car and dips to look at me in through the open door.

"If Savannah wants to go, then okay. But there is school tomorrow."

"Great, c'mon Bryan. Race you to the car." Over his shoulder he yells, "See you all at Ruby's."

I close the door and start the car. I'm going to get there before them there so I don't have to walk in alone.

Conversations and confrontations barrel through my mind, all unlikely, but possibilities. Absent mindedly I hurry to the square and park near the tracks. Jackson and Savannah pull in next to me and we all meet in front of the cars and start across the park.

Walking across the square everyone laughs and jokes—except me. I'm lugging my bowling ball. I let Jackson and Savannah walk in front, hiding behind them. Light from Ruby's pours onto the street and reaches out to us. Jackson opens the door and ushers Savannah in. Cheers of "hello" and "Savannah" swell to pull us into the warmth and light. I maneuver to stay behind Jackson but forget my discomfort when Ricky steps forward, grabs my daughter and kisses her hard, right in front of everyone.

And she kisses him back!

She snuggles an arm around his waist and I move in front of Jackson to try and catch her eye, but she avoids me. What happened to "I'm through with him. I don't like his crowd. He wants me to do things?" All the good feelings I developed in the past couple hours about Savannah are dispersing like the steam from the coffee cups sitting around me.

I slide with my back to the counter into the nearest booth and reach up to tug on Jackson's jacket. "I want a cup of decaf and pie. Something chocolate." He nods and I let go of his jacket. I slide all the way to the wall and wrap my arms around me tight. Savannah makes the rounds. I guess I should say Savannah *and Ricky* make the rounds, as they are attached.

Bryan joins several friends at a table across from Susan and Griffin. Laney and Shaw aren't here yet with the newly crowned queen whose picture duties lasted longer than those of the other girls. Angie and Susie Mae sit in the booth with Susan. Missus holds court near the counter. Other folks fill nearly every seat and I realize I know most everyone's name.

"Can I join you?" FM asks as he slides in beside me.

"Sure, I guess."

"Not in the mood to party? Why aren't you there?" he nods toward Susan's table.

"We, we, uh, kinda had a falling out. Why aren't you over there with your wife?"

"I got questions she won't answer."

"Really?" I ask and lean toward him. "No, wait a minute," I shake my head. "I don't care. I'm through getting in the middle of everyone else's business."

"Gonna be hard to do that here. Gossip's pretty much the number one pastime in Chancey."

"Don't I know it."

"Hey, FM, good to see you." Jackson sets down our pie and shakes FM's hand. "Can I get you some pie or coffee?"

"You know, I'd appreciate that. I got a question or two I need to ask your wife if you don't mind."

"Sure, any kind of pie in particular."

"Apple would be good and a cup of tea. Anything decaf."

Jackson pauses but then nods and walks back to the counter and I turn to my seat companion with little patience. "What?"

FM pushes his glasses down and rubs his chin with his hand. "That night, the bonfire night, what was the ghost waving at the train?"

"Seriously? With all I have on my mind? I... don't know. A stick?"

"Think about it, really think about it and concentrate." FM stares at me, waiting for me to think.

"Okay." I close my eyes and remember the kids on the bridge running towards me. I see the train, the light and the ghost. I have trouble calling that ghost Tommy because Tommy is who I talk to at the river, not the kind of ghost running around shouting at trains and scaring people. So the ghost was standing there by the tracks waving at the train. "I don't know, a stick or something."

"Was he saying anything?"

"No. I started to the door, heard the train, and saw him heading straight for me. Then I heard the kids shouting. By time I got the door open the ghost was gone and the kids crowded onto the porch."

FM stares at me his lips pressed together tight. He sighs and asks, "That story Savannah told, or acted out tonight, where'd she get that?"

"She says it's from stuff Missus knew or had and then from

books at the library. What are you wondering about? What's going on?"

"Here you go." Jackson sets a piece of pie and tea in front of FM.

"Thanks much," he says as Jackson slides into the other side of the booth.

FM takes a big bite of pie and I pull my saucer to me. A large piece of old-fashioned chocolate pie practically spills over the edges. "Thanks, honey, this looks great." We eat in silence and just as I start to ask FM again what he's worried about, the door flies open.

"Introducing Miss Whitten County, Jenna Conner!" Shaw announces as Jenna sashays through the entry. She's closely followed by Laney and it truly is as if royalty has descended. Cheers and clapping greet her and her family and they take places at the center table. Savannah welcomes Jenna with a hug. Angie and Susie Mae are in line for hugs as are the table of cheerleaders that follow Jenna around. Laney wades through the crowd to her sister and they greet each other with a hug and then some serious whispering. I thought I belonged with them. But they're small town royalty, not my scene. As I look around the room, I recognize store owners, the recreation board, the historical society leaders, the folks that have run Chancey for years. What are the Jessups doing here? Lots of people in Chancey aren't here tonight. People who live here and go to school here, but don't run with these people. We moved in and they wanted our B&B so they made us a part of this club. Well, they can have it. I'd rather not be a mover and shaker.

"I'm finishing this and then we need to leave." I pass my decree on to Jackson. "Bryan has school tomorrow."

"Yeah, I have to be on the road to Columbus first thing in the morning, too. Savannah's got her car if she wants to stay longer."

FM looks up at Jackson then over at me. He shakes his head, lifts another bite to his mouth and mumbles, "I gotta get to the bottom of this."

I ignore both FM's muttering and Jackson's questioning look

and speak up, "Okay, well, Bryan will want to ride with you, so I'm going to head on home." I finish my pie in two bites and wash it down with lukewarm coffee. "Excuse me, FM, but I'm exhausted." I add a weak smile because I know I'm being rude, but I have to get out of here.

I walk out Ruby's front door and the cold darkness comforts me. To be there in the light and crowd you have to play games. Games I'm not good at. I turn to find Savannah in her rich blue dress seated between Missus, the town matriarch, and Jenna, the town beauty queen. Behind her, his hands laid on her shoulders, is Ricky, the star quarterback.

I sigh, turn, and walk away from the light.

# CHAPTER 25

"Can you be here at noon? I'll get some sandwiches brought in and we can talk over lunch. Marney just told me she wants to use her vacation as part of her two week notice so she'll only be here one more week."

"Sure, I can be there." I drop the dish cloth I'm wiping the table with and reach for a towel to dry my hands on while telling Ida Faye goodbye. My hand places the phone on its hook, forms a fist and pumps into the air. Talking over lunch is a very good sign and Ida Faye seemed relaxed. Maybe she's forgiven me for letting Missus help Savannah. Savannah did do great last night.

I run up the stairs and take a detour into Savannah's empty room where her stereo plays and her lamp is still on. Clothes lie on every surface and her mango body spray hangs in the air. She came in late last night, but she was up and in a good mood this morning. "Ricky is good," is all I got out of her this morning before she left for school. I guess they're dating again.

Nothing illegal or overtly immoral (except for the Victoria's Secret ad on her desk) catches my attention so I turn off her stereo, snap off her light, and close the door behind me.

A cool breeze meets me upon entering our bedroom. Jackson loves fresh air at night and so we sleep with the window cracked, even on cold nights. I cross the room and close the window. The river is visible through the trees now and this morning it is a muddy greenish-brown. I wonder where Tommy is and shiver.

Savannah, as Mettie, talked about wandering the riverbank looking for a ghost. This morning the riverbank looks ghostly

221

itself, mist clings to the bank, drifts under trees and wraps around bushes huddled together in the cold. Gray skies press down on the trees already heavy with wet, brown leaves.

With a shift of my head to see the bridges, I catch my breath. Someone is on the walking bridge. A man leans on the railing looking away from the house. His hair is long and pulled in a loose pony tail. His jacket hangs half-way down his thighs and is army green. He's smoking and the cold morning doesn't seem to bother him. He looks relaxed, contemplative.

Visitors to the bridge usually hang around long enough to see a train or two. I'm sure this guy will be gone by time I leave the house for my interview.

But, wait, how will he leave? There wasn't a car out front a minute ago. In Savannah's room when I lifted her blinds, I looked down at the front yard and drive. It was empty except for my van. Another shiver runs down my back. Just a wanderer probably. However, the idea of someone hanging out so close to the house, especially since Jackson went out of town again this morning, isn't appealing.

I drop my head against the window frame. What an awful morning. Jackson left angry, but I can't do this B&B thing anymore. He thinks I owe Laney and Susan an explanation, but he doesn't understand how angry they are. No, I just need to push forward.

Once things get back to normal, no one will remember the B&B ever existed.

"So, you want to start tomorrow?" Ida Faye brushes crumbs off her mauve knit top and smiles at me.

"Really? I... I think so. Yes. Yes, tomorrow would be great."

"You'll do fine and I understand. Getting wrapped up with Shermania Bedwell just sometimes *can't* be helped. It *is* a small town."

Anxious to please, I nod. "Missus is rather overwhelming. She desperately wanted the B&B for the grant money. They'll just have to find another way to make it happen." I beam at my new boss and breathe deep. Knots in my shoulders magically release. The job is mine. The B&B is over, done with. I'm calling and canceling the reservations we have as soon as I get home. Then calls to Laney and Susan, hopefully they'll be gone and I can just leave messages.

"That grant was a pipe dream all along. Laney Shaw writing a grant? Please! That girl's never done *anything* but chase boys. She caught Conner Shaw and you'd think that'd keep her happy, but *no*. She displays what God gave her all over creation. I'd say *half* the divorces in Whitten County are Laney Trout Shaw's responsibility."

My mouth suddenly goes dry. I've been thinking bad things about Laney all night, but this... "Well, um, Laney is attractive."

Ida Faye crosses her arms across her pillowy, mauve front and leans on her desk. "You'd *think* her mother and sister would make her behave, but they just whine and moan about it all. A couple of sisters-better-than-you who want everyone to think *they're* perfect. But I'm here to tell you, they're not. Oh, far, *far* from it." Her voice drops to a whisper, "And that *sweet* little Susie Mae? You won't *believe* what I heard."

I squirm in my seat and smooth my hands down the front of my tweed skirt. "Ah, what time tomorrow should I be here?"

Ida Faye pauses at the interruption and looks down at her calendar. "Oh, right. Ten is good. I want you learning the front desk *immediately*. Saturday we're hosting the St. Mark's quilters in the Barberry Room upstairs. I'll need you to help run the front desk all day since I'll be busy with the quilters." She stands and holds out her hand. "Welcome to the Chancey Library."

I stand and place my hand in hers.

She pats my arm, "You'll find we're like *family* here."

I loosen my grip, but she tightens hers and leans toward me. "I *heard* what happened at Ruby's last night. It must've hurt something *awful* to be treated like a vegetarian at a barbeque by *that* group." Her gray eyes gleam like wet river stones. "I called you this morning as *soon* as I heard. Believe me, you're not the first or last to be shunned by *that* group."

"Thanks." My mouth is dry *and* tastes bad now. I pull my hand away and step toward the door. "See you in the morning."

Of course my ex-communication already hit the phone lines. I hate small towns.

# Chapter 26

Outside the library, I pause and look around. The library is in a two-story, gray stone block building across from the end of the park. Kelly green trim and window boxes show that someone tried to liven up the imposing façade. At one time, it housed the city offices, fire and police departments, and the library. Ten years ago, the new city hall was built on the edge of the park and the library was left to occupy the cavernous structure alone.

The library faces a row of single-family homes where railroad workers probably lived at one time. Behind the row of homes are the railroad tracks. I look to my left; the sidewalk I'm on passes in front of Missus' front porch. To my right, the sidewalk ends at the corner. The neighborhood past that point features large yards, one-story homes, and old trees. Carports, aluminum siding, and blonde brick denote the decade the homes were built. Tricycles, swing sets, and trampolines speak to the ages of the families there.

What to do now? I need to cancel the upcoming reservations for the B&B, but I'm dressed up and I don't want to go home.

Lunch with Ida Faye featured lukewarm, grilled-cheese sandwiches sent over from Ruby's. I picked at mine partly due to nervousness but mostly due to a dislike for congealed cheese. My stomach growls and I think of all those places in the suburbs where you can eat an entire meal without one person asking about your ghost or your daughter's sex life.

I check my phone and see that I have three hours before the

kids come home from school.

Applebee's, here I come.

Twenty minutes. That's all it took to be down the highway, on the interstate, parked and seated in a booth at Applebee's. Twenty minutes.

I keep saying that to myself. I don't know why I'm fascinated with that fact. The clock on the dash tells me that only one hour and fifteen minutes ago I left the library. In a little over an hour I went to lunch where no one knew me and am back at the Chancey welcome sign.

"Welcome to Chancey, Georgia. Holler if you need anything!"

Was it really only twelve weeks ago Savannah and I sat in this very spot reading that sign? Seems like I've lived in Chancey forever. Susan, Laney, the B&B, the pageant, Missus, Tommy. It's time to slow this down and my new job will make it possible to lose myself in the books, the catalog files, the quiet. There will be time to read because all those people won't need to talk to me. No pageant teas, no bonfires with the city council, no teen-age work crews. It's time to do Chancey on *my* terms.

Coming upon the elementary-school, I notice the line of cars out front, so I slow to a crawl. Children rush out the doors holding papers. I see familiar faces and laugh watching a sister and brother fight over the front seat. They don't care that they're holding up at least a dozen cars behind them.

Out of the school zone, I speed up and decide to make a stop at the grocery store. I need to stock up on some easier meals now that I'm working again. The parking lot is nearly empty. I meander the aisles and smile when I realize I'm humming the Air Supply song on the speaker system. A sense of calm and peacefulness have enveloped me since accepting Ida Faye's job offer. The return to familiar territory allows me to breathe.

At the check-out, I look around for Angie before realizing

she's still in school.

"Here, hon, I'm open even if the light isn't on. Bulb burnt out last week and no one's gotten around to putting in a new one." A gray-haired lady in a blue shirt and red apron calls to me.

I maneuver the cart to her register and empty my purchases onto the moving belt.

"Your daughter did real good last night. Sorry she didn't win, but her heart didn't really look into it at first. But, boy did she ever nail that skit." The clerk whips the groceries across the scanner. "I know you all were real proud."

"Yeah, we were."

"Pace Langston is my sister-in-law's niece so I went mainly to watch her, but it's always a good show."

"Oh, I know Pace. She's such a nice girl."

"Yep, she sure is. And she sure loved staying at your hotel up there at the river. Said it's got train stuff an' all. My husband is a train nut and he says he hopes you all have an open house sometime so he can come see it. Says he can't hardly see paying to stay a night in his hometown." She rolls her eyes, "'Course we been married now 33 years and he can't see a need to stay overnight much of anywhere outside his own bed."

I laugh, "That's understandable. Maybe we will have an open house. That's a great idea." I place my last bag into my cart. "It was good to meet you."

"You, too. Glad your family's liking Chancey so much. It's always good to have folks move in that have big dreams. Reminds the rest of us what life is all about."

Now why did I talk like the B&B was still functional? Maybe it will be again someday. It's Jackson's dream. When he's going to be home more he can open it back up. He's the big dreamer, not me. Nope, not me.

The drive up the hill takes me past Susan's house. Only two days have passed since we loaded all the fair stuff and I never did get to see the exhibits. Maybe we'll go back later in the week, since Bryan wants to go back to the fair.

I'm not sure I agree with Ida Faye that Susan thinks she's better than everyone, but she sure does have definite ideas.

Making the kids work in the garden. Bossing the youth around, working on the B&B rooms. She does think she knows what's best for everyone.

Crossing the tracks at the house, I look both ways, not only for safety, but also to see if there's train coming anytime soon. My automatic impulse makes me laugh. My rail fan husband trained me well. There is a head light in the distance, so I drive across and stop in the driveway. Out of the van, I walk around to the back where I lean on the rear bumper and wait.

The mist has drifted away, but left gray skies that hang close. Rusty leaves and wet brown bark stand out against the gray. The brighter colors, red and gold, need sunlight to make them glow. It's so quiet and I barely hear the rumble of the coming train. With a deep breath, I smell the waning exhaust from my van, the fishiness of the water, the mustiness of the fallen leaves. I fill my lungs again and again.

The chugging of the train engine grows louder as I wait for the rush of pure power when it charges past. As the mountain of steel and energy comes toward me, the noise fills the damp air. The engines bring with them a wall of wind. The commanding presence of tons of metal and movement awes me. All of that is riding on those two little ribbons of steel. Cars rush past me and the romance of railroading fills the air around me. I remember standing like this with the children and watching their faces. They let the train get to them, Jackson did too. But I always tried to hold back. Keep the noise and bigness at bay. But not today. Today I let the train fill me up. When the last car passes I walk toward the tracks to watch it move on to other crossings, other bridges, other towns.

Standing on the track, I watch until the final car turns around the bend past the river. Why did I let the train get to me today? Things are finally getting things back to normal. Tomorrow I'll be in the library. Tomorrow my life takes me away from my home on the hill and the river. Away from my willow tree and my ghost. Tomorrow I get my life back.

Maybe the train was just a way to say "good-bye."

# CHAPTER 27

"I *know* you don't have any clean underwear. That's why I'm doing laundry at eleven o'clock on a Sunday night," I shout up the stairs.

Thursday, Friday, and Saturday were full work days. Today I slept in, while Jackson and the kids went to church. The rest of the morning I spent in blessed solitude and silence. Eating the huge container of fried rice from the Chinese restaurant, took up the rest of my energy, so I took a nap. Maybe I'm not tired as much as I'm avoiding the mess in this house.

I forgot what working away from home means. It means there's no one working at home.

Savannah vacuumed under threat of death yesterday, but then Bryan spilled a bag of chips in the living room. The bathrooms were also on Savannah's to-do list and she did clean them—with toilet tissue. Bryan swept the kitchen and raked the front yard. Of course, half the leaves he raked followed him into the house. So much for the sweeping.

Dirty dishes stack up every day because no one can remember who is supposed to unload the dishwasher. Of course that argument can only be settled by a parent and there's only one parent coming home at night.

I forgot that when I worked in Marietta Jackson didn't travel. He was home to help put things in order. He can yell at the kids as well as I can. Probably better.

So tonight I'm in the basement doing laundry at eleven o'clock and Jackson is trying to pack to go out of town. However there's nothing clean to put in his suitcase.

The basement is unfinished and has several rooms I've not been in since moving day. It's not a spooky basement as there is lots of light from hanging fluorescent fixtures in the main room. The back wall is above ground so windows let in light during the day. A door on the side by the driveway is easy access to the yard. Jackson has talked about opening up that end and making a drive-in garage down here, but that sounds like a lot of work to me.

The walls are stone, but host several coats of white paint. Pieces of carpet lay scattered throughout. So while it's not uncomfortable, I don't choose to hang out down here. Except tonight I have so much laundry to do and the house above my head is still a wreck. So I'm chilling in the basement going through boxes of unpacked magazines and books.

"Mom, you down here?" Savannah calls from the top of the stairs.

"Yeah, what do you need?"

"Is my white hoodie clean?" She descends the stairs and stands staring at the mounds of clothing surrounding the washer and dryer.

"It's clean, but not dry yet. It will be by morning, though."

"Okay."

"You got anything special going on this week?"

"Not really." She steps over a clothes-basket and comes to look in the box I'm going through. "What's that? Stuff from the move?"

"Uh huh." She's got something on her mind. She's doing that floaty thing that means she wants to talk. It's when kids kind of hover around, counting on a parent's curiosity to finally get to the desired subject. William did this a lot. I would hardly see him for days and then he'd come sit by me on the couch. Just sit and wait for me to ask the right question. Savannah, however, rarely plays this game.

"So, about the talent thing last night. You think I was really good?"

I lay down the books I was sorting and lean back on a stool

sitting beside the washer. "Yeah, I did. Everyone did."

"Auditions for the spring play are next week." She tests her weight on an unopened box.

"You can sit on it, it's just books. Are you trying out?"

"Should I?" she asks.

Peeking up at me, I see the scared girl from the stage last night. I smile and nod. "I think you should."

"Okay." She rocks slightly, but doesn't move to get up.

I'm not sure what topic is next on the agenda, but I'll give it a try. "So, Ricky?"

"Yeah, we're back together."

"What about the rock throwing and him expecting you to, ah, to party with him?"

"Oh, I set him straight on that. I told him the partying stuff was a lie, a rumor. So that's not a problem." She banishes her bad reputation with a wave of her hand. She sighs and smoothes down the flannel leg of her pajama pants several times. "He's really upset about Susie Mae, though."

"How is Susie Mae?"

"It's bad and she can't handle it. When everyone talked about me, I kinda liked it and just laughed about it, but Susie Mae keeps crying. It's like everyone wants the bad stuff to be true because she's so good."

"People like to see angels fall. Have you talked to her yet?"

Savannah shakes her head and presses her lips together. She looks around at the boxes. "Can you believe we only moved here this summer?"

"I was thinking that last week. Sometimes if feels like we've lived here forever."

"Do you like your new job?" she asks and I suddenly feel this is what we're talking about.

"Yeah, I'm figuring it out."

"So what about the B&B?"

I shrug, "What about it?"

"Is it closing? Everyone wants to know?"

"Everyone, or just Missus?" The dryer buzzes and I get up to take the clothes out and put more in.

"Can I do it?"

"Sure, grab that basket."

"No, not the laundry. The B&B."

"What?" I straighten up and turn around to face her. "What are you talking about?"

"We were talking, me and Angie. We want to run the B&B. You keep telling me I need a part-time job. I bet we could get Missus to help and Angie's mom says she'll help with the reservations and stuff like she's been doing."

"You've talked to Laney?"

"It just kind of came up when we were at Angie's Friday night after the ballgame."

"No." I turn around and start pulling clothes out of the dryer. "I'm tired of my house being full of strangers."

"Dad thinks it's a good idea. He said he'd at least like to try it so we can keep the reservations we already have." She stands up and opens the washer. "Do you want all these in the dryer?"

I straighten up again, my right hand fisted on my hip. "And all the laundry. You're telling me that you and Angie will do all the laundry?"

"Yes. We'll keep track of our hours and Miss Laney says she'll take care of the books so we get paid."

"Take a look upstairs at your cleaning skills. You cleaned the bathroom with tissue. The B&B would have to be spotless."

"But it would be my job, so I'd do better. Really. Just let us try."

"I don't know. I have to think about it." I jerk out the lint filter and pull off the layer of lint. I shove it back in. "Where does Missus come in?"

Savannah folds her arms and cocks her head at me. "She wants to do our PR and, well, she had some other ideas."

"Like...?"

"Well, some tours or teas or... well... ghost walks." A grin breaks through.

"Ghost walks? Like in your story last night? Mettie walking the river bank looking for Tommy?" I shake my head, "That woman has lost her mind. She's obsessed with this ghost thing."

Then my thoughts jump to Charles asking me why I was so worried about the ghost. *Why are we all so focused on him?*

"Missus is really ticked off at you for closing the B&B. She says she worked too hard to get Tommy attention and it's not fair for you to... ah..." My daughter stops talking and starts taking clothes out of the washer.

"Not fair for me to what? Tell me what she said."

Savannah looks up at me, her blue eyes dancing. "She said it's not fair for you to just close up shop and sit on your behind at the library with Ida Faye Newbern. I won't tell you *exactly* what she called your new boss."

"Why do those two hate each other?"

Hands loaded with wet bundles, she leans toward me to put them in the dryer. She throws them in and then stands. "I don't know. I was so excited about doing the B&B that I forgot to ask. So, can we?"

I pick up the basket, take it to my chair, and drop it in the floor. "I don't know. I'll have to talk it over with your dad." I sit down and pull the basket to me. "I do hate to cancel out on people. Especially since some of them are your dad's friends."

"Excellent. I'm going to go call Angie. She's waiting for me to talk to you."

"Hey," I call out to my daughter already heading to the stairs. "Put the rest of the clothes in the dryer and then let's see if you can figure out how to start it."

She has the grace to look embarrassed, "Sure."

It only took three tries before she had the dryer going and could race upstairs.

The tumbling of the dryer and repetitive motions of folding clothes lulls me into calmly thinking about Savannah's proposal. I'll be working every Saturday, so I won't have to deal with the weekend guests. We could try it until Christmas and not take any new bookings. Laney does a good job handling the books, despite Ida Faye believing she has only one talent. However, if Missus gets a toe hold in this place... could be hard to ever get rid of her. If that's my biggest concern, then...

Apparently, I can't think of any real objections.

# CHAPTER 28

"So you're *letting* that woman hang around at your house? Your husband must be *thrilled*." Ida Faye stretches the word *thrilled* to four syllables and her eyebrows lift to meet her poufy, gray bangs. Her hair is super-short on the sides and back, but she makes up for that with a hanging curl of bangs. Marching out of her office she wants to restart a conversation we've run into the ground ever since I told her the new plan for the B&B.

"Laney's not after Jackson. Besides, the girls are always there." I turn my chair away from her and look through the top drawer of the library desk. "Do we have Post-it pads? I need to mark these held books."

She rolls her eyes and takes a deep breath. "In the supply closet, near the bathrooms."

My chair spins back as I jump up, "Great. I'll get them while you're up here to watch things. Is that okay?"

"Sure." Ida Faye sits down in the seat next to mine, still shaking her head. She clicks her tongue in concern, "You're playing with *fire*. Laney Troutman has always been trouble and now, well... get those Post-its and we'll *talk* when you get back." She mutters, only partly to herself, "Laney working with Missus is something I *never* thought I'd see. Talk about forgive and forget!"

Her words cause me to pause at the counter. After two weeks working here, I know that Ida Faye holds the dirt on everyone in Chancey, however it's not reliable. It's the normal recipe for small-town gossip. One part truth, one part wishful thinking and a dash of horrific detail. Being Southern, she sandwiches all this between "Bless her heart" and "God love her."

She realizes I'm listening. "Bless her heart, Laney can't *help* being attractive. I guess it's just a family curse." Ida Faye's head bows under the strain of untold secrets.

"Okay, so what's-"

The door flies open and Bryan and Grant run into the library.

"Hey, Mom. Hey, Mrs. Newbern." The boys have red clay ground into the knees of their jeans and their faces are flushed.

Ida Faye's face contorts. "Boys, don't lean on the counter like that. You're all sweaty."

"We were playing football in the field out in the park. Can we have money for a Coke?"

Back behind the desk, I sit in my chair and pull my purse out of the drawer I keep it in. "Sure. Change for the machine?"

They nod and I hand over several quarters and a couple of dimes.

"Grant, how is your sister? I haven't seen Susie Mae lately." Ida Faye's eyes widen to express her deep concern.

"Fine, I guess." Grant shrugs and the boys begin sorting the money.

"Bryan, did you tell Savannah you were playing football after school and didn't need a ride home today?"

"Nope, she told me to find a ride 'cause she was leaving school early for some B&B guests." They move toward the door as they divide their money.

"Today? It's Wednesday."

"Okay," Bryan says over his shoulder. "We'll be back for a ride at five, okay?"

"Yeah, five is good." I dig for my phone and hit the home button, but no one answers the house phone. I next try Savannah's cell phone, but she doesn't answer. I text her "call me," and drop the phone in my purse.

"Trouble?"

"I'm completely out of the loop. They never tell me anything." I look up and see the shine in Ida Fay's eyes and cough. "No, no trouble. I, uh, I guess I forgot to look at the booking calendar."

I set my purse in the drawer and stand. "I'm going to get those Post-it notes."

My stride doesn't break until I'm across the entrance and down the hall past the children's section. Turning the corner, out of site of the front desk, I lean against the wall. Savannah left school early. That's not good. Mid-week guests? Laney knows better. I should've brought my phone back here to make some calls and figure this out without gossip-queen listening. I tip my head back and push away from the wall. It's gone well so far, but this can't take over Savannah's life. With a jerk of my hand, I open the closet door and find my supplies.

Back at the front desk. Ida Faye pushes out my chair for me. She watches me sit, then pulls the sides of her lavender sweater together at her throat. "I'm not surprised Grant doesn't want to talk about his sister." She shakes her head and her gray, bangs slide side-to-side. With a sigh, she pats her chest, "Although, wonder if the poor boy even knows."

"Knows what?" I grab my phone from my purse and check for messages. *I need to talk to Savannah.*

"She's pregnant."

I stop breathing, "What?"

Ida Faye nods, "Susie Mae, God love her."

My phone is suddenly way too heavy and my hand falls into my lap. "That can't be true. I have to leave. I have to, ah, I need to go home." I clutch my phone in one hand while my other hand fumbles with the straps of my purse. "I have to go."

Ida Faye frowns, "But you're on duty until five. I need you here. Also, aren't Grant and Bryan getting a ride from you?"

Oh, yes, the boys. And even if this is true, I can't do anything about it. Susan and I aren't talking.

*Wonder if Savannah knows?*

I plop in my chair and look up at Ida Faye. She's waiting for me to ask. She has stories to tell. So I nod and take a deep breath, "How did you find out?"

"She threw up at school yesterday morning and went to the *clinic*. My daughter's mother-in-law, Bertie Goodman, works there—in the clinic. Susie Mae came in and this girl *jokingly* asked Susie Mae if she was *pregnant*. Well, Susie Mae broke down sobbing. Bertie, took her back to the sick room and sat with her while they called Susan. And *then* in the front office when they were signing out, my neighbor's son heard Susan tell Susie Mae she'd made a *doctor's appointment*."

Relief creeps down my back and my chest relaxes a little. "That doesn't mean she's pregnant. She probably just has a stomach virus."

"Oh, *really*?" my boss shakes her head at my silly delusion. "Griffin Lyles shirks his council duties for his children's *stomach virus*? Wanda Brandstetter, you know the lady that reads all those smutty romances from the paperback bin? Well, she works in the *mayor's* office. Wanda told me Griffin called up the Mayor yesterday and explained he wouldn't be at the council meeting last night due to, and I quote, *a family emergency*.

I press my lips together. Griffin and Susan must be reeling. Poor Susie Mae. I press my lips harder trying to not let the sadness in my chest out. My eyes burn and my nose runs. I swipe at my nose with my palm.

Ida Faye stands and walks behind me. She leans down and squeezes my shoulders in her large, doughy hands. "I'm *so sorry* I had to be the one to tell you this. I know you worry *constantly* about Savannah ending up pregnant, bless her heart, she's so pretty and popular. And that Ricky Troutman... well, he *is* his father's son. You know the boys' mama left 'cause she couldn't trust Scott Troutman farther than she could *throw* him. Well, you can *always* talk to me. You're part of *our family* now." She leans down and presses her cheek to mine.

She squeezes me one more time and steps away from the back of my chair. "I'll be in my office if you need *anything*, or if you want to talk." Ida Faye's voice fades as she walks away. "Poor Susie Mae. *But* if you lie down with the dogs, you're going to get *up* with fleas."

Picturing sweet, tiny Susie Mae crawling with fleas makes me want to scream. I want to pound the counter with my fists and yell at God. Susan and Griffin spend every Sunday morning in that big, red-brick church. Why would this happen to their daughter? I look to the ceiling. *God, what's wrong with you? Why would you let this happen?* My eyes narrow and my jaw tightens. *You're not making any friends down here, you know.*

# Chapter 29

Bryan and Grant slam the car doors and run into the Lyles house. Only a couple of weeks ago I would've put the car in park, turned the key and walked in that front door behind them. I would've called Susan's name and made my way back to the kitchen, following the smells of dinner preparation. We'd sit at the kitchen table and chat while the boys found Bryan's jacket.

Today, however, I sit in the car as the autumn sun hangs behind the tall trees in their back yard. Golden sunlight fills the air, flowing through the line of walnut trees. My window is down and I breathe deep the smell of decaying leaves. There is hardly a chill today as the time hasn't changed, so the evenings stretch into hours of maize, pumpkin, and amethyst skies. But winter is coming. Underneath the warm earthiness, I feel the cold.

In the purpling air, Susan's home exudes warmth. Lights from deep inside and textured cushions on the front porch rockers beckon. I know the smells and sounds to be found in her kitchen. But no more. That door is closed. She closed it.

It's for the best—all for the best.

My eyes sink shut and barely slit when the front door open. Susan holds the screen door wide. Bryan pushes around her and dashes for my car. Susan nods at me and I... I shut my eyes.

This really is the best way.

Cars fill our driveway and every window spills light. I park in front of the house, where visitors to the bridge usually park.

Bryan opens the back door of the van to retrieve his backpack and pauses after he slings it over his shoulder. "I think they're out back."

"Yeah, Savannah said they were going to have a wiener roast for dinner."

"Cool!" Bryan strides toward the backyard.

After closing the car doors, I walk to the end of the driveway to check the mailbox. Shoving the mail into my purse, I survey the cars. When I finally reached Savannah this afternoon she told me who our guests are. Lou Taylor, the mayor's dad, is back with a couple rail fan buddies from North Carolina. Dorothy came too but she's staying with Jed and Betty and her six grand children. My stroll up the drive takes me past the mayor's red truck, his parents car with North Carolina tags, and another car, also with a North Carolina tag. Laney's mustang convertible sits nearly in the back yard, next to Missus' boat of an old Cadillac. Savannah's car and Ricky's truck are out near my minivan. I walk up the sidewalk and onto the porch. Reaching the door, I feel an overwhelming impulse to ring the doorbell. Like a stranger.

Why can't we go back to our old life? Because my family refuses. They purposely ignore the fences I'm trying to build to keep this new life out.

Looking down, I gaze at my hand on the screen door handle. Opening the library door—that feels right. This, this is strange. I sigh and pull open the screen door.

Laughter in the kitchen belongs to my daughter. It leads to her and Ricky.

"Hey, Mom. We're trying to make more lemonade but we can't find the mix." Savannah is on her knees on the counter digging through the top cabinets. Ricky is behind her with his hands around her waist.

"You can't find it because we don't have any." I drop my purse in a kitchen chair.

"Catch me," she says as she leans back into Ricky's arms.

He easily swings her around and puts her feet on the ground.

She tugs her shirt down. "Dinner's going good. You ought to get out there before the hot dogs are all gone."

"You never gave me a real good reason why you came home early from school today."

Savannah's face hardens, "I needed to get ready for the company and, well, we had an assembly I didn't want to go to."

"Who left early with you?" My eyes flit to Ricky before I can stop them.

Savannah tucks a stray bit of hair behind her ear and nods, "Yeah, Ricky came with me. Um, but Mom. Nothing happened. We just hung out and... ah... talked."

With a shake of my head, I stand up and head for the living room. Contrary to everything I've been trying to do—stay quiet, listen, and pay attention—I'm walking away. "Whatever. I'm going to change my clothes."

Ricky slides toward the back door and Savannah moves with him. "Okay, I'll save you a hot dog." They leave the kitchen and step onto the deck. The door shuts quietly behind them. I pause, then turn, cross back across the kitchen and look out at the bonfire.

Orange flames outline adults and teens alike. Bryan is roasting a hot dog, his second I'd guess by the way his cheeks jut out. Angie is leaning against the condiments table talking to a boy I don't recognize. Lou is surrounded by his rail fan friends, I assume. I stretch, but don't see Laney and Missus.

"Looking for us?"

I turn around to find them coming from the B&B hallway. "Honestly? Yeah."

Laney walks behind me to the sink and turns on the water. "We were just checking out the girls' cleaning." She pumps soap into her palm. "Wish Angie'd clean like this at home. But I guess I'd have to pay her."

Missus pulls out a kitchen chair and sits down. "They did well. However, it never hurts to check. Sit down, Carolina. I never heard your thoughts on Savannah's performance in the pageant." She lays her hands on the kitchen table, one on top of the other. "Of course, I mean the talent competition. Her overall demeanor was surprising and rather disappointing."

"I'm really tired and I need to change." I push past both women. They will not suck me in again.

"How is it working with Ida Faye?" Missus' accent fades and the words are dry, humorless.

"Fine."

Laney laughs and I spin around. "What's so funny? Ida Faye? She sure doesn't think you two are funny."

"Of course she doesn't." Laney is leaning on my counter looking very at home. She has on well-fitted jeans, a cherry-red sweater that hangs mid-thigh and adorable fawn-colored suede boots. Her hair is tied back with a red bandana. "Ida Faye wouldn't know funny if it was a file in her card catalog. I'd say she's jealous, but she doesn't have the sense to be jealous. She's just mean."

"And a touch crazy." Missus pronounces her diagnosis and smiles. "Carolina, I'm happy you are enjoying the library, but we need you here. Your daughter understands the importance of this place. You seemed to understand it at one time yourself. Now, sit down and tell me why you are hiding at the library."

"I'm not hiding at the library. This is a three-ring circus and Savannah's only in it for the money. She'll see what a pain it is." I spread my arms out, "This can't be my life. It's too... too chaotic, too unpredictable."

Missus tilts her head at me, "But that is what life is. Unpredictable. Messy..."

"Fun!" Laney grins wide and points outside. "Look out there, kids and adults toasting marshmallows at a bonfire; high on a hill overlooking the river." She holds her hands out to me, "You created that. You made that possible."

"No, I had nothing to do with all this. It just happened. You two, Susan, Jackson and even my kids. This mess is y'alls fault."

Laney's arms drop to her sides and she shakes her head. "Mess? Your husband's happy, your kids seem fine." She squints at me, "You do know that Savannah is fine, right? Ricky's crazy about her and she's making him behave. He's actually doing well in school now, believe it or not. I do wish you'd never led us to believe she was so out of control, but we know now." She smiles and holds out a manicured hand, palm up. "Don't be mad, come out to the fire. Enjoy it. Lou and his buddies from North Carolina are a lot of fun, although I don't understand a word of that train stuff."

I shake my head at her. "Have you talked to Susan today?"

Laney's smile disappears. She drops her head, walks to the door, and opens it. She starts to step out on the deck, but stops and looks at me. "Yes, I've talked to her. That's what we're trying to tell you. Life is messy." She moves through the door and closes it behind her.

In the silence, I wonder if Missus knows about Susie Mae. We both stare at the French door Laney just walked through until Missus stands up and turns to me.

"Honey, Ida Faye sits in her perfect library and judges the rest of us. If you feel that is where you belong, I wish you well." Missus reaches out and takes my hand.

A smile flits to my mouth when I look down and see she doesn't have her white gloves on, but her dove-gray leather gloves perfectly match her slacks and sweater.

She pats my hand. "I'm going to find someone to get my car out of the driveway so I can go home. I'll be by in the morning with muffins from Ruby's. I suppose you won't be at our committee meeting for the B&B tomorrow?"

"No, I work all day."

"Pity. However, as my Aunt Evelyn always said, 'People do what they want.'"

She leaves and I drag myself up the stairs, arguing with myself all the way. "Life doesn't have to be messy. It wasn't in Marietta." I ignore the voice reminding me of Savannah and Parker. I ignore the voice saying I avoided messiness by always agreeing with Jackson. I ignore the voice telling me those boxes of books in the basement is where I kept my messes contained.

I pull off my black slacks and cream sweater and put on jeans and a navy turtle neck. From the back of my bedroom door, I grab my red West Georgia University hoodie. There's white stuff all over the back of it. Powder, baby powder I realize as I smell it. Where did baby powder come from? I step into the bathroom and shake it out over the tub. When did I wear this last?

I put on the hoodie and then slip my feet into my brown, fake Lands' End shoes. Halfway down the stairs I remember wearing the hoodie at the pageant sleepover. The night I hurt my back and when we all saw the ghost. I step off the last stair and I'm at the front door. It rushes back to me. That night the thing the ghost held up was shiny in front of the train. It was metal, not a stick like everyone keeps saying. I open the front door and think of what I saw that night.

The ghost rushed up the porch steps and... and... what is it? I step onto the porch. Chilly night air greets me and I try to put myself back to that night. The train, the kids' yells, the ghost running toward me. He stepped up on the porch and... and he grabbed the porch railing. That's it! That's what didn't fit. Why would a ghost need help getting up the stairs? To steady himself? To keep from falling?

"A ghost wouldn't need the railing," I say and wonder what it means. My stomach grumbles. The smell of the fire, toasted marshmallows, and roasted hot dogs floats from the back yard. I step into the living room feeling good that I'd finally remembered what bothered me about that night. I grab a Diet Coke from the refrigerator and head out to the fire. Hope they saved me a hot dog.

# Chapter 30

"You know how to make coffee?" I stumble into the kitchen to find my daughter measuring scoops of coffee into our coffee maker.

"Angie showed me. She worked one summer in the baseball field concession stand and learned there." Savannah pours the water in and flips the "On" switch. She walks to the table and sits down in front of a notepad covered with writing.

"What's that?" I sit down across from her.

"It's our check list. Angie and I made it up so we don't have to remember what all to do." She places a couple checks on the sheet and then lays down her pen. Her dark complexion lets her tan without burning, but it also gives her dark circles under her eyes when she's tired.

"How did you sleep?"

"Alright."

"What's on your mind?"

"Nothing."

"How's Susie Mae?"

"Good, I guess. She left school sick Tuesday and wasn't there yesterday."

Savannah's eyes stay glued to her list. I don't know what to say. "There are rumors going around," I finally venture.

"I know." She looks at me. "Are they true?"

"I don't know. What do you think?"

She shrugs and looks at the microwave clock. "Angie was supposed to find out last night and call me this morning, but..."

she shrugs again. She folds her arms on the table and slumps her head on them. "It's not fair. Those boys are slime." She lifts her head and looks at me. "They've been bragging for weeks and now they're all saying 'Not me, not me." Her head drops, "I hate them all."

I move over to sit next to her. I lay my arm on her shoulder and smooth her hair with my other hand. "Honey, I don't know what to say. I'm just so sorry for everyone. I feel so sad and I don't know what to do."

"Angie says Leslie really hates me. She talks all the time about wishing we hadn't moved here. But Ricky says that doesn't make sense. I wasn't even there that night. He and Angie were, but they're family, so of course Leslie can't blame them."

"There's nothing you can do. Just stay out of it, I guess."

She turns her head to lay sideways on her arms so she can look at me. "Really? I, uh, I was thinking of going over there today after school and trying to talk to Susie Mae or her mom."

I shake my head and frown. "I think you should stay out of it. It's really not our problem. They have lots of family to help."

Savannah thinks for a moment then sighs, "I guess. I'm just glad I have Ricky."

"Really?"

"Yeah. Ricky and my job here. They keep my mind off everything. And there's play auditions on Monday."

"Y'all did a great job last night. I loved the fire and you can't beat a roasted hot dog."

She sits up, "It was fun, but it's kind of weird having Miss Laney and Missus here instead of you. You still like the library?"

"Yes, I do and I think that coffee is done so I'm going upstairs to get ready for work." Savannah and I both stand and stretch. She has on jeans, Sperry Topsiders and a white long-sleeve t-shirt under a Georgia Tech t-shirt . "You're already dressed for school."

"Yeah, can you make sure Bryan is up so we can leave on time and tell the guys on the front porch that the coffee is done?"

"They're already out there watching for trains?"

Savannah is arranging spoons, sugar and cream beside

the coffee pot. "Yes, they were going out when I came into the kitchen. I told them I'd make coffee and Missus is bringing muffins around 8:30."

"Okay." Almost to the front door, I stop and turn back. "Do you have any plans for the weekend?"

"There's a party, but with Susie Mae... everything's kind of on hold. Doesn't seem right to be having fun, you know?"

"Well, your dad will be home tonight and maybe I'll get pumpkins for everyone to carve. You think Lou and his friends would enjoy that?"

She laughs, "Careful, Mom, that's B&B business. But it might be fun, I'll check with Missus.

While I'm wiping down the kitchen counters before leaving for work, the phone rings.

"Hello, Carolina? Power is out in town so there's no need for you to come in yet. This place is dark as a dungeon and the computers are down. Why don't you come in around eleven?"

"Sure. I'll be here. Call me if the power comes back on."

"Okay, but apparently a work crew hit a pole with a transformer on it and they say it will take a couple hours to repair."

"Oh? Okay, I'll see you at eleven."

I press end on the phone and lean back against the counter. The kitchen is clean, breakfast finished. Lou and his friends enjoyed muffins and coffee on the front porch. Then they left to chase trains toward Dalton and Tunnel Hill. Brisk winds picked up overnight and we're expecting a cold front later but so far the temperature is comfortable. They left early to get a full day in before the weather turns. I heat up the leftover coffee in the microwave and step out on the deck. Savannah's coffee is good, but I can't decide if I should be surprised or not.

My brown corduroy pants and ivory fleece tunic feel good

out in the breeze. I lean on the railing and sip my coffee. The wind sends leaves high in the air and shafts of morning sun dart through the clouds and catch them every so often. My willow tree sways and tosses as it conducts the show like a grand maestro. I drain my coffee cup, leave it on the railing and step onto the grass. It's been a while since I've journeyed down the hill to visit Tommy.

Soon, my walk takes me to the tree line and the trees tower over me in their wild dance. I duck out of the wind under the willow branches. Morning light doesn't stop me from remembering Savannah's soliloquy at the pageant.

"Tommy, it was amazing. She really captured Mettie." I walk around the trunk. "Savannah's acting surprised me— surprised us all. Jackson and I started the night fighting about me taking the library job, but forgot to finish arguing after her performance." The memory causes me to smirk as I lean against the tree. "I guess I won since I took the job. Of course, Jackson and I never finish a conversation these days and, well, we used to never argue. Now..." I think about our fight this morning and hang my head. "Now I argue with everyone. I can't get comfortable at work, at home—anywhere."

I push away from the tree and walk to the edge of my circle, where the willow branches form a swaying wall. The river flows past me on the other side of the curtain of leaves. "I've fenced myself off. I was in such a hurry to be rid of all this, I never thought I'd miss it. I miss Laney and Missus. I miss the ladies on the B&B committee, I miss the kids and I really miss Susan."

"The library held out hope, but I don't know." Gathering a handful of branches in each hand, I pull them to the sides like a hung drapery. "I don't like it. I keep telling everyone it's great, but I hate it." Tugging on the branches, I feel the strength of the tree. "I don't belong anywhere and it's all my own doing." I open my hands and the branches swirl away from me. Quickly, the wind starts them dancing again.

My voice drops to a whisper, "Were you this good of a listener in life? I've told no one else all this. I'm stuck in this, like quicksand. I've got to accept that this is my life and deal with it." I clench my fists. "Focus. I need to focus. Tommy, I'm sorry but you mess up my concentration. I need to stop talking to you, okay? You've been great, but I need to get past all this... this daydreaming. I have to fix my own problems, not waste time talking to a ghost." I dig my fingernails into my palms and nod. "Thanks, Tommy, but goodbye."

I turn and walk away from the river. One last caress of the willow's trunk as I pass by. The sooner I forget all this, the better.

One foot in front of the other, I make it up the hill, onto the deck and through the door.

I park the van behind the library and look up. Lights weren't on at Ruby's, so I bet the power is still out. But intermittent clouds may allow enough light in to work in the children's section. We're creating a new space for reading time and several shelves have to be moved. I bustle along the side of the building to the front sidewalk. Rounding the front corner, a gust hits me and pushes me back a couple steps. I regroup and struggle on to the library's front entrance.

"This wind will sure knock you around." FM shouts to me from his and Missus' front yard. He's on his knees working in his garden. "Power's still out."

"I thought so." I look in the door at the dark library and decide to visit with FM. I continue up the sidewalk. "Hey, you got a minute?"

"Absolutely." He stands and brushes off his pants. He slides his gloves off and drops them on the lawn beside him. "How are things? Missus says you got a house full again up there. Lou Taylor's back, I hear. Repeat business already is a good sign."

I shrug. "I guess. Hey, you know you were asking me to think about that night with the ghost? Last night something came to me. Whatever he was shaking at the train wasn't a stick. It was metal. I remember the headlight hitting something shiny."

"Yeah," FM rubs the back of his neck. "That's what I was thinking."

"Really, why?"

He peers up at me for a moment, "Well, I need to talk to Missus first. She's over in Dalton this morning where they're announcing the grant. She, Laney, Jed, and Charles left at the crack of dawn to get over there for the Chamber of Commerce breakfast."

"Oh, that's today? They didn't mention it last night."

"That newshound, Charles, told them to keep quiet so he could break it in a special edition of the paper he's planning on running this afternoon. 'Course, if the power don't come back on..." FM grinned. "Boy that'd tie a knot in his tail."

"They feel like we're going to get it?"

"That bunch don't think anybody can do anything as good as them, so of course they're absolutely positive they can't lose."

"Must be nice to be so sure of yourself," I mumble. FM shrugs, but doesn't offer an opinion. I tuck my hands in my coat pockets. "Well, I need to get to work. So we'll talk about the ghost after you talk to Missus? I'll be at the library all day."

"Unless the power don't come on, 'cause it would get cold quick in that old building."

"True, talk to you later." I step back. "Have fun in your garden. Your house sure is beautiful." Even with the flowers lost to last week's frost, the burning bushes at the corners of the porch display flaming red leaves and the crepe myrtles add touches of red and gold. The thick layer of fresh pine straw is cinnamon brown. My eyes roam across the porch with baskets of newly planted pansies as I turn. But I stop, and look back. That curtain on the second floor moved, like how I let the willow branches fall out of my hand this morning. I swing to look at FM but he's busy putting his gloves back on.

*Who could be upstairs at the Bedwell's?*

# Chapter 31

"Hey, y'all like working in the dark? Where are you?"

"Back in the children's section," I shout. I get up off my knees and walk toward Charles' voice. "There you are. You're back from Dalton?"

"Yeah, but it's not good news. We didn't get the grant."

"What?" That possibility never entered my head. How could someone tell Missus and Laney, 'No'?

Charles follows me back to where Ida Faye sits behind a table sorting books. I point him to a kids chair and I kneel back down at the pile of books I'm putting on the shelf.

"You can lay your coat on that table," Ida Faye tells him. "So, no grant money, huh?"

"No grant money and I think I'll hang onto my coat. It's chilly in here." He squats down onto the chair. "And, you know, Missus and Laney, being queen bees, don't rightly know how to accept second place. It wasn't pretty."

"Collinswood won, I suppose." Ida Faye sighs, "Whoever thought Laney Troutman Shaw could write a grant deserves to lose. But that money would've been wonderful for the town. Of course, Missus probably would've denied the library any share, so it's fine with me. 'Bout time someone took those two big-headed divas down a notch or two."

Usually it's just library staff around when Ida Faye rants. I wonder if Charles is waiting for me to come to Laney or Missus' defense. "So, uh, any news on the power coming back on?" No surprise, I'm a big ol' chicken.

"Nope, some part on the transformer was bad and they have to send over to Cummings to get it. May be a couple more hours."

"Well, that does it for me." Ida Faye drops the book in her hands. It smacks the table. "We're closing, Carolina. I'm cold and can't see to mark these books correctly." She stands, "So Charles, did they throw a fit? You said it wasn't pretty."

"Missus glared at everyone, you know, and didn't speak a word until we got out of the room. But Laney did the whole sugarcoated stink-bomb thing she's so good at. Left them all squinting in confusion at how they ended up being flattered and insulted in the same sentence." He grimaced and un-folded his legs from the short chair. "However, on the way home, you know, they blasted the ears off me and the mayor."

"Just leave these piled in the floor?" I interrupt and wave my hands across the mound of books in front of me.

Ida Faye doesn't even look at me she's so busy grinning at Charles. "Yes, we'll take care of them in the morning. So, what did they say? I bet Miss Laney can curse like a sailor."

Charles attention has shifted though and he stares at me, "Ah, well, no cursing. They, well, they were just disappointed. You know, I need to get on to, you know, I've got some things to look into."

Ida Faye sets her mouth and harrumphs at Charles then marches back to her office.

Charles leans toward me and whispers, "I forgot how much she hates those two, almost gave her an early Christmas gift. Hey, so them two, along with your girl and Laney's daughter are running the B&B now?"

"Yeah. It's just not my kind of thing." I stand and we walk back toward the front.

His eyebrows steeple, "And this is?" He gestures toward Ida Faye's office. "How's it going with her?"

My grimace happens before I think not to. "Not bad. I just ignore her."

His grin lifts his mustache, cheeks and glasses, "Then you're a better man than I. That's one woman I couldn't put in a good hour with, much less a whole day." He pats his hands on the counter and steps back. "Well, better get back to the salt mines."

"Okay, see you. Thanks for letting us know what happened."

He waves then pauses as he lays his hands on the door. He turns to me, "Carolina, we mighta pushed you a little much when you got here, you know. I think you were doing just fine with the B&B."

I cough and try a smile, "Thanks, but this really is better."

He turns to look past me and in the midday gloom he surveys my surroundings. He meets my eyes and sadly nods. "If you say so." He pushes the door open and leaves.

I sigh and take a cleansing breath. Behind the desk, I get my coat and purse as Ida Faye comes out of her office.

"So, any more news on Susie Mae Lyles being pregnant? They keeping the baby? Bless her heart, what did Susan say?"

"No one knows anything for sure." I turn away from her as I put my coat on. I mumble, "It really is a private matter."

"That's what the Troutman's *always* say, 'It's private'. They don't hesitate to judge the rest of us in public, but when it comes to them? It's private. *Believe* me, if it was Savannah Jessup that was pregnant, Laney Troutman Shaw would be talking a blue streak about it. Susan Troutman Lyles would be spreading it like wildfire on those *prayer chains* of hers. Sanctifying gossip is all those prayer chains are *good* for, I tell you."

My stomach rolls over, whether from hearing Savannah's name and pregnant in the same sentence or swallowing another dose of Ida Faye's bile, I'm not sure. I press my purse against my mid-section and head for the door. "See you tomorrow at ten, okay?"

"Sure, keep your ears open. See what Savannah hears at school today, okay?"

All I can manage is to wave and nod. In the fresh air, my lungs gasp and draw it in deep. Usually, I do that upon entering a library or book store, the smell of books intoxicates me. Now I'm associating books with Ida Faye's garbage. I stomp down the sidewalk to my car. *Why don't I speak up?* She vomits her vileness all around me while I smile politely and step over it.

Back and forth, I twist my neck to loosen the knots along my shoulders and try to forestall the creeping headache. I stretch my shoulders and work my head side to side.

*Where should I go?* I drive toward home, but at the flashing light I turn to the left and head to the Piggly Wiggly. I'm not sure if they have power, but I need some ibuprofen and we're out at home.

In the parking lot, I drive close to the store and see light inside. Hallelujah, electricity. The weather forecasters were right. A cold front has descended on north Georgia.

Hot cider simmering on the stove when the kids come home from school strikes me as a great idea. A gallon of cider, spices, cinnamon sticks, and oranges go in the cart. Hot chocolate mix and marshmallows join them. A family dinner would be nice. It's been hard with going back to working full-time. Stew beef with mushroom gravy, mashed potatoes, and broccoli with cheese sounds wonderful. By time I get to the check-out the cart is full. My headache is fading some. Maybe because I'm relaxing. Maybe because I tore into the box and popped three ibuprofen in the medicine aisle. Jimmy Buffet calls ibuprofen the "drug of choice" for our generation. It sure is mine.

Fresh baked apple bread from one of the apple barns in Ellijay sits near the check-out. My stomach rumbles and I put two loaves in my cart as I maneuver into a lane.

"Hey, Mrs. Jessup."

"Angie, hi. Today your early release day for work study?"

"Yeah. Did you hear? Susie Mae's not pregnant."

"Oh my, really?" My mouth drops open and tears jump to my eyes. The knots in my neck and shoulders unravel.

Angie's face is red and her eyes wet. "I'm just so happy. She's, she's..."

Relief and happiness propel me around the end of the counter to hug Angie. I wrap her in my arms and she starts shaking. I pull away and see she's laughing.

"Laughing to crying. I can't seem to make up my mind," she says. She wipes her eyes with a tissue she pull out of her pocket. It's covered with black marks, the make-up she applied so carefully this morning.

I realize how beautiful and soft her eyes are without all the dark lining. "Look at your beautiful eyes, Angie Shaw."

"I know, I know. We found out at lunch today and by time lunch was over my make-up was gone."

"Does Savannah know?"

"Yeah. She, uh, well she'll tell you. She went to see Susie Mae today. That's how we found out." Her eyes dart toward a lady heading to the registers with a full shopping cart. "We better get you checked out."

"Oh, yeah." I go back around and start unloading my cart as Angie concentrates on scanning and bagging my purchases. My chest feels so light and I can't imagine how good Susan and Griffin must feel. Not to mention Susie Mae.

A manager comes to help Angie bag my groceries and so we don't get to talk anymore. *Savannah went to see Susie Mae?* She'll be home in less than an hour and what's better than talking over a cup of hot cider.

"Lou and the boys are still out looking at trains, but I need to get my walking shoes from his room." Dorothy Taylor greets me from my own front porch as I trudge up the sidewalk. "I didn't realize no one would be here to let me in. Forgot you give the guests a front door key with their room key." She reaches for my purse and a bag of potatoes in my hand. "Here let me help you."

"Hope you weren't waiting long. It's getting cold."

She follows me up onto the porch. "No, I just got here." Dorothy holds the screen door while I locate the right key.

I turn the key, push open the front door and we take everything to the kitchen. We load down the table. "Help yourself to your shoes. Lou's staying in the same one you stayed in before, The Orange Blossom Special."

"Yes, that's what he said, but can I help you with the groceries first?"

"No, I've got them. Thanks." I block open the screen door so it will be out of the way and make two more trips to the car. After I set down the final bags, I go back to release the screen door.

Dorothy comes from the B&B rooms into the living room. "Whew, just putting on my shoes is a chore these days. I'm just too short and too round to have to tie shoestrings." She sits down in a wing chair near the front window. "Are things as glum over here as they are at Jed's house since they didn't get the grant?"

I close the front door and sit in the chair opposite hers. "I don't know. I feel bad for Jed and Missus, but that's about it. So, Jed's taking it hard?"

"That boy of mine takes *everything* hard. He feels like he let down the whole town and he's scared to death of Missus and Laney. He loves being mayor, though only the Lord knows why, and he's afraid they'll take it away from him."

*Missus and Laney again.* "Dorothy, I need to put cider on for the kids, but I want to ask you a couple questions. Can we go in the kitchen or are you headed someplace?"

"I'm all yours. When the kids get out of school we're going to the pumpkin farm, but that's not for an hour or so."

In the kitchen, Dorothy takes a seat at the table and I kneel down to root through the bottom cabinets looking for my big pot. "It seems to me Missus and Laney get along fine, but I keep hearing they have fought in the past. What is the deal? Do you know?" I pull out the pot and my head and turn to look at my guest.

Dorothy is seated sideways in her chair, one arm lying on the kitchen table. Her golden red hair is teased a little in the back and catches the sunlight coming from the living room. Her eyebrows are also golden red and furrowed over delft blue eyes. Her lips, hard-set in the folds of her pale, Dutch face tell me I asked the wrong person.

"Carolina, I believe that would fall under the heading of gossip. Gossip about two people I hear you no longer associate with?"

I unfold myself from the floor and put the pot in the sink to rinse out. "Just thought I'd ask." *Really, what am I doing asking about them? Trying to get back in the middle of this Peyton Place? I'm out of it all and good riddance. Right?*

"Am I correct? Have you removed yourself from association with the Troutman girls and Missus?" the school marm seated at my kitchen table demands.

What is up with her? Water runs through my fingers and into the pot. "I'm working at the library and they're running the B&B with Savannah, but that's all." I shut off the water and hold the silver pot upside down over the sink. "But, why shouldn't I want to know some of their history? I don't want to get involved with them, but I feel so out of the loop."

"It's a quandary, isn't it? Living here, but trying not to get sucked in."

The pot slips into the sink and I whirl to face her, "Exactly. I feel off balance, like I don't know what I'm supposed to do." I turn back to the sink and pick up the pot. "Maybe my balance will come back working at the library. This B&B is too much for me. This just isn't what... well, what it was supposed to be."

Silence greets my confession. I pour the apple juice into the pot and am almost done before Dorothy speaks up.

"Pardon me, Carolina. But that's baloney"

A splash of apple juice hits the floor. "What?"

"I said, 'baloney'. I know this seems sudden and I don't know you that well, but since we were here last month I've thought and thought of how you remind me of myself when we first moved to Chancey. I was so determined to be unhappy."

"You think I'm determined to be unhappy?"

"I think I had everything I needed to be happy and turned my back on it. I'm afraid, from what I've heard, you might be doing the same thing."

"Of course, everyone is talking. I'm so tired of that. Why do they have to talk about *me* and *my* decision? I don't belong here. They don't know me."

"But they might want to."

I wring out the soaked dishcloth, lay it across the sink and then shake my head. "I don't think so." Turning away from her, I open the cabinet, pull out the cinnamon sticks and cloves, and put them on the counter.

"Here let me help. I ought to make some of this for the kids tonight." Dorothy joins me at the stove, opens the cinnamon and takes out two sticks. Breaking them in half she drops them in the cider. She pours several whole cloves into her palm and turns her hand to let them fall in the pot. "Do you have an orange?" She picks up the long wooden spoon I'd laid on the counter and begins stirring.

"Sure, you put an orange in your cider?" I take an orange from a bowl of fruit. "Peel it or what?"

"Slice it with the peel on and put it in. Gives the cider a nice citrus touch and looks pretty in the pot." She sighs and continues stirring, "Guess I'm being an old busy body, but I'm concerned about you and don't want you to make the same mistake I did. I gave up on Chancey way too quick." She squints at the stove controls, "Is this on 'high'?"

I check the stove indicators, "Yes, I want to get it going quick and then I'll turn it down. We can sit and wait on it."

Dorothy takes the spoon out of the cider and lays it on the Rock City spoon rest on the stove. "After our visit here, Lou couldn't stop talking about Chancey and it forced me to see how happy he'd been here. And Jed. Jed loved it here but I made up my mind after my first fight with Missus that I couldn't get out of this town fast enough." She shuffles back to the table and sits down with another sigh. "And you think you're in the center ring? Lou was high school principal. Education was only a tiny part of his job. If the football team didn't make it to the playoffs, he was responsible. If the clarinets were featured over the flutes in the Christmas parade, he should talk to the band director. If Cindy Lou Who got dumped by Bobby Joe Studmuffin between classes, then he wasn't patrolling the halls appropriately." She shudders and covers her face for a moment with her hands.

I put glasses of ice water on the table for us and sit down across from her. "I can't imagine. But you say Lou loved it here?"

Her hand smacks the table. "Yes. He loved knowing

everything about every child and family. Like Jed, he felt responsible for all of them and loved every minute."

"But just because he loved it doesn't mean you automatically have to love it."

"Right. That's what I kept telling myself. That's his job and has nothing to do with me. I didn't want everyone thinking they could just come up and talk to me. I didn't want to hear what the spring play should be or where the janitor didn't clean every time I went to the Piggly Wiggly."

"And yet you lived here for ten years?"

"Yes. And for nine and half of those years I lived behind walls. My job as the school secretary over in Collinswood helped me stay isolated. When not at work, I practiced my music. Playing the piano for hours and yet every hair on my body would bristle each time someone asked me about teaching piano lessons. *Teach piano to these hillbillies?* No way. So I never went to school sporting events, concerts, or open houses. We attended church but I only went to service because as the principal's wife that was my duty. No Sunday School class or pot-luck dinners for me. Just bided my time until Jed graduated, because I'd promised Lou I'd do that. I just passed time here waiting until I could move and finally be happy."

Dorothy's stiffness disappears and she lays her arms on the table. Her plump face falls like a heavy cake around her blue eyes and thin pink mouth. "I wasted ten years. I see that now. Coming back here, I see all the things I hated and realize they aren't evil or stupid. They just are. I wasn't any happier in Raleigh. There Lou was just one of many high school principals. There was no automatic status or recognition. No one knew me, my wish come true, and yet. . ."

She smiles at me, "And you know the worst part? I found the same people there as here. Some were loud and vain and thought they owned the world. Others were sneaky and quiet and stabbed folks in the back. I didn't see good in anyone and apparently it didn't have anything to do with the size of the town, except in a small town I couldn't hide my contempt. Chancey people wanted to know me. The people in Raleigh left me alone. But wasn't that what *I* wanted?" She stretches out her arms in a question and then lets them drop to her sides.

Plops of cider sizzle as they overflow the pot so I jump up to turn down the burner. Thick, spicy steam warms my face and I draw in a deep breath.

"Law, look at the time!" Dorothy rises from the table. "I told Betty I'd be home well before school let out." She moves into the living room and picks up the flats she'd traded for her walking shoes. "Carolina, I'm sorry if you feel like you've been preached to this afternoon. But there's no reason for you to make the same mistake I did."

Following her into the living room, I open the front door. "No, I enjoyed talking to you and, and I'll think about it, but you're such a different person that I am."

Dorothy places her hand on my arm, "No, honey, I'm not. That's what I've been trying to tell you. I'm different now, but that's because I choose to be different. You don't have to wait as long as I did to wake up. This is it, your one life. And looks like you're going to be in Chancey a while. So give it a try. That's all."

I pat her hand and smile, "I'll think about it."

Dorothy pulls her hand away, steps through the door and laughs. "Pshaw. Quit thinking so much and just do it."

Laughing with her, I wave as she waddles down the sidewalk. I pull the screen door shut, but stand behind it looking out. The earlier clouds have rolled past but the autumn sun doesn't provide much warmth. As promised, the cold front has dipped into the Georgia Mountains. A whistle sounds so I step back out onto the porch. Roaring across the bridge a train barrels toward me then shoots past the house. All the trains I've watched with Jackson and the kids. Was I really just biding time?

# Chapter 32

"How was I to know you were here waiting with hot cider? I don't check to see what cars are parked in the driveway?" Savannah dashes down the stairs and rounds the corner into the kitchen. "And don't yell at me," she grunts. "We have guests."

"I yelled at you because you don't come home after school and then when you do decide to show up, you head right upstairs to your bedroom. If you'd come in and say 'hello' like a civilized person then I wouldn't have to yell."

She flips her dark hair, "Whatever. What do you want?"

"I want to know if you always leave Bryan here alone after school?"

"He's in eighth grade. He's not a baby."

"Where did you and Ricky go?"

"It's the one day he and I both don't have practice. We went driving around. Out to the Sonic and stuff. And why were you home early?" She pushes past me, "Is the cider still hot?"

"Yes, but we're having dinner in half an hour."

"I'm not hungry. We ate at Sonic and besides we're all going over to Jamie's tonight to make junior shirts. The senior girls keep showing up in stupid shirts on Fridays so we're making shirts for tomorrow. Can I take our iron?" She pours a cup of cider and turns to lean on the counter.

Her jeans hit low on her hips and the lacy edge of a cami rides along the belt loops. Over the cami she wears a button-up menswear shirt in peppermint pink with tiny green stripes. She leans over the cup and blows on it before taking a sip.

"You're doing iron-on's?"

"Yeah, Ricky took me to that new super Wal-mart and I got all the letters."

"When are you going to Jamie's?"

"Around seven. Can I take the iron?"

"I thought since I'm home we'd have a family dinner, but I guess not."

"How was I supposed to know you'd be home early today?"

"I know," I sigh and add some hot cider to my cup. "The power was out so the library closed early. You went to see Susie Mae, I hear."

"Oh, yeah." She brightens up. "She's not pregnant, but she's still pretty upset. I'm not sure why." Savannah shrugs and crosses the kitchen. "The iron?"

"Yes, you can take the iron. That's all you have to say about Susie Mae?"

"Yeah, I guess." She leaves but as she passes into the living room, she stops and pokes her head back in the door, "Thanks for the cider."

The front door opens and I hear Savannah talking to Lou and his friends. The men pile into the kitchen.

"We hear there might be some cider in here if we hurry."

"Yep, I heard you talking and I've already poured a couple." I hand the mugs to the first two men. "Everyone want some?"

"Absolutely," the youngest in the group says. "It's getting downright chilly out there. Thanks."

"You're welcome to have a seat in here or the living room. Give yourselves a chance to warm up."

Dave, a tall man with a tailored hair cut and a leather coat pulls out a chair. He sits his mug on the table and then pulls off his gloves. "We're going to set up some equipment outside tonight if that's okay."

"What kind of equipment?"

Lou grins and shakes his head at me. "If you weren't a railroad wife we'd be leery of telling you since you'd think us crazy. We want to record the sound of several trains on the bridge. If we do it at night we don't get cars and such in the background."

"Just the sound? No pictures?" I put the empty cider pot in the sink.

"Right. We took some video today, but Dave here is a sound guy. He's put together lots of old recordings of steam engines in his studio and has several albums out."

"I'm working on putting together some cd recordings. My new collection is trains on trestles or bridges. The last one I did was trains in tunnels."

The men all nod and I bite my lower lip to keep from giggling. "Can you tell where the train is? Which tunnel or bridge?"

"Sometimes, but mostly it's just a place a rail-fan wants to go. They've seen the pictures so now they can hear it."

The younger man shakes his head, "I think you can tell where the recording is a lot of the time by how steep the grade is or how long the tunnel is. Of course, there are variations with the train, like if the train is hauling full cars or empty."

"The weather can make a difference," Lou interjects.

"That makes sense," I agree. "Do you need anything from us? Jackson will be home soon and I know he'll want to help any way he can."

Dave shakes his head, "We've got it covered. We're thinking of setting up some chairs and a portable heater out on the bridge."

"You're going to stay out there?"

"Some of the time. We'll be real quite when we come in so we don't disturb you."

"Oh, you won't disturb us. Matter of fact Jackson would probably be right out there with you if he didn't have to work tomorrow."

Lou frowns, "We could wait until tomorrow night? What's the weather supposed to be like?"

"Got it here," the biggest man holds his phone out. "Might be a little warmer tomorrow night with some cloud cover, but no chance of rain."

"You say Jackson should be here soon?" Lou turns to the men. "Jackson is a good one, guys. He works for CSX. Can you believe that? Gets paid to play with trains every day."

"Lucky man," Dave admits. "I don't make enough on my train recordings to eat, so I'm stuck working in advertising."

The youngest man runs his hand through his thick brown hair. "My dad worked for the railroad and I thought it was the worst job in the world. I wanted to work in an office where I wouldn't come home dirty and exhausted. Now I sit in an office practicing law and I'd give anything to never wear another starched shirt or tie again." He laughs, "The older I get, the smarter my dad gets."

"Well, let's get out of Carolina's way men." Lou says and they all stand, drain their cups and file past the sink to put them in. "We're going over to Jed's tonight for dinner. Betty and Dorothy took the kids to the pumpkin farm and are stopping at McDonalds, grandma's treat. Jed smoked a venison roast for us men. He wraps it in bacon and it is some kind of good."

"Sounds like a full night for everyone." I stir the boiling potatoes on the stove. "When Jackson gets here I'll tell him to check in with you about tomorrow night, okay?"

"Sure thing. Thanks again for the cider. It hit the spot."

# CHAPTER 33

Every morning since Lou and his friends arrived, Missus has brought over a basket of muffins from Ruby's. She picks an assortment of eight and being men they eat every single one. I get to see the muffins, smell the muffins, but get nary a bite of even a leftover one in the evening.

Today I'm not counting on them being tired of the muffins. I'm going to Ruby's myself and having one before work. Chocolate-chocolate chip, or maybe a Cheddar-Bacon, or Pecan-Pumpkin?

My last time in Ruby's was the night of the pageant, now over two weeks ago. Seems like a lifetime away.

Warmth, coffee, delicious aromas mix to form a welcoming blanket when I walk in the front door. Several folks wave or nod along my path to the counter at the back. I slide onto a padded stool and lean against the chrome edging of the counter.

"Hey Sugar," Ruby greets me. "Long-time no see." She stretches her neck to look behind her. "And you didn't bring in that big-haired, loud-mouth friend of yours this time, I see. Laney still moping about the grant?"

A smile jumps to my lips when I try to imagine Laney moping. "I don't know. Haven't seen her lately."

"Me either and I feel almost dull-witted when I don't have her to wrestle with ever so often. What can I get you?"

"Muffin and black coffee. What's your best muffin today?"

Ruby twirls her pen in her fingers and studies the case of baked goods. "Pecan-Pumpkin with a dollop of whipped cream cheese. Yep, that's what I'd order if I was sitting out there instead of trying to make a couple bucks back here."

"Sounds great. I'll just stay here at the counter if that's okay."

"Sure," she says, sitting a plain white cup and saucer in front of me. "And there's a pot of coffee just finishing so I'll bring you fresh. How are Lou Taylor and them men enjoying your house?"

"They like the house okay, but the trains they love. They're actually recording the trains tonight. Just sound recordings, no video."

"What for?" She pours my cup full of rich brown coffee.

I lift my cup and blow ripples across the top to cool it. "For rail buffs to listen to, I guess. My husband would love to be right out there with them, so I can't make too much fun of it."

"Shoot, find a good man that'll work hard and come home at night, I'd let him record hippopotamus love-making at the zoo, if he wanted."

"What are you two talking about?" Libby Stone stands at my side with an empty coffee pot. "Hippopotamus love-making?"

Ruby laughs and takes the empty pot to refill, leaving me to explain.

"We were just talking about how crazy men can be. How's Cathy doing? Savannah says she's a lot of help with the cheerleaders."

Libby sighs and rests her arms on the counter, "Cheerleading is all she wants to do. Forrest started full-time pre-K this fall and Bill told her she needs to get a job. But she doesn't want to. She keeps telling her daddy and me that she needs to be available for all the cheerleading practices and games."

"Does the school pay her?"

"No, she's not the sponsor. That old Mrs. Myers, the home ec teacher, gets the little bit the school budgets. Cathy's just a cheerleader wannabe that won't go away." Libby's eyes rise to mine, "You've heard how she had to leave her senior year?"

"Yeah. It's a shame that he got to go on with his life and Cathy couldn't."

Libby jumps, like I'd poured coffee on her, "Couldn't? Wouldn't is more like it. Me and Bill wanted her to go on to college. We would've raised Forrest. We had it all worked out and she was accepted to several colleges." She plants both fists on her skinny hips and rolls her eyes. "But she didn't make their cheer squads since she'd just had a baby. So she came home to sit on my couch and watch *Nickelodeon* and the *Disney Channel*."

Ruby sits the full pot in front of Libby and a cinnamon-brown muffin on a dark green saucer in front of me, "Yeah, Cathy's cute, but cute don't pay the bills."

"True. Oh well, didn't mean to bend your ear like that. It's just I'm worn out from the fighting between Bill and Cathy." She picks up the pot, turns and smirks, "I might just need to book me a room up there on the hill with you."

Beside my muffin Ruby sits two small bowls. "Here's some butter and cream cheese, but try the cream cheese first." The sleeves of her gold sweat shirt are pushed up to her elbows and a huge sunflower appliqué sits mid-chest with a name embroidered on each petal.

"Those your grandkids?" I ask as I break open my muffin.

She pulls her shirt away from her body and looks down, "Yeah, all five belong to my Jewel." She scrunches up her eyes and looks at me, "Have you met Jewel?"

"I don't think so."

"She's a hard worker. She's not always been a good girl, but we handled it all together. Her daddy never was part of her life so the two of us always stuck together." She watches Libby taking an order at a front table, "Funny how parents act when things happen with their kids, isn't it?"

"What do you mean?"

"Like Libby and Bill with Cathy. They tried to make Cathy something she wasn't. Anyone that ever saw Cathy with a pompom and a football player knew she had everything she ever wanted. My Jewel got pregnant in high school, too. I just accepted that she'd moved on to adulthood. Now she's married to a guy over in Dalton that sells cars and who treats the three young'uns that aren't his, just like they are. Then there's Susan Lyles."

"What about Susan?" I can't help it. Just like with the muffin, I say I won't eat it all, but I do. I say I don't want to know what's going on in Chancey, but I do.

"She swore her kids would rise above all this. Not run around like her sister and brother. No one would ever have reason to gossip about Susan and Griffin's children. Yet that Susie Mae of hers has been talk of the town all week." She jerks upright, looking over my shoulder, she mumbles, "Speak of the devil."

I turn to see Susan push through the door.

She spots me, pulls her purse strap tight and marches my way. "Ruby, I need a dozen smaller muffins and four coffees, to go."

"Sitting in the pumpkin patch today? I'll get it together." Ruby walks to the other end of the counter.

"Hi, Carolina."

"Hi. Pumpkin Patch?"

"Down at the church, the youth and parents sell pumpkins in October to fund the youth program for the year." She twists in front of the stool next to me and sits down. "I'm headed there now. We need to talk. Can you come to the Pumpkin Patch later?"

"I work until five today, will you still be there?"

She sighs and I recognize weariness in the tightness of her mouth, the downward pull of her eyes. "Yes. I've been doing other... other stuff all week, well, you know. So I'll be there until we close tonight."

"Here you go." Ruby sets her tray of coffees and bag of muffins on the counter.

Susan looks at the ticket and digs money out of her jean pocket. "Keep the change. Around five then?"

"Sure."

Susan gathers her tray and bag. She strides across the floor with no wasted motion. She never swerves, but powers to the door in total efficiency.

I hurry to finish and go before Ruby gets back. I'm tired of our conversation. One muffin, one cup of coffee, and I'm swimming in Chancey's deep-end again.

Believe it or not, I'm ready for the library. At least with Ida Faye she talks *at* me, not to me.

# Chapter 34

Warmth and sunlight flood the old gray-stone library. The cold front brought clear blue skies. Fall colors are peaking and the view from the small, narrow windows behind the check-out desk lights up the entire first floor. Across the street, the park looks like the setting for a Southern Living article, "Autumn in a Small Southern Town."

I'm stuck inside all day.

But aren't most people? Am I so different? Why feel sorry for myself? All those weeks on my hill by the river spoiled me, right?

My cell phone rings. Grabbing my purse, I also check the lights on the library phone. Yep, Ida Faye is still on the phone in the office.

Checking my display I see its Jackson. "Hey there."

"Hey. You at the library yet?"

"Yeah. Where are you?"

"Out near Kingston checking that new crossing. I forgot to tell you last night that I'm picking up a couple pounds of barbeque at a place out this way and bringing it home for dinner tonight. Lou told me about it and said he wanted to buy dinner for everyone."

"Great. Are you getting fixings to go with it?"

"Yep, should have everything we need. Well, except drinks."

"No problem. I made a gallon of sweet tea last night. We're good. What time will you be home?"

"Hoping to get through early and be there around five. What about you?"

For some reason, I hesitate at mentioning I'm meeting Susan. "I get off at five but have some errands to do. Shouldn't be too late. We can eat around six?"

"Good. I'll let Lou know. Recording is going to be great tonight. You're sure it's okay with you I hang out there with them?"

"Of course. Got to go, Ida Faye's off the phone. Bye."

I stand up and see Ida Faye working at her filing cabinet. She's been on the phone all morning, but I need to find out what she wants to do about the mess we left in the children's section yesterday. The desk is busy today so one of us needs to stay in the front area. I walk to her door and knock lightly then push it the rest of the way open.

"I wanted to check on what we should do with the children's area. I can clean it up, but we're pretty busy out front."

She surveys the stacks of papers on her desk, "I suppose I *could* bring these reports out there and work on them. I'm not making much progress because the phone just won't stop ringing." Ida Faye's peach top and pants are velvet textured and she has a dark brown turtle neck underneath. The turtle neck sticks out at top and at the end of each sleeve. She looks like a big dollop of peach congealed salad with toasted pecans around the edges.

She glides, like Jell-O sliding off a plate, around to where I stand, "Everyone calling wants to know if I've heard anything about, well, you know."

"What?"

She bends her head toward me, shaking it slowly side to side. "It's terrible what that family is going through. No one doubts that they made the right decision, but..."

Here I am again. She's dying to tell me something and my stomach says don't listen. "Okay. Good." I say and back away. "I'll get started with the kids stuff and you'll do the desk? Great."

I turn and flee. In the children's section, I start piling the books according to where they'll be moved to. It's slow, tedious work but mindless, so there's nothing for me to do but wonder what Ida Faye wanted to tell me.

For three years in elementary, Savannah played soccer both spring and fall. She didn't like it and never even tried to learn the game. She just wanted to be with her friends. On the field, she ran along the edges of the field never attempting to touch the ball or engage the other team. Those were excruciating seasons for Jackson and me. To sit at games week in, week out; drive back and forth to all the practices; pay the registration and equipment fees. All so our daughter could run along on the edge of the field.

That type of frustration builds in me now about this situation. A decision, get involved or quit playing, must be made. Trying to play on the edges isn't working. Being a *little bit* involved won't work.

Dorothy quit and now she regrets it.

I got involved and got burned.

But I have to go one way or the other and quit hanging out on the sidelines.

Book after book makes its way onto the correct shelf. I put the last one in place and still don't know what to do.

"All done?" Ida Faye calls out to me as I walk around the corner.

"Yep, everything in order. You had a good idea for changing those shelves around. Makes a lot more sense."

Ida Faye Peach Parfait. That comes to me when she stands up behind the counter and now it runs around in my head while I try and listen to her flood of words. Ida Faye Peach Parfait. Then one word stops the silly rhyme cold.

"What? Who?"

She gives me her disapproving librarian stare, "Aren't you *listening?* It's the only thing that could've happened, don't you think? Sure she's back at school today, but *really!*" She stacks her papers and then straightens them by hitting the bottom edge on the counter. "I tried asking you about it *earlier,* but you were in *such* a hurry to get the children's section organized."

I walk behind the counter and sit down. "You think Susie Mae had an abortion?"

Ida Faye lifts one hand to her chest, "It's not *me* thinking that, it's everyone else. I just, well, I *can't see* any other answer to how she can be pregnant one day and *not the next*."

"Maybe she never was pregnant," I try.

"*Honestly*, Carolina, you're just too close to the situation to understand and then having your *own* daughter running *all over* the country side with *Ricky Troutman*. I see why you *want* to think that. Bless Susie Mae's *heart*, I hope what you say is true, *but...*"

Her voice trails off as she bends down behind me and squeezes my shoulders. "You'll see after you live here *awhile*. It's just how the Troutman's *are,* honey. *Always* have been, *always* will."

"But..." what do I know? Nothing. Maybe she's right. Maybe she's wrong. Maybe I wish this was all just a story in a book I could close and stick on the shelf.

# Chapter 35

Finally. I walk out the front door and breath deep. All day Ida Faye barraged me with fake concern. First for Susie Mae and her poor, poor baby. Then for Savannah and the road to ruin she's riding in the front seat of Ricky's truck. Every so often she'd interrupt the "bless her hearts" with tut-tuts and sad shaking of her head over Susan and Griffin's lack of parenting control and obvious disregard for their first grandchild.

She "regretfully" informed me after one call that Susan was definitely pro-life as her old station wagon had a pro-life bumper sticker. It had taken a couple hours to track down that information but finally someone who followed Susan in a caravan to scout camp five years ago remembered it word for word. "Sad, but *true*," the peach parfait lamented.

Political calls began after lunch. "Should such a breach in his personal beliefs lead to Griffin resigning his post on the Town Council?"

I don't know what wore me out more, ignoring her obvious enjoyment of the situation or keeping track of the reverberating consequences.

Several times I tried to say we weren't sure she had an abortion or was ever pregnant. Ida Fay looked at me the way she gazes at a patron who explains the computer must be wrong, because they most certainly returned the overdue book last week.

My van offers refuge from the day's barrage and I slump in the front seat. As much as I dread talking to Susan, Ida Faye caused me to pray for the clock hands to move faster. I start the car and punch the air conditioner button. The cold front blew through town leaving us with temps in the low seventies this afternoon, but the humidity is stifling. I also lower my window before twisting around in my seat to find a water bottle in the van floor behind me. There's always a bottle of water rolling around somewhere back there. Snagging a half-full one, I unscrew the top and down the contents. Germs from your own family don't count, right?

Half-bottle of lukewarm water, fresh air from the window, and cool air from the vents all refresh me. Absence of a certain gossip-laden peachy dessert causes my shoulders to relax. I back out of my parking spot and turn left on to the side street and then with another left I'm cruising pass the front of the building. Ida Faye is working late tonight with one of the high school girls. Her office light is on and she'll be fielding phone calls late into the night on this breaking story. National Enquirer doesn't realize the gold mine they missed in her.

Lights are coming on in the homes and buildings around the square. Large trees and surrounding mountains make night fall faster in town. The Bedwell's house comes up on the left. FM did a lot of work on the front gardens today. I check out the upper windows, but they are dark.

"Hey, Carolina."

FM's greeting startles me, then I see he and Missus seated on the front porch. My brakes squeal slightly as the van stops. "Hi there. Beautiful evening for sitting out there."

"You're welcome to join us—oof!" FM ends his invitation with an elbow in his side.

Their sideshow causes me to chuckle. "Thanks, but I've got an appointment."

"Where you going?" Missus hollers.

Now Missus wants to talk to me. Of course. That's why I used the word appointment. Just to get to her, because she can't stand to be out of the loop. "Nowhere important. You all have a good evening."

Missus lifts her wrap from mid-arm and drapes it across her

shoulders, "You, too, and tell Susan we said, hello."

I lay my foot on the gas pedal and laugh. Of course, she knows where I'm going. I hate small towns.

Dinner time anywhere finds lights glowing from kitchens and dining rooms. I drive past homes settling into their evening routine. Routine that's what a small town is all about. Everyone worships at the altar of Routine. Or Tradition. What was, is and always shall be. Disrupt it at risk of your own peril.

Okay, maybe the lengthening mountain shadows of an October evening bring out my inner drama queen.

I pull in behind the church where the staff and Pumpkin patch workers cars are parked. The front lot is for customers and when I walk around the side of the building, the busy crowd surprises me. Parents corral excited children to and from cars. Teen-agers working their shifts welcome the newcomers or carry newly purchased pumpkins to the cars. Susan is standing at an open car door talking to the person in the driver's seat. When she turns to say good bye, she sees me. She waves and holds up a finger to say "one minute." I sit down on the front steps to wait.

Up the small hill Susan trudges like she's carrying the weight of all Chancey on her shoulders. Her jeans are faded to a light blue but her long-sleeve tee-shirt looks new.

She pushes the Kelly-green sleeves of her tee shirt up as she joins me on the steps. "Thanks for coming."

"Looks busy. Y'all make a lot of money with this?"

"Enough to run the youth program all year. It's a lot of work in October, but we don't have to do any other fund raisers."

Silence settles into our conversation and we both let it rest there.

Susan stretches her arms above her head, then drops them back in her lap. "We've had a rough week."

"Yeah, I heard. Sorry about that, I wanted to talk to you but... well, I didn't know what to say or if you'd even talk to me." My voice fades out and I sigh, "We've caused your family so much grief. I feel awful and I know Savannah feels really bad."

"No, don't say that. Don't--,"

"But it's true. Poor Susie Mae, going through all this."

"I know. You feel bad. Savannah, Angie, and even Jenna, all feel responsible. Ricky can't sleep at night and Laney is sick with worry. Griffin thinks he spent too much time with Leslie and her college applications. Everyone feels guilty."

I shake my head. "It's just that we all care for Susie Mae and it's not fair for her to have to deal with all this, especially since I'm sure none of it was true."

Susan stretches her legs down the steps and then bends them up so her elbows sit on her knees. She opens her hands and rests her forehead on her fingertips. "Susie Mae was pregnant."

"Oh, Susan."

"Last spring."

"What?"

"I found out when she lost the baby in April. And as for this fall, I figured she wasn't pregnant because I put her on birth control in May."

My gaping mouth won't close. Susie Mae? Finally, I clear my throat and choke out, "I don't understand."

"Me either. I swore this wouldn't happen to my kids. Laney's or Scott's? Maybe. Probably. But never mine. There would be *no* talking about my kids, *no* whispering about them seen with blankets out at the railroad tracks or steamed windows on the back roads. No way. Not *my* kids."

"We all feel that way."

She sits up and stares at me, "You didn't. You talked about Savannah having problems. I've never heard anyone be honest about their kid like you were. I thought Savannah moving to town and being so wild would keep everyone's focus off Susie Mae. And then you tell me she's not who I wanted her to be. I was so angry at you, at her. At everyone. Plus," her shoulders fall, "I knew Susie Mae was sneaking out again."

"Sneaking out? But the kids, I never heard anything. No one suspected anything."

"Of course not, she's Susan and Griffin Lyle's daughter. The boy she's been with is just a kid and he's scared to say anything to anyone. And well, honestly... I covered for her. Can you believe that? Me, the one everyone trusted. I hid everything from everybody." She waves a hand towards the folks on the lawn below us, then clinches her open palm into a fist. "Even Griffin."

Oh, I breath in and then release with a whisper, "I bet he's really upset."

She relaxes her hand and pulls it through her hair. "We've all been in heavy-duty counseling this week, but I'm not sure he'll forgive me. I'm not sure he should." Her gaze wanders off to the area of trees to my right and I watch as memories tear across her mind. "Susie Mae finally couldn't take it. At school, Leslie threatening people to stay away from her, the girls and Ricky all sick with guilt, and then the boys from that night being called liars—and worse." She breaks her gaze and turns to me, "Did you know Ricky got into a fist fight with one of them?"

"No."

"Susie Mae couldn't stop crying. The boy Ricky tried to beat up was in one of his classes. One day he had that class right after he'd seen Susie May having a panic attack in the hallway and he attacked him. Of course, that made her even more upset and the more she cried the more everyone felt sorry for her. More miserable she was, the guiltier everyone felt. It was a vicious circle. Once everything came out and her daddy and sister knew the truth, she started getting better. Me and my secret-keeping caused it all." Susan drops her face back into her hands.

I slide closer and put my arm around her shoulders.

Susan raises her head and her tears mix with laughter, "You're just my warm-up act." Her voice breaks, "Now I have to tell my sister and brother. I've judged them and their kids so harshly. You've no idea. My kids were better, my life was better."

Horror rises in my chest as I think of how Laney will act upon hearing her sister has been lying to her all this time. Laney doesn't strike me as the forgiving sort.

Susan's voice squeaks, "So, can you forgive me?"

I pause because, well, I'm not sure I can. My arm around her now feels wrong, it was just an impulse to comfort her, but forgive? No one has ever asked me point blank to forgive them. Usually people don't admit they're wrong. If they do admit it, they say "sorry" and just move on, assuming forgiveness.

"Honestly, Susan, I'm not sure. I've tried really hard to untangle myself from all of you and I don't know what I feel. I'm pretty sure I'm angry, but I'm not good at knowing my feelings. I need some time."

Susan tilts her head at me, "Are you sure you're Southern? Most Southerners would say, "Sure, honey. I forgive you. Then they'd spend a good portion of every day reminding everyone of how disappointed they are in their good friend who lied to them about her poor, poor daughter, bless her heart."

I laugh but then the "bless her heart" plunges like an icicle into my soul.

Ida Faye will be unbearable.

I jump up from the steps. "That stone is cold. I need to go and think about all this, okay?"

Susan's confused look makes me sad, but I have to get away from all this. I can't stand it. "When are you talking to Laney and Scott?"

"Tonight. Mama too, but Mama's always been embarrassed by Laney and Scott so she'll understand. I don't think they will. And then Laney will have to talk to Jenna and Angie. Scott has to talk to Ricky. You can decide when and what you want to tell Savannah. I just want it all out before I get too scared and start hiding again.

"But what about Susie Mae? How will she deal with people knowing this stuff?"

"The counselor says part of Susie Mae's problem is my expectations are so high and written in stone. No room for a do-over. Because I couldn't face the truth, one mistake led to another and another and all the time I ignored what I knew was going on. Susie Mae needed me to help her stop and I turned the other way." Pain slashes across Susan's face and she clamps her eyes shut for a moment." Taking a deep breath, she opens her eyes and relaxes her mouth into a small smile. "Vickie, that's our counselor's name, she's a Christian counselor and she keeps talking about grace and mercy and forgiveness. All stuff I was raised on and teach every week. But when it's my daughter? my reputation? Well...." She shrugs. "It's been an eye-opening week."

I'm no longer stunned into a block of stone and my feet are itching to walk. To get away from here so I can think through this turn-over of the Chancey fruit basket.

"I've got to go. People to feed at the house, you know."

"Sure, hope you're okay and if you need to talk, just holler." Susan smiles and for a moment peace flashes across her face.

With that flash, I realize she'll eventually be okay and the ache in my heart is soothed a little.

"I'm going inside," she nods behind her at the sanctuary doors. "We're meeting at Mama's at 6:30 so I've got some time to work on this mercy and forgiveness bit."

As she stands, I walk. Down the sidewalk and around the church. At the rear, I collapse against the brick wall, letting it hold me up. This is all too much. Susan? Susie Mae? I straighten up and walk to the car. In the van, I pull my cell phone from my purse and dial home with shaky fingers.

"Hey, I'm going to be a little late. Go ahead and start dinner, okay? You've got everything you need for the barbeque, right? I won't be long. Bye."

Now where?

Now what?

# Chapter 36

Jackson finds me out on the bridge leaning against the railing and staring out at the bruised sky. The water is pushing its way past the bridge in a hurry to get wherever it's going. Leaves of burgundy, mud-red, and brown hang on for one more day before falling to become compost. Finally the landscape around here fits my mood.

"Didn't know you were home until I started out here with the lantern." He leans beside me and we both face the river.

"Everyone ate?"

"Yeah, it was good. There's plenty left for you. So, what's going on?"

There are no words. Driving around for the past hour didn't help me sift through the new information or what it means to me.

"Oh, I'm not sure. Except, except that the people I looked up to, the ones I thought had it all figured out are just as messed up as the rest of us."

"Susan?"

My head jerks toward him. "Why did you say Susan?"

"C'mon, honey, you've had her on a pedestal since we got here. You two hit it off and it's obvious you think she's special, and don't get me wrong. She is special. I like y'all being friends, she just leapt to my mind as someone that has it all together. And the way you talk about Susie Mae and Leslie it's obvious how much you want Savannah to be like them."

"I do not!"

"Now, don't get mad. I'm probably wrong. But they are good kids and have it all together. Why wouldn't you like them? Okay, so *who* are you talking about that's as messed us as everyone else?"

My smile won't be held back. "Susan." I turn back toward the railing.

He puts one arm around my shoulders and snuggles close. "Wow, I was right. I'm getting good at this husband thing. You should keep me around."

Why I married Jackson rushes over me and I move closer to him. "Thanks for loving me. I know I've not been too lovable lately."

"No more than usual. Just joking," he adds when I play like I'm pulling away from him. He tightens his arm around me and kisses my hair.

Another smile bubbles up and I let this one settle in. "You're making me feel better. Get this, Susan said I was a good mom because I talked about Savannah's problems. Susie Mae is, well, she's got some issues she's got to deal with and Susan admits she didn't handle it well. Boy, did she not handle it well. She covered for Susie Mae sneaking out with a boy. Even put her on birth control without telling Griffin." My body tenses and anger rises up in my chest, "She let us think she was perfect. Perfect when her daughter, who is only fifteen, is out running loose. How dare she---."

"Wait a minute, from what I've seen she only acted how everyone expected her to act. I've got to admit, you were right about small towns. Since we've lived here I can't believe how much everyone knows about each other. Maybe Susan got typecast in the role of "good girl" as a kid and she was just filling that role." Jackson steps back a little and shoves his hands in his pockets, "Maybe she's tired of being perfect."

Tired of being perfect? Isn't that why I always fought being on display? My anger begins to dissipate. "Could be. I know it's hard for me to stay mad at her. My anger boils up and then it kind of fritters away." I step away from the railing and nod to the chairs and heater at the end of the bridge. "So the guys have everything ready for the recording session tonight?"

"Yeah, they're in getting long johns on and packing up their supplies. Should've seen us at supper. It was like Will and his friends getting ready for a Boy Scout trip. Oh, and thanks for getting out my sleeping bag. I didn't know you'd found it."

"You found your sleeping bag?"

"You left it on the couch, didn't you? That was where it was when I got home. I thought Bryan put it there, but he said he didn't know anything about it."

"No, it's been missing since we moved. I decided Will accidentally took it back to school with him. How did it get on the couch?"

He shrugged, "Maybe Bryan doesn't want us to know he had it."

"Maybe, but Bryan isn't a good liar. He has trouble even playing a practical joke, he's so honest." I shake my head, "It was on the living room couch?"

"Yep, well I need to get changed, or do you want to talk some more?"

He's a good one, isn't he? Willing to talk when he's practically jumping out of his khaki's wanting to get on with his little outing with his train buddies. I grin and reach out my arms.

He steps into my arms and closes his around me. "Carolina, you've got to stop beating yourself up. Be happy, okay?"

It *is* me beating myself up, not Chancey, isn't it? Why can't I just relax and enjoy my life? Night has crept out onto the bridge with us and behind Jackson's shoulder, the moon rises over the trees. Moonlight hits the water and sparkles form a path leading right to where we stand. What if I decide to be happy? All the ingredients for happiness are already mine, aren't they? I lean back and with moonlight on my face, I gaze into my husband's eyes. "Kiss me. That will make me happy."

My face burns from Jackson's beard and I snuggle closer to his side as we walk toward the house. "What's Savannah doing tonight?"

"She'd already left for the bus to the game by time I got home."

"Oh, the game. How could I forget?" Just when I start feeling good about my mothering skills...

"Yeah, they're playing over in Paulding County, so they'll be late getting back tonight."

"Susan said she was going to meet with Laney and Scott and her mom tonight to talk about Susie Mae. That's odd that none of them are going to the game."

"It is pretty far. Plus maybe this is more important."

"More important than Chancey football? I don't think so."

We both laugh and step up onto the porch. Jackson pulls open the screen door, "I know it will be tough for Susan. I'll be sure and say a prayer for her. For all of them."

I stop with my hand on the door knob and turn to look up at Jackson, "You've never said anything about prayer before."

"Can't hurt, can it? Besides you're the one who dropped out of church, not me."

The door jerks open and pulls me with it. Bryan is on the other side and he steps aside as I stumble in.

"Mom, can I hang out with the train guys and Dad tonight. Mr. Lou says it's okay with him if it's okay with you and Dad."

"I guess. Wait, why don't you call Grant and see if he wants to spend the night?"

"His mom won't let him, remember?" Bryan stares at me and shakes his head like he can't believe how dense I am.

"She might now. Give it a try if you want."

"Really? Cool." Bryan races up the stairs. He's missed Grant. Um, I've missed Grant. I've missed seeing all the kids. The summer with them here all the time was fun. What about it did I hate so much?

Jackson starts up the stairs behind Bryan, "Hope Grant can come over." He gets a little farther up and stops to look down at me, "You know you've got beard burn?"

"Yes, I know. It's your fault. Go get ready to play with your little friends and your trains and leave me alone." Joking with Jackson feels unbelievably good.

In the kitchen, there are cartons of pulled pork, coleslaw and some fried potatoes. I fix a plate of pork and potatoes and heat it in the microwave. My stomach rumbles and I stick my fork in the coleslaw. Delicious. It's cold and crunchy and now I'm starving. After I pull my plate from the microwave, I add a helping of slaw and grab a Diet Coke from the refrigerator. Placing everything on the coffee-table in the living room, I look around for the remote. Hope there's a chick-flick on, 'cause the TV is all mine tonight.

# Chapter 37

*What is that sound?* My head is crammed into the arm of the couch at an angle that has my neck screaming. I blink several times at the TV screen and try to focus. Harry had just met Sally for the first time when I closed my eyes for just a minute. Harry and Sally apparently continued meeting while I slept. Now Kevin Costner is on the screen wearing a baseball uniform and making a really annoying sound.

Wait, that's my cell phone. I push to sit up and shake my head. The house is dark, the only light coming from the TV. My phone has quit chirping or singing or buzzing or whatever it does. I've got to try and remember what the different sounds mean. Text or call or message. Currently, I can't even remember where my phone is.

Digging in the couch I find the remote and then mute the movie. In the kitchen, where I've stumbled to, a new search begins, this time for my purse. With phone in hand, I stare at the last text message.

"dont wry, ething gd."

Is Savannah texting me to not cry, or is that to not worry? "What?" I manage to text back. I see that I've missed several calls from her but she didn't leave a voice message. Kids don't believe in voice messages anymore. They believe actually having to listen to a message is too much trouble. Smart kids. I lay my phone on the table and pull out a chair before turning to the kitchen.

With a fork from the silverware drawer in hand, I take the

coleslaw container out of the refrigerator. Might as well finish off the slaw while I wait for her to text me back.

Elbows situated on the table I eat and wait—true mother-mode. Maybe Savannah's with Leslie and Susie Mae and she's telling me everything is good with them. Or her and Ricky? I don't think they're fighting, but who knows.

The slaw is gone and she hasn't responded. Silence fills the house like moonlight floods in the back windows. I didn't change from work so I still have on my gray slacks and black sweater. My plan to start the movie and eat before changing into my robe didn't seem to work out. I slide my feet into Jackson's work boots, which he left by the back door and step onto the back deck.

There is not a bit of breeze. Everything is still and silent. I walk to the edge and lean on the side rail of the deck. Automatically I scan the edge of the woods. Tonight is different, though. Usually I look to convince myself there is no one out there, tonight I'm hoping to see Tommy. I've seen him most often skirting along just inside the tree-line. Maybe I am like those people on the TV shows that learn to live with their ghosts. Tommy makes me feel at home here. Shoot, I flat out miss him. Why *did* I stop talking to him?

There he is! On the edge of the woods at the corner of the house. Branches are swaying and a pale arm moves in the moonlight. I step away from the railing and stay in the line of shadows on one side of the steps. On the first step Jackson's boots almost make me fall. *Should I take them off?* I'd be faster and quieter, but that grass looks wet and cold. Boots stay.

At the bottom of the steps, I slide off to my right. I'll come from the other side of the house by the driveway. It's difficult in the work books, but I tip toe across the gravel drive and then stop at the corner of the porch. After a peek around the corner, I creep out to the porch stairs. Shadows from the house are deep and I stand in total blackness next to the porch.

The men are sitting in a circle in the corner of the front yard down near the tracks. Looks like more than four, they must've picked up some closet rail-fans. They are sitting in full moonlight and the heater glows red. The boys are lying in their sleeping bags but their upturned faces say they are far from sleep. Apparently my falling asleep meant missing Grant's arrival.

Where the woods come almost to the far side of the house I watch for the ghost. Branches move, but shadows lie across that part of the yard so I don't see the gray figure yet. Then he comes out of the woods and starts walking between the men and the house.

My heart is coming out of my chest. He's going to head for the porch like usual and I'm right here to meet him. I'm going to see Tommy, face to face.

"Look! There's the ghost!" Lou shouts.

I swing my head at his shout, but he's looking across the tracks. He's not looking at the ghost. What? Then I realize Tommy has stopped walking and is staring across the tracks also. I follow his gaze and they're right. Between the tracks is another ghost who is hurrying toward the front yard.

Bryan and Grant struggle to get out of their sleeping bags but stop when they see the ghost by the house. "A ghost!" they shriek. The ghost from the tracks comes to a sudden stop when he sees the ghost in the front yard. Then both start running towards me.

Behind the gray men rushing at me, the men and boys are yelling and running. I fall against the railing and understand where the saying "my knees turned to jelly" came from. The ghosts reach the steps at the same time and both sets of eyes widen in their white faces when they see me plastered against the porch. One ghost is old but he takes the stairs two at a time, the younger ghost looks confused. Maybe he's haunting the wrong house. I'm sure the older ghost that came from the woods is Tommy and he's winning the race until his feet fly up in the air and he lands flat on his back. The other ghost stumbles over him and ends up lying in a heap, half on-top of his haunting buddy. Grant and Bryan are first from the front yard circle to reach the collision site. Right behind them is Jackson who dives in the front door and turns on the porch light.

"Mr. Peter, it's you!" Grant yells.

Tommy sits up on his elbows and squints into the light. "Hey, Grant. Didn't know you were going to be up here tonight."

"Sure am glad I gave James here a ride up tonight. You two look this way." Charles says as he snaps pictures.

The other ghost is keeping his face hidden by staying curled-up, face down. But then a voice yells, "Ricky, are you alright?" from out near the tracks. He cringes, but doesn't turn around.

"Charles, what are you doing here?"

"Hey Carolina, I brought James out here for Missus. He's that reporter doing the story for Railroads & Railfans."

"Well, no more pictures until we figure out what's going on." I test my knees to see if they're steady and step onto the sidewalk.

Savannah bounds past me and up the stairs, "Ricky, Mr. Peter, you okay?"

I realize what I smell. "Baby powder. You two are covered in baby powder."

Jackson steps to the railing, "Carolina, what's going on? What are you doing down there?"

"I was following the ghost, the first ghost, the Mr. Peter ghost and other than that I don't know anything."

"Why, Peter Bedwell, I thought I recognized you. What in the world is going on?" Lou Taylor demands in his best principal voice.

I stare at the long, white face and recognize the man I saw standing on the bridge a week ago. "You're Missus' and FM's son."

"Nice to officially meet you, Mrs. Jessup." He says and nods at me. He shifts his eyes to my daughter, still in her cheerleading uniform, "Savannah, you might as well go ahead and call Mama."

"Can I go? This is embarrassing." The heap, better known as Ricky Troutman, whines. He rolls over and partially sits up. He has yet to show his face.

I clunk up the stairs in Jackson's boots, "I want to know what's going on."

"Please, Ms. Jessup, let me go home. I did this for Savannah, that's all. Mr. Stone, you aren't going to put this in the paper, are you? Having my girlfriend beam me with rocks in the park was bad enough, but I'd never live this down." Ricky does all his talking with his knees pulled up in front of him, his arms crossed on top of his knees and his face hidden behind his arms.

Lou bursts out laughing, "Lord, that's Scott Troutman's son, isn't it? Son, you are a spitting image of your daddy and I can't even see your face. This is just like something your father would do. Try to impress a girl and end up looking like a fool. Being his principal was a true challenge."

"This was my idea, I admit it." Savannah holds her hands up in confession, she drops them as she adds, "Of course it wasn't my idea that he screw it up so bad."

"Yep, that's Scott's son." Lou shakes his head and chuckles, "Boy, you've got to learn to just say 'no', no matter how good looking she is."

All the men are laughing now and Ricky's head hangs lower.

Savannah has a hand on her hip and is staring at Jackson, "Dad..."

"Okay, Ricky, go home." Jackson finally relents. "But we'll talk tomorrow, right?"

"Yes, sir." The love-sick quarterback gets up and leaves without once letting his face be seen in the light.

That boy might truly make it in professional sports one day.

"Let's go inside. It's cold out here." I push past my daughter but throw at her, "And do like he said, go ahead and call Missus and whoever else you're in cahoots with. Bryan, go get some towels for Mr. Bedwell to sit on and then you and Grant can go up to your room. Your night outside is over."

"Guess our night recording is over, too," Dave says when we've all trudged into the living room. "Sounds like more folks will be coming."

Jackson nods, "Yeah, I'm sorry guys. But you're welcome to stay out there. Shouldn't really be that much more car traffic."

"Go on back out." Lou winks at his friends and takes a seat in the middle of the couch. "I'll get the story and fill you in later."

Charles and James show their intent to stay for the whole story by taking a seat on either side of Lou.

"Seriously?" Savannah's hip is jutted out so far I'm afraid she's going to fall over. And can you roll your eyes so far back they get stuck? "We're going to have this conversation with two reporters right here?"

I kick Jackson's boots off across the living room and the release of energy feels good. I've been played by my own daughter. I point at the indignant cheerleader and match her attitude. "You go change into something a little less cute, call whoever needs to be here and get downstairs inside five minutes. You don't want reporters here, funny, but I get the feeling this is all about the reporters."

She whirls around and stomps up the stairs, but I yell after her, "And if you don't want folks knowing what you're doing—then don't do it!"

Bryan and Grant pass Savannah at the top of the stairs carrying a stack of towels. They scurry down the stairs.

Grant grins at the tall, lanky ghost and hands him a towel. "Here, Mr. Peter. I can't believe you're the ghost."

"How do y'all know each other?" Jackson calls from the kitchen where he's making coffee.

Grant spills. "I went to the Bedwell's with Savannah and Angie one day. Mr. Peter helped me shoot my bb gun. He got his out of the attic and we did target shooting in his backyard. Plus, I remembered him when he came and worked at the museum a long time ago. I liked the bugs and we set up the display."

Spreading out the towels, Peter nodded at Grant, "That was fun, wasn't it? I haven't gotten to go into the museum the whole time I've been back. We can look into adding some stuff now, can't we?"

"Can I help?" Bryan asks. "I have some bug books and stuff."

"Sure," Peter sits on the towels. "I'm sure the display needs to be cleaned. Maybe this weekend?"

"I guess since your haunting days are over you have time on your hands?" My voice is shrill with anger. I stare at the ghost now seated in our recliner and remember some of the stuff I told Tommy down at the willow. I swallow, but my throat is tight and dry. "It's been you all the time?" squeaks out.

Peter nods and looks down at his hands. He brushes off the powder in light strokes.

Sweat breaks out down my back. My sweater is hot and prickly. Less than an hour ago, I stood on the back deck and congratulated myself on adapting to living with a ghost. But a live human being? That's just creepy and a shiver follows the sweat rolling down my back. "I'm going to change."

On the stairs, I look down to see Charles explaining to the magazine writer the history of our ghost. Peter is still rubbing the powder off his hands. Grant and Bryan have staked out a place behind the couch, hoping to be unseen participants. "Boys, come on up now. If you want a snack get it 'cause you're in for the night."

Bryan looks up to start his plea for staying, but Jackson is already rousting them.

I step into my room and close the door. Wish I could just crawl into bed, but no. I throw off my sticky black sweater, spritz myself with body spray, and then pull on the first tee shirt I come to on my closet shelf.

In the hall, I knock on Savannah's door and open it. "Come down now."

She's sitting on her bed, cell phone in hand. She's changed into pajama pants and a hoodie. "Mom, did you know about Susie Mae and Gib Rollins?"

"Is that the boy that... um?"

"That she's been sleeping with? Yes. Angie called to see how things went over here and told me. I can't believe it. Susie Mae?"

"We're not going to talk about this right now. Tomorrow, okay? Susan told me all about it today. Tomorrow I'll tell you everything I know."

Savannah unfolds off the bed and walks into the hall in front of me and we hear the door opening below us. Missus starts talking before she's fully in the room. Savannah stops and I bump into her.

She peers down the stairs, "Woah, Missus is on fire. Guess

everyone's secrets are coming out today, huh?"

"Yep, and it's about time."

# CHAPTER 38

"I'm not leaving. I asked you point blank this summer if you had anything to do with the ghost business up here on the river and you lied to me. Lied right to my face." Charles glares at Missus from his place on the couch.

"This is none of your business. It's private. Good, there you are Carolina. Tell this bunch it's time for them to leave." Missus has on a full-length fur but when she turns to address me, I see her ankles are bare between the coat and her shoes. She's rushed out and just put her coat on top of her night gown.

"First, let me take your coat so you can get comfortable."

She looks at my outstretched hand and then meets my eyes. "No, uh, no thank you, Carolina. I'm still chilly after being summoned by your daughter in the middle of the night."

She knows that I know she's only wearing her nightgown.

With a nod of her head she acknowledges my winning of round one. "I demand the reporters and Principal Taylor leave."

"Mama, sit down and let's just get this all out. I'm tired and want to go home."

"Peter, I will not have an employee of my newspaper—"

"Who's newspaper?" Peter shakes his head at his mother.

Missus pulls her shoulders back and her head tall, then backs into the rocking chair by the front window. "Fine. I'll just sit here quietly and let you people ruin everything."

Charles coughs to cover his snort of laughter and then points his reporters pad at Peter, "You own the paper?"

"Yes, I do."

The editor of the paper cocks his head. "Hmm, I didn't know that. Okay, so what are you doing running up and down the riverbanks covered in baby powder?"

"It was my idea," Missus announces.

"So much for sitting quietly," Jackson whispers in my ear as he places a chair from the kitchen near the stairs for me to sit on. Savannah has taken a seat in the floor next to the couch.

I giggle at Jackson as he goes to get a chair for himself and get the boys moving upstairs. The boys dart behind me and up the stairs waving at Mr. Peter as they go.

Missus clears her throat and speaks louder, "Like I said, it was all my idea last summer. This house had sat empty and kids were having parties out on the bridge. When Peter showed up back in town, I asked him to play the part of the ghost to scare them away. That's all. It might've gotten out of hand lately, but it was just an attempt on my part to do the parenting this generation is failing to do. If the parents weren't allowing their children to run wild, all this would not have been necessary." She makes her decree and clamps her lips together. They snap back open when she finally looks down from her pulpit. "Charles, if you are so intent on getting this story, why did you not write that down?"

"I don't believe a word of it."

"Mama, give it up and quit preaching." Peter smiles and looks around the room, "Folks, I've been living out here in the woods since last spring. I've wandered around homeless for..."

"Peter Tecumseh Bedwell, you were never homeless! You always had a home with your father and I, you *chose* to live in the woods."

"True. That is true." Peter leans forward, his elbows on his knees. "I knew Mama would welcome me with open arms. So I did have a home. I just didn't want to live in that home and be who I'd have to be living there." He looks at his mother, "Is that better?"

Missus tightens her lips and shakes her head.

"So, I was camping out here and the ghost rumors..."

"Wait a minute," the reporter from Railroad & Railfans

speaks up. "Your middle name is Tecumseh, like in William Tecumseh Sherman? Isn't Sherman hated down here?"

Charles and Lou grin and swing their heads back to Missus.

"Young man, that is none of your business. And you two stop grinning like a couple of teenagers looking at a girly magazine."

Peter bites his lip to keep from laughing, "Mister, uh,..."

"Harralson, James Harralson."

Peter nods, "Nice to meet you, Mr. Harralson. My name is part of a long family legacy and an even longer story. Though, now that you mention it might be a good feature story for folks around here. Don't you think so, Charles?"

Missus gasps, "Not in my paper."

"Whose paper?" her son asks with raised eyebrows. "Anyway, the rumors started when the kids would spot me down in the woods, usually after they'd been drinking. Mama showed up out here one day and stood on the bridge yelling my name."

"I've never yelled in my life. I called your name and you came." She sniffs and looks away from her son. "When this house belonged to my aunt and uncle, Peter practically lived in the woods here. So when I heard the ridiculous story of a ghost, I knew it was my son. My Harvard-educated son, camping out like a hobo."

"Wondered how long you'd go before throwing the H-word into the conversation." Peter's smile shows straight white teeth and now that most of the powder has fallen off, his good looks are more evident. "And I don't mean hobo."

Savannah sits up onto her knees, "Tell them about the trap door. That's how he kept disappearing."

"Like Mama said, I know all about this house and land. There's an opening where coal used to be dumped into the basement when the furnace was coal-burning. It's on the front porch, but if you didn't know it was there you'd never find it."

"So that's why you always ended up there," I shake my head. "But why go to such measures to haunt up here."

Peter drops his eyes, but then looks up at his mother. "The grant. It was all about getting the grant." He smoothes his hand down the side of his face. "It just got more complicated once y'all moved in."

"I saw the interest the ghost created and decided it was good for Chancey." Missus waves her hand at Savannah and then Peter, "And these two can say what they want, but..." her face crinkles into a smile. "The whole thing has been great fun!"

Savannah rocks forward, "I met Mr. Peter at Missus' house that day he shot BB guns with Grant and then the next day is when I saw the ghost in the yard. I knew it was him right away. So Missus let me and Angie help because Mr. Spoon kept saying it was a person that fell off the train and Missus thought tourists would like a soldier ghost more."

"Yes, Charles, why were you so obstinate about the ghost being a hobo?" Missus demands.

"Just yanking your chain. I knew, just knew, you were behind the whole ghost bit. Even thought it might be Peter, you know, but I couldn't get anything solid. However, I've got to tell you, that night of the bonfire when we saw you in the train lights waving that sword. Man, that was something else. Good job."

"Charles Spoon! You knew it was a sword?" Missus leans up and her fur falls open a little, showing light blue satin. "Why didn't you put that in the paper instead of all that nonsense about a stick? I went to a lot of trouble to get that sword and then you call it a hobo's stick. I wanted to strangle you."

"I'll tell you, when she handed me Daddy's sword, I knew she meant business. That sword hadn't left the fireplace wall in decades. You writing it was a stick just strung it out longer. That was supposed to be my last night, but Mama wouldn't let my spirit rest until everyone knew the ghost was a confederate soldier."

Missus gathers the front of her coat shut and juts her chin out. "This is a good place to end this conversation. Due to my persistence, Savannah made her acting debut at the pageant. A rather pleasant outcome, if I may say so myself." She tilts her head at Savannah. "I insist on being mentioned in your acceptance speech at the Oscar's. That is all the thanks I want from you and your parents. Come along, Peter." She stands and marches across the living room.

We all stand. Questions race through my mind, "How did Ricky get involved?"

Savannah comes to her father's side and leans against him. "That was me. I knew the reporter from the magazine was coming tonight but Mr. Peter had said he was done."

"And I was. That's why I left the sleeping bag on the couch. Sorry about taking it, but the nights started getting chilly at the end of summer."

"So I got Ricky to fill in. We parked off the street over near Miss Susan's house when we got home from the game."

"And then, of course, Mama convinced me to haunt y'all one more time." He bends his head down, but lifts merry eyes. "Mama's right. It was fun. I'd run up the porch, hit the little door and slip right down into the basement into that corner room y'all just have junk in. Then I walked out the back door. Simple."

Lou clears his throat, "Carolina and Jackson, I'm giving James here my room. I'll go down and stay at Jed and Betty's with my wife. James, this place isn't always this exciting, but it's a fine bed and breakfast place for rail fans."

James laughs, "I'm not sure what I'll do with all this. Even I can't wait to read my story!"

I hold open the door for everyone to leave and then follow them onto the porch.

Savannah steps out and gives me a hug. "Mom, we'll talk tomorrow, okay?" She waits for me to nod and then darts back into the house.

Jackson, Charles, James, and Lou walk over to where the heater still glows. Missus clutches her coat around her and slides into the driver's seat of her Cadillac. Peter walks along behind her brushing off his shirt and pants. He says something to his mother then turns back toward the house. He walks up the sidewalk and stops at the bottom stair.

I look down at him and wait.

"You don't need to worry, Carolina. But we need to talk."

My stomach rolls, "I think I've talked enough to you."

"I know, the willow, but you don't understand and I need

you to understand, okay? Can we meet tomorrow? Wherever and whenever you say."

Why not? I've told this man more than anyone ever, including my husband. "Sure. I work until noon."

Peter gazes straight into my eyes, "Think we could meet under the willow?"

"No, that place is..." I pause and look away. "I started to say haunted."

He smiles and bows his head.

After a deep breath, I nod. "Sure, under the willow. Why not?"

"Okay, see you then." He turns and strides to the passenger door of his mother's car.

Numb, I walk into the house and up the stairs. The alarm clock will be ringing in a few hours and I'm exhausted.

# CHAPTER 39

If Ida Faye had asked me one more time what I thought was going on with the Troutmans, I swear I would've taken that cordless phone she was carrying around in her pocket all morning and shoved it in her slobbering mouth. Slobbering, salivating. She smells blood in the water and the bloody victim is a Troutman, she thinks. And that's my saving grace, she doesn't actually *know* anything. Yet.

My head is pounding and walking down the hill to the willow, I try to forget the four hours at work today. Chancey's vultures are circling, but they can't quite figure out where to find the road kill:

-Griffin and Shaw, *only* in-laws, represented the older Troutman generations at the football game. Shocking.

-Susie Mae didn't cheer, but she was at the game. Conflicting reports on possible weight gain/loss. Confusing.

-Charles Spoon was only at the first half of the game. Later he was seen with a stranger. Suspicious.

-Missus' pulled into her drive in the wee hours and she had a stranger with her. Unconfirmed suspicion he was the man seen earlier with Charles Spoon. Concerning.

-Ricky Troutman left straight from the team bus and didn't even go to the locker room. This news carried with it an expression of sympathy and assurance that Ida Faye was trying *so very hard* to keep Savannah's name out of all this.

I blamed bad hot dogs eaten Friday night on my constant escaping to the bathroom all morning.

Only good thing about Ida Faye's digging and supposing is that it kept my mind off meeting with Tommy, er, Peter.

Nearing the bottom of the hill, I see him sitting at the far edge of the willow. He's facing the river and sadness pulls at my chest. I missed talking to him when I thought I could pick it up anytime in the future. Now that I know it's over...well...

"Hi there."

"Oh, hi, here sit down. I pulled out your table cloth. Hope that's okay."

I step in front of the folded mat and sit down. "You clean up good."

Peter chuckled, "Yeah, but I don't smell as good as last night, no baby powder. Here." He hands me a bottle of peach ice tea. "Thought you might need a drink after spending the morning with Ida Faye."

"I need something stronger than this." I unscrew the lid and take a drink. "So you know Ida Faye."

"Yeah, she and I don't get along too well."

"I know she's not a fan of your mother."

"No, Mama stood up for me and Ida Faye's daughter when we, well when we were kids. We dated all through high school. Mama thought it wasn't a good idea, but she knew better than to forbid us. Ida Faye didn't have any use for me until I came back from college, but I'd moved on by then. Some of the stories Ida Faye told about me were real doozies."

I lift my bottle to my mouth but catch the look on Peter's face.

Staring at the railroad bridge off to our left, confusion washes his face and then pain. "Why in the world would I want to move back here?"

After a long drink, I shake my head, "Believe me. I'm the last person that would know why anyone would want to live here. Where else have you lived?"

"All over, but mostly outside Chicago. I ran a newspaper up there but when the owner's son got old enough to take over they pushed me to the side."

"You coming home to do that to Charles?"

"What?" He looks over at me. "No, not at all. I just want to make a life here. Always knew I'd come home and since I'll be fifty next year, it's time. Not sure what I'll do after getting the museum squared away." He starts to take a drink of his tea, but stops with the bottle lifted, "You know, I wasn't just playing with the boys, we're going to bring that place to life." He stands up, forgetting to take a drink, "A train's coming."

He takes a couple steps toward the water and we both watch the train charge across the bridge. When the engines come into view with the blue autumn sky providing background, rippling green water beneath and the sun-lit leaves dancing in the foreground, I'm reminded of a calendar picture.

"That's why I love this riverbank."

"You're another train nut?"

He laughs and turns his back to the river. "Kind of. But mostly I was a nut about getting out of here. Catching a ride on a train sounded like a fun way to leave town. Or leaving by boat would've worked too."

He holds his hand up to shade his eyes and looks up the hill, "I always thought I'd buy your house. It was the only place in Chancey I could see me living."

"It sat empty forever from what I hear." He wanted this house? My headache flashes back. "Why didn't you buy it then?"

"Angry, Carolina? Wishing I'd bought it before you did?"

"Honestly, yes. It's obvious we don't belong here. You belong here."

Peter drops back down beside me, "How can you be so blind?"

"Me blind? You're the one saying you should've bought this house when you had the chance."

"No, that's not what I said." He turns, facing me. Dark brown eyes stare and beg me to pay attention. "You belong here. I said I thought about buying this house, but something always stopped me. What stopped me is this. It isn't my house. It's your house."

"I know it's my house. I just wish it wasn't."

"No you don't."

I push up from the ground and brush off my gold corduroy pants. "You think you know me because I've talked to you so much. But I was only rambling because I thought you were a ghost. You don't know anything about me." I bite my bottom lip to stop its trembling.

"You don't have to worry about what you told me. It's all safe."

I walk away from him.

"Wait, Carolina, what I mean is that I didn't listen to you. After the first time I always stayed away when you came down here. Sometimes you heard me around you, but I was always leaving."

I stop and turn around. "I don't believe you."

"Because you felt like someone was listening to you, right? I saw you when you'd walk down the hill, burdened, unhappy, worried and then I'd watch you walk up the hill, lighter, cares gone, happier. You felt like you'd really connected with someone and left your burden here. Right?"

"You didn't hear me? Never?"

"Not after the first time."

I step to the willow trunk and lean against it. "Why does that make me sad? I was mad and embarrassed and now I'm sad. Face it, I'm a mess." Tears burn my eyes and my head pounds.

"Listen to me, I believe you were heard. Me and God always had our best talks right here on this riverbank."

My eyes blink back the tears, "God? I don't know. That feels even more creepy."

"Creepy? Why?" His bright teeth shine at me. "I tell you your ghost counselor who never spoke back isn't real and you're sad. I tell you God was listening and you're creeped out?" Peter stares at the air in front of him, then drops his head between his arms which rest on his knees. He takes a deep breath and reaching behind him, pulls his dark-brown hair out of its pony tail and smoothes it with his hands. After tucking it behind his ears, he claps his hands once then opens them toward me. "You know, I've told you what I wanted to tell you. Take it or leave it. But I want us to be friends, okay? I really like you and Jackson and I need some friends who have seen the outside world." He stands up and finishes his bottle of tea. "Folks from the great beyond, which is anything outside Chancey, are in great demand here. You are quite the popular lady."

The river flows past my gaze. *Really? Susan and Laney liked me because I'm not from here?* Somehow that rings true. I never thought of it that way.

Turning around, I look back at Peter and reach out my hand to shake his. "Okay. Friends."

He pulls me into a hug and we laugh. Then, I playfully push him away, "One thing I know is that I got to talk a whole lot more when you were a ghost."

"Aw, that hurts. Now I'm going up to see if I can help Jackson with sealing up that secret door on the front porch. Don't want Bryan and Grant using it and getting hurt."

I relax against the willow and watch him walk up the hill. The boys see him and come running down the hill. Savannah is sitting on the deck in the sun talking on her cell phone. The front-yard maples tower over the house and shade it with burnt-orange leaves. I can't stop a laugh remembering Lou and his buddies recording trains well into the morning hours. Always something happening here, that's for sure.

Peter could buy the house. The thought jumps across my brain. Yeah, maybe that's the solution to everything. No more Ida Faye, no more Chancey. I pat the tree trunk, maybe God does talk to me down here. Seems I've found the answer I've been looking for. Okay, I'll try. "Thanks, God. I appreciate you fixing all this."

I walk up the hill, lighter, more carefree, happier. Peter might know what he's talking about.

"We're going? Right? C'mon, Mom let's go." Bryan meets me half-way up the hill after my talk with Peter.

"Go where?"

"To the apple place with Grant's family. Everybody's going?

Dad said we had to check with you."

"Bryan!" Jackson yells from the deck. "I told you I'd talk to your Mom. Besides we're not going anywhere until you finish cleaning up that mess you and Grant made in the kitchen this morning."

I grin and tilt my head at my son who will probably be taller than me by this time next year. "It did look like something exploded in the kitchen this morning. What did y'all make?"

"Chocolate-chip Banana muffins. We wanted to eat them while the chocolate was still gooey. We forgot to clean up." He darts ahead of me and then turns around to jog backwards. "Please say we can go. Please?"

"I'll see. Hurry and get done with the kitchen."

"'kay." He twists around, runs up the rest of the hill, and then leaps onto the deck.

Jackson lets him in the door, closes it, and walks to the railing to lean on it.

I join him and get a quick kiss for my efforts.

"You were gone by time I got up this morning. How was Ida Faye?"

"Please don't get me started. She was unbearable."

"Well, we missed you. Grant and Bryan made muffins but they tripled the chocolate chips so it was like eating handfuls of melted chocolate laced with chunks of warm banana all topped with a nearly burnt crust. I'd forgotten how Saturdays use to be with you at work. I've lost my breakfast making skills."

"So Bryan's lining up a trip to the apple barns?"

"Yeah, Susan called. They're riding over to Ellijay to buy apples and then going on a picnic at Carter's Lake. What do you think?"

"But the apple thing was always just our family." I whine.

"Yeah, I know. But, well..."

"What? Tell me."

"In Marietta, *everything* was just our family. We didn't really have friends, you know. It's weird having people want to be with us, isn't it? Before we just kind of worked and the kids went to school and, well, you know."

I really, really want to argue with him. Names and faces pop up but they won't come together in my mouth. Probably also not the time to tell him I've figured out a way to move back there, is it? My laughter bubbles over, because for the very first time the truth hits me between the eyes. My family won't leave Chancey, even with a bulldozer.

Pushing away from the railing, certainty of my fate grows. "Sure, let's go to the apple barns and on a picnic with the Lyles."

I keep laughing because everything inside me is crying.

# CHAPTER 40

"So, the Troutmans have you back wrapped around their little fingers I hear." Ida Faye greets me at the front desk Monday morning.

I ignore her, shrug off my coat and carry it to the work room. We spent every available moment with Laney and Susan and their families this weekend and apparently that fact made the phone circuit. My coat goes on the rack and I set my purse on the table. Squatting down to put my lunch in the small refrigerator, I first take one of two apples from my bag and then close the bag back up. Stashing the bag on the middle shelf, I unbend and stand up. The door swings shut after being hit with my knee. My first bite of my Fuji apple is crisp and sweet. Fuji apples became my favorite this weekend and I've eaten at least a dozen since Saturday afternoon.

With the bite comes the crisp smell of hot cider, the laughter of Griffin and Jackson chasing our bag of chips blowing down the hill towards the lake, the beauty of teenage girls sitting in the autumn sun singing camp songs and the joy of an afternoon of nothing, and yet everything. I tried to stay wrapped in my cloud of self-pity, but that wasn't easy to do when Laney greeted me with a rib-crushing hug and tears.

"*So* King Peter is back in town." Ida Faye breaks into my memory. She leans on the wall outside the work-room. Her arms are crossed against a gray wool jumper, shiny with wear and everything is topped by the floppy white bow at the neck of her blouse. "I'm sure he plans on just *taking over* Chancey as Lord of the Manor and his mother will let him. Jed Taylor better watch out 'cause he won't be mayor for long with the *favorite* son back."

"Really?" I choke out and chomp down on my apple to stop the defense of Peter jumping in my throat. I made up my mind last night to limit my vocabulary at work to "Really?" and "That right?"

"That reporter *still* up at your house?" Ida Faye in her school marm outfit follows me behind the desk.

"Yes." Okay, I hadn't thought of how to handle direct questions. I sit in my chair and open the drawer I stash my purse in.

"Having a reporter staying in your home just isn't *normal*. When's he leaving? How did he like your place?" She looks down over her double chin and straightens the loops of her bow. "I bet Laney put on a *show* for him. You *know* how she is with strange men."

"He'll be leaving tonight." I stare at the calendar in front of me, willing her office phone to ring.

"So he leaves and *that's it* for your B&B?"

I nod, "Yes, Jackson and I decided last night we'll wait until he retires to try it again. Savannah's wants to get a part in the school play, and so she'll be busy with that, besides I think she's tired of her part-time job running the B&B. So, yes, we decided to wait. I better get the dropped off books from the weekend checked in." I stand and turn right into Ida Faye's open embrace.

"You've been *so* supportive of your husband's dream, bless your heart. And dealing with that *witch* Missus and trying to keep Laney and Susan Troutman happy. I know you are just *worn out* from all that craziness."

My face is pressed against her iron gray hair and one side of the stupid bow. She's patting my back with one hand while her arms shackle me to her. "Thanks," I mumble and wiggle out of her grip. "Thanks, but..." The glee on her face stops my words more effectively than a mouthful of apple.

"Poor Carolina, I know how *unhappy* you've been. Now you

can put *all* that behind you." She pats my back one last time and shudders. "Those people were just *using* you and you're so fortunate to be rid of them."

*She's happy, she's really happy. But why?* I blurt, "Why does this make you so happy?"

"Oh, no. No. I'm not *happy*. I'm just pleased for *you*. The Troutmans and Missus and now that *Peter's* back, well they all just play with people. It's not *normal* how they think they belong in the middle of everyone's business." Ida Faye tugs on her bow and straightens her shoulders. "Honestly, a B&B in Chancey? How *crazy!*"

"Mr. Harrelson, the man from the magazine, says it's a perfect location. He thinks we're crazy to *not* do it now." So much for limiting my vocabulary.

She waves her hand in the air. "He's a *stranger*. He doesn't know Chancey like I do. *Nothing* here ever changes. The Troutman girls are trouble, Missus thinks nothing of ruining people lives, and outsiders *never* fit in."

"Outsiders like me?"

The double chin comes to a rest on top of the bow and Ida Faye's little gray eyes narrow. "Of course I don't mean you. *I'm* helping you fit in. Now, I need to get to work. I'll be in my office." She tromps to her office and is on the phone before she even sits down.

I fall into my chair and rest my head on my hands. A tiny chime rings on the desk clock. Nine o'clock, time to unlock the front door. I dig the key out of my desk and walk to the doors. Leaves sweep across the street and into the park. For a moment, it appears like it did the first time Jackson and I came here. When we sat in the gazebo and talked about Ruby's and dreamed about the old houses. What about all that causes me such fear? I turn the key and then push open the door to make sure it unlatched. Pocketing the key, I grab the mat to move it outside onto the sidewalk. Once the mat is in place, I step down the sidewalk to check the window boxes to see if they need water.

"Morning, Carolina."

FM walks, half-jogs toward me. "So, it's all out in the open now, huh?"

"Maybe," I push my fingers into the window box soil. "Ida Faye doesn't seem to know Peter was the ghost."

He tilts his head and rubs his moustache. "Really? Well, doesn't much matter." His eyes twinkle. "Sure am glad to have him back. He's something, isn't he?"

"Yes, he seems really great." My smile feels good after the tension with Ida Faye. I check the other box and then shake the dirt from my fingers.

FM grins. "Yeah, we do know how to raise good people here. That's for sure. I'll let you get back to work. Don't want Ida Faye after me."

We laugh and I walk back to the front door. He waves before ambling back down the sidewalk. I grip the tarnished, gold handle and pull open the heavy wood-and-glass door. I sigh, "Back into my prison cell." Catching a glimpse of Ida Faye at her office door I realize she looks more like a prison matron than a school marm. When the door slams behind me she looks up.

"Good, you *remembered* to open the door. Last week you were late and the Henry kids almost *froze* to death. With their father on the library board that was a mighty poor lapse on *your* part."

I pull the key from my pocket and lay it on the desk. "Ida Faye, I quit." I march around the corner and get my purse from the drawer. "I'm going home to my B&B."

Ida Faye scurries after me when I stride into the work room. "No *notice*? This will ruin your reputation, you know."

"Not as much as working with you." I pull on my coat, grab my lunch and stand face to face with my boss, my ex-boss. "You wouldn't talk any better about me if I gave you a two-month notice. You are hateful and arrogant and small-minded. It just dawned on me. I don't hate small towns, I hate small people." Squeezing past her, I practically run to the front door, push it open, take a deep breath, and look to my left.

"Hey, FM. I just quit my job!"

FM stops his raking and stares at me for a moment. Then

he lifts his rake in the air and shouts, "Good for you. Welcome back from the dark-side!"

I shove my lunch bag under my arm and find my cell phone. Jackson took the day off to hang out with Mr. Harrelson today. "Hey, where are you?"

"Hey, uh, we're having coffee at Ruby's. What's up?"

"Nothing. I'll see you there in a minute, okay?"

I whirl around and head for the café. FM is no longer in the yard and as I get to his sidewalk he comes out his front door with Missus in tow.

"Carolina. You've quit Ida Faye? Where are you going?" Missus has her fur coat on again, and this time her feet are bare.

I laugh and point, "You are the only person I've ever heard of that uses a fur coat for a bathrobe."

Missus scrunches down, "Does that hide my feet? Now, you've really quit Ida Faye?"

"Yes. I don't know why it took so long. I'm going to Ruby's, you all coming?"

FM nods, "I am."

"I have to get dressed. But all I really want to know is what about the bed and breakfast?"

I dance away from her, "Wellll, I am out of work now..." I wrap my arm around FM's and we continue down the sidewalk. "Did you really not know the ghost was Peter?"

He places his other hand over my hand crooked in is his elbow. "Truth is, I was afraid to hope. When Missus took my sword I thought if she gave it to anyone other than Peter then I'd have to put her away in the asylum, but I wasn't sure."

"So that's why you kept asking me about it?"

"Yeah. So why'd you quit?"

"Look around, the folks here are crazy. Missus wearing a fur coat over her nightgown on the front sidewalk, you chasing her around town looking for an old sword, Laney church swapping every week, Susan entering two car-loads of stuff in the fair, the mayor's brother, a senator-wanna-be, fooling around out by the train tracks with his wife the judge. Top it all off with a ghost? The library was the only sane place in this town."

317

"I guess I never thought of it that way. If you're used to things being quiet and, well, normal."

"Right. Normal. That's all I've ever wanted in my life. Normal. Problem is I realized this morning if normal is Ida Faye, then I'm joining the crazies."

He pats my hand and grins, "Welcome. So, what about the bed and breakfast?"

I cock my head at him, "Does it sound normal to rent rooms named after railroads to train nuts? Does it sound normal to live with your kids and husband on a hill over-looking the river and a train bridge? To hang out with a man that was once a ghost, to build bon-fires for every teen-ager in town to make out at? If all that sounds normal, then it's not for me."

"I'm old and my brain doesn't work as fast as it used to. What did you say?"

I step to Ruby's door and open it wide. With my free arm I wave FM into the crowd. I step inside behind him and smile at my husband seated on a barstool at the counter. "Yes, the Bed and Breakfast is here to stay and, you know what? We need a name for it."


The End


*Want to name the Bed and Breakfast? Visit my website at kaydewshostak.com and sign up for my quarterly newsletter to receive information on the Naming Contest!*

# Acknowledgments

This book begins and ends with my husband and best friend, Mike Shostak. He's always believed in me and thought I could do whatever I had a mind to. And he not only thought that, he told me so every day.

But even before Mike, my first blessing was to be the daughter of Linney and Evelyn Chancey Dew who knew how to raise adults. While we had the most fun childhood, they never forgot what they were doing, making adults. Adults with the ability to not only dream, but make those dreams come true. Mama and Daddy you gave me, Linney and David everything we needed to make the world a better place, and we did.

The adults Mike and I got to raise have filled our lives with so much joy. Robert, Ryan and Lizzy, you never once thought I couldn't write a book. (Or at least you never said so, even as teenagers.) You never once acted like it was silly or a waste of my time. You acted like it was normal, and I thank you for that. And we thank you for the wonderful people you've found to make our lives even better. Carrie, Casey, and Michael, thank you for making dreams come true in our children's lives every day. Especially those dreams named, Cas, Liddy, and Tucker!

Many years ago (when surely I'd be published any day now), I asked a group of ladies to be Prayer Support for my writing. They each agreed and while at times it felt indulgent, they prayed for me and my writing whenever I asked. They will never know what that has meant through these long years. Ann Holley, Cindy Webb, Sherry Bruce, Stephanie Newton, Mary Ann McCoy, Joni Mohr, Chris Keith, Meg Matthews and Juanita Tatum, thank you ladies. I knew I was never alone.

Then there are the friends from college who made the journey fun and boosted me when I didn't even know I needed a boost. Jane Bays Conner and Connie Bowman Smith, thank you for knowing me then and now and never letting me down.

So many others have supported this dream and now celebrate this book. You know who you are and the smile on your face as you picked up this book, tells the world who you are. Some of you are writers who helped me become a better writer, especially Cec Murphey. Thank you, Cec, for pushing and prodding and always teaching. I'm so proud to call you my friend and mentor.

Hope you enjoyed your time in Chancey and will be back soon. Remember, just holler if you need anything!

# Author's Note

Kay was raised by small-town Southerners in the South. However, none of them stayed only in the South or stayed only in small towns, and that is how this book came to be.

Taking a look at the familiar and loved from new perspectives lets you see the absurd, the beautiful, and the funny. In Kay's world, that gave her something to write about.

After having several stories in compilation books and spending a few years in journalism, Kay wandered into Chancey and found it hard to leave. She currently is working on the fourth book in the Chancey series and living in Fernandina Beach, Florida.

CPSIA information can be obtained at www.ICGtesting.com
Printed in the USA
LVOW11s0534311215

468561LV00005B/11/P